BOOK OF ISAIAH
A Commentary

THIS VOLUME WAS MADE POSSIBLE THROUGH THE EISENDRATH

PUBLICATION FUND, INSTITUTED ON THE TWENTY-FIFTH ANNIVERSARY

OF RABBI MAURICE N. EISENDRATH AS PRESIDENT OF

THE UNION OF AMERICAN HEBREW CONGREGATIONS

THE JEWISH COMMENTARY FOR BIBLE READERS

BOOK OF ISAIAH

A Commentary by Solomon B. Freehof, D.D.

UNION OF AMERICAN HEBREW CONGREGATIONS

NEW YORK · MCMLXXII

LIBRARY OF CONGRESS CATALOGING IN PUBLICATION DATA

FREEHOF, SOLOMON BENNETT, 1892–
  Book of Isaiah.
  (The Jewish Commentary for Bible Readers)
      Bibliography: p.
      1. Bible. O. T. Isaiah—Commentaries. I. Bible. O. T. Isaiah. II. Series: Commission on Jewish Education of the Union of American Hebrew Congregations and the Central Conference of American Rabbis. The Jewish Commentary for Bible Readers.
  BS1515.3.F74   224'.1'07   72–2156

COPYRIGHT, *1972*
by Union of American Hebrew Congregations, New York, N.Y.
Printed in U.S. of America
Designed by Andor Braun

IN AFFECTIONATE GRATITUDE FOR HER UNSTINTED HELP,

WITHOUT WHICH THIS AND MANY ANOTHER BOOK

COULD NOT HAVE BEEN WRITTEN,

THIS COMMENTARY IS DEDICATED TO

Esther S. Tyrnauer

EDITOR'S INTRODUCTION

WITH THE APPEARANCE of this volume, the Union of American Hebrew Congregations is proud to present the seventh in its Bible Commentary series. The history of this series commenced in 1927 when Emanuel Gamoran, of blessed memory, educational director of the Commission on Jewish Education, suggested that a series of commentaries on biblical books should be published. The recommendation was accepted and the commentary series was launched.

Dr. Solomon B. Freehof prepared the first of the commentaries on the Psalms and Preface to Scripture which is a general introduction to the entire series. The others are on the Five Scrolls (1 volume), Kings I, Job, and Proverbs. Commentaries to others are in preparation.

The impetus for the creation of this series comes from the recognition that the Bible is the wellspring of our heritage as Jews. Out of its deep reservoirs of wisdom flow the commentaries of the centuries. Commentaries have been created in every age to clarify the biblical text, to teach the biblical message, to derive new meanings from the perspective of contemporary idiom and insight. New commentaries are needed in our day as well so that students of the Bible can understand the text from the perspective of Jewish tradition.

The original mandate of the committee engaged in formulating the criteria for preparing the commentaries is still relevant: "While thoroughly abreast of modern research, the writer is instructed to utilize especially the Jewish tradition as it speaks in the works of the great classical commentators and in the midrashic literature. The writer is required to bring out the ethical and religious significance of the book wherever possible. This commentary, while aiming to increase knowledge, also aims at edification so that a reader will be helped by it ethically and religiously. The commentary should also call attention to literary beauty. The purpose of the commentator should be to bring out the meaning of the content of the book as a literary religious classic, irrespective of time."

Jack D. Spiro

CONTENTS

Editor's Introduction   vii

Introduction   3

The Prophet Isaiah (*Chapters 1–39*)   9

The Second and Third Isaiahs (*Chapters 40–66*)   197

Bibliography   333

BOOK OF ISAIAH
A Commentary

Introduction

READING the Bible "from cover to cover" was not a Jewish habit. It became part of modern, spiritual self-culture through the Protestant Church, which rested its authority upon the bond between the individual and Scripture. Of course the Bible was studied from ancient times among Jews. It was the subject of instruction of children: "These words . . . thou shalt teach diligently unto thy children," and the Talmud records numerous incidents in which a child passing by is halted and asked to recite his verse. But, from the Middle Ages and on, the child was introduced early and directly to the Talmud. So there was no broad knowledge of the total Bible in the life of the average Jew, any more than it was in the life of the average Catholic.

Nevertheless, the average Jew knew a large portion of Scripture, even though he did not have the habit of reading it "from cover to cover." The source of his biblical knowledge was the prayer book and the ritual of the synagogue; and, since this was the channel through which he learned Scripture, we can understand why certain books of the Bible were best known to the average Jew. Of course he knew the Torah (the Pentateuch) best of all. Each year, in the synagogue, the Torah was read in its entirety, Sabbath by Sabbath; and it was a duty, generally fulfilled, for each man to prepare for this synagogue reading by reciting at home twice the scriptural portion and once the Targum, the Aramaic translation. Thus there developed among Jews a fluent reading knowledge of the Aramaic language and there was a ready-made audience for the great and popular mystic book, the Zohar, when

4   Introduction

it appeared. Because he learned the Torah through the weekly reading, the average Jew, when quoting a verse, cited it not by the chapter division (which developed in the Middle Ages in Europe) but by the weekly portion in which the verse was found.

The Bible book which ranked next to the Torah in the knowledge and awareness of Jews was the Book of Psalms. Their knowledge of the psalms came directly from the prayer book. Perhaps fully half of the actual contents of the daily and Sabbath services were chapters and verses from the Book of Psalms. Besides its prominent presence in the service, the Book of Psalms became a beloved book of personal devotion, read regularly and at times of special emotional stress and family trouble. The Kabalists, who ascribed to the Psalms a special power in affecting the events of life, added to the popularity of the book. The five scrolls too were fairly well known, since each one of them was read in the synagogue on a certain occasion—the Song of Songs on Passover, Ruth on Shavuot, Ecclesiastes on Sukot, Lamentations on the Ninth of Av, and Esther on Purim. Of these perhaps the best known was the Song of Songs because many pious people read it every Friday.

After the Torah, the Psalms, and the Song of Songs, there can be little doubt that the best known biblical book was the Book of Isaiah. This, too, was due to the reading from the Prophets at services in the synagogue. The Prophets were not read consecutively as the Torah was, but choice and appropriate selections (i.e. the Haftarot) from the various Prophets were a regular part of the Sabbath and holiday services since ancient times. Thus the average Jew acquired a knowledge of the prophetic books, not totally or consecutively, but selectively. The reading list of the Haftarot, the prophetic selections, constituted a choice anthology of the prophetic writings. In this list of synagogue prophetic readings, it is to be noted that there are two from Amos, four from Hosea, nine from Ezekiel, nine from Jeremiah, but nineteen from Isaiah—more than twice as many passages from Isaiah than from either of the other two major prophets. This is due partly to the fact that the Book of Isaiah is somewhat larger than the other two major prophetic books and partly to the fact that already in ancient times, when this list of synagogue readings grew up, the Book of Isaiah was a favorite because of the message of comfort and redemption in its latter part. At all events, the people, Saturday after Saturday, year after year, heard more of Isaiah than of any other prophet.

Then about a century and a half ago, when under the influence of the Mendelssohn school and the Haskalah movement a more complete study of Scripture became popular, the new Hebrew literature which arose was almost entirely biblical in its diction. The first Haskalah writings were almost a mosaic of biblical phrases, and in those days Isaiah was clearly the favorite book. Some of the novels of that period such as those of Mapu seemed to be an echo of the language of Isaiah.

In the Christian tradition Isaiah always had a special place, owing to its messianic predictions and especially because of the chapter on the "suffering servant" which older Christian theologians refer to the founder of Christianity and his career. In modern times when Christian theological studies developed into the scientific study of Scripture, the Book of Isaiah was subjected to intense critical scrutiny. Words were emended, verses were shifted, and soon the entire book was broken up into sections, many of which were dated later than Isaiah ben Amoz. Of the sixty-six chapters of the book at least half were attributed to later authors.

Besides chapters forty through sixty-six, which all agreed were by later writers, there is substantial agreement that the following chapters or parts of chapters were not of Isaiah's authorship:

Chapters two: 2-4; four: 5-6; eleven: 10 through fourteen: 23; nineteen; twenty-one; twenty-three through twenty-seven; thirty-three through thirty-five; thirty-six through thirty-nine. (See Cornill, *Introduction to the Canonical Books of the Old Testament*, New York, 1907, page 266.)

Also there is a general consensus among critical scholars that the following chapters are to be deemed indisputably authentic: one; two: 6 through four: 1; five; six; seven through eight: 18; nine: 7 through ten: 4; ten: 5-15; seventeen: 1-11; eighteen; twenty; twenty-two; twenty-eight through thirty-one.

This extensive modern critical study is of course important to a full understanding of the book. Yet in a commentary such as this, much of this work is not directly relevant. This commentary (as are all the commentaries published by the Commission on Jewish Education) is meant to be a reader's commentary, which means of course that it is directed to the average reader, to help him in the understanding of the Book of Scripture which is commented upon. The fact that this is not meant to be a technical commentary determines the degree to which the critical studies of Isaiah are relevant to it.

The scientific commentary would be greatly concerned with the Hebrew text, the errors that have crept into it, the possible correction of these errors, and a new translation of certain verses based upon these corrections of the text. A reader's commentary, however, basically accepts the text as it is, in this case the Jewish Publication Society translation of the Prophet Isaiah. Of course this translation in itself is a sort of commentary, having been based upon a choice among the opinions of older commentators as to the meaning of each verse and perhaps, also, occasionally taking advantage of certain acceptable emendations. It is this text which is before the reader and which the commentator must try to explain. Where this English text is in itself obscure and where an emendation suggested by some scholar might clear up the obscurity, reference will be made then to this emendation of the original Hebrew text. But generally, wherever possible, and it will be possible most of the time, the text as it stands in the English will be accepted as basic.

Therefore what was usually called "lower criticism," namely emendation of the Hebrew text, is only of minor concern in a reader's commentary. But what was usually called "higher criticism" has considerably more importance. This "higher criticism" tries to date the various passages and chapters and therefore to determine which of them could not have been written by the prophet to whom they are ascribed if they were written at a later date. The attempt is then made to determine at which date the passage in question was written. The resulting stratification of the book is essential to the full understanding of it as an historical document and must be constantly dealt with in the commentary. For this purpose the commentator made use of the erudite and complete work of Otto Eissfeldt, *The Old Testament—An Introduction.*

But even this broader study of the structure of the book and the dating of its various parts is of limited use in a reader's commentary. In the first place, many of these datings and, therefore, the meanings of certain chapters are still the subject of vehement dispute among scientific biblical scholars. For example, the famous Chapter Fifty-Three, the "suffering servant," is still hotly debated. Scholars differ as to the time of its composition, and various proposals have been made and are still being made as to the identity of the "servant." Clearly, in debates such as these, the commentator must content himself with the majority of present opinion whenever there is such a majority.

Besides, even when certain datings of certain chapters have been fairly well agreed upon, the stratification of the book is not of primary concern in a reader's commentary. This is not an essay on Isaiah ben Amoz and therefore we are concerned only with what can be scientifically authenticated as his own writing. It is a commentary on the whole Book of Isaiah as it has come down to us and has been part of Jewish life, worship, and study for over two thousand years. When a book is twenty centuries old, it is meaningless to derogate parts of it as "inauthentic." To those who have loved and love the book, it is not of too great moment that a certain chapter was written, not twenty-seven hundred years ago, but only twenty-five hundred years ago. The unknown writer who wrote a certain "inauthentic" chapter twenty-five hundred years ago is also an important contributor to biblical literature. G. Buchanan Gray, the author of the commentary in the *International Critical Commentary* on the first part of this book, speaks of the value of these nameless authors of the "inauthentic" passages. He says on page xi of his preface: "But there is yet another [task]: and that is to do justice to other contributors to the book and above all to approach with sympathy the work of, perhaps, many nameless writers that now form so large a part of it. No full justice can be done to a book which is a great monument of Jewish religion after the Exile if all our attention is devoted to determining whether this or that passage is 'genuine' and dismissing it as not 'genuine' if it is not the work of Isaiah. In reference to work such as the Book of Isaiah, the term 'genuine' is indeed misleading. None of these nameless writers may have possessed the religious genius of Isaiah, but together they represent the play of the earlier prophetic teaching on the Jewish church." (See also Eissfeldt, p. 318.)

For the average reader the critical dating and rearranging and the occasional emendation of the text are of importance only as they are of help in the understanding of the passage involved. But it is the entire book as it has come down to us, with all its various strata, which has achieved its unique status for readers of the Bible.

For this reason the classic (ancient and medieval) commentaries have a special value. They present the historic Jewish reaction to the Book of Isaiah. Thus the basic part of this book will consist of the opinions and reactions of the historic commentaries—The Targum (third-century Aramaic translation), the Talmud, Rashi (of twelfth-century northern France), Ibn Ezra (Rashi's contemporary itinerant Spanish commentator), David Kimchi (of thirteenth-century Provence), the Malbim (much read Orthodox commentator of the last century; Malbim is the acronym from the initials of his name, Meir Lebush ben Yehiel Michel), Arnold Ehrlich (Randglossen), Samuel Krauss (contemporary Jewish scholar), Tur Sinai (Torczyner) and Menahem Haran (two modern Israeli scholars).

It is hoped that the Christian scholars may find this book of value precisely for the reason that it presents the comment of all the chief Jewish commentators. The various opinions of Jewish commentators to the Book of Isaiah through the ages will, in a sense, serve as a reflection of the spirit of Judaism and the psychology of the Jewish people. If, for example, a certain verse refers to a happier time, each of the classical commentators may define the happiness in a different way. Rashi might say that the verse means that the people will cast away its sins and rejoice in the Lord; Ibn Ezra might say that the verse refers to the joy over the miraculous victory over the invading Assyrian army; Kimchi might say that the achievement is the blessedness of the messianic day when evil and violence will vanish from the earth. These three different reactions would reveal three leading moods in Judaism: moral responsibility, confidence in God's protection in history, and the conviction of the coming of an age of righteousness and peace. In this way the marshaling of the classic Jewish commentators displays the spectrum of Jewish thought and feeling. Perhaps we might say that the purpose of this commentary is to record the ongoing dialogue between the Book of Isaiah and the people of Israel.

The Prophet Isaiah

VERY LITTLE is known specifically about the career of the Prophet Isaiah ben Amoz. However, certain facts and certain dates become clear. Isaiah was married; he calls his wife "the prophetess." (Isaiah 8:3) Whether or not she was a prophet cannot be known; perhaps he merely meant, "the prophet's wife." He had, at least, two sons (7:3, 8:3) to both of whom he gave symbolic names prophesying the future events of the nation's history. There is a tradition in the Talmud (Megillah 10b) that his father Amoz was the brother of King Amaziah, the father of King Uzziah, at the end of whose reign Isaiah's prophecy began. Whether or not the talmudic statement is factual, it is nevertheless apparent that he was a man of honored social status. This is evident in a number of ways. When he comes before King Ahaz, no one challenges his right to be present. He speaks to the king boldly. When he writes the scroll of prophecy, he calls Uriah, the priest, and Zechariah as the two witnesses. He could call for the cooperation of the leading men of the kingdom. Finally, though he preached often in a tone of bitter denunciation, he was never molested (as far as we know) as Jeremiah was. Apparently he was well known and respected at court.

His career stretched over the reign of four kings, Uzziah, Jotham, Ahaz, and Hezekiah. Generally the dates of his active career are thought to be from 746 B.C.E. to 701 B.C.E., namely for forty-five years. This period was a time of great historical disturbance. The first event which he records was the siege of Jerusalem by an alliance of Syria and the Northern Kingdom (Syro-Ephramitic war). Then there came the rebellion of the Northern Kingdom against the Assyrian king, Shalmanezzar, and the destruction of the Northern Kingdom by Sargon in 722 B.C.E. King Hezekiah's attempt to make various foreign alliances to protect himself against the Assyrians and the alliance was smashed by the capture of Ashdod by Sargon. And there was the siege of Jerusalem by the Assyrians under Sennacherib in 701 B.C.E. It was in these eventful years that this child of Jerusalem preached his message against the policies of his own kings and the character and life style of the nobility.

The Message of Isaiah

ISAIAH had a firm confidence in the validity of his prophetic mission. He spoke with the conviction that it was God's word which he was bringing to his people. Amos, who was an earlier contemporary and the first of the literary prophets, disclaimed the status of the prophet. He said: "I was no prophet . . . but I was a herdsman and the Lord took me from following the flock and said to me, Go prophesy unto My people Israel." (Amos 7:14-15) So, too, Jeremiah, when the call to prophecy came to him, said: "Lord God, behold I cannot speak for I am a child, and the Lord said to me, Say not: I am a child. Whatsoever I command thee, thou shalt speak." (Jeremiah 1:6) But there was no such hesitation or self-doubt with Isaiah. When he heard the words of the Lord: "Whom shall I send?" and "Who will go for us?" he answered at once, forthrightly, "Here am I. Send me." (Isaiah 6:8) This forthrightness characterizes all his prophecies. He spoke to the people and directly to the king, and always without hesitation. For that reason his message is clear and can be summarized without too much difficulty.

His concept of God was broad and deep. God is constantly referred to as "Holy," demanding a holiness of ethical living from all His children; and that to Isaiah meant that all humanity had the duty of righteousness because the Holy God was a Universal Presence. "Holy, holy, holy, is the Lord of hosts; the whole earth is full of His glory." (6:3) History is the area where God's holiness works in the actions of peoples: "He will lift up an ensign to nations from afar." (5:6) "O Asshur, rod of Mine anger, I send him against an ungodly people." (10:6f.)

Yet, although all the nations are part of God's plan of worldwide holiness and righteousness, the people of Israel owes God a special obligation for it was the first trained by Him to know Him and to live according to His laws. Israel is described thus: "Children have I reared and brought up, and they have rebelled against Me." (1:2) Or, in Chapter 5, Israel is described as God's vineyard, carefully prepared and protected. Since Israel was especially nurtured and the first to know God and His holy way, its sins are especially grievous and deserve greater punishment. It is to be the voice of God's rebuke to Israel, His rebellious child, that Isaiah visualizes as his essential function as a prophet.

The sins which Israel has committed are clearly stated and frequently reemphasized. First there is the sin of the relapse into idolatry. The prophet looks forward to the time when the training will be successful "and the idols shall utterly pass away." (2:18) This message emphasized by Isaiah's older contemporary Hosea in the Northern Kingdom of Israel is heard in the words of all the preexilic prophets and is the one lesson that was completely successful, because after the Exile all idolatry passed away from Israel and was rarely heard of again.

But this general prophetic campaign against idolatry is not the central message of Isaiah. To him the chief evidence of Israel's treachery to God is not in the field of worship primarily but in the field of social justice. The injustices which he denounces are primarily those of the upper ruling classes who oppress the poor through perverting the processes of law: "What mean ye, that ye crush My people and grind the face of the poor?" (3:15) "Seek justice, relieve the oppressed, judge the fatherless, and plead for the widow." (1:17) He denounces the riotous living of the oppressors: "Woe to the crown of pride of the drunkards of Ephraim" (28:1) and also the luxurious living of the women of the upper classes: "Moreover, the Lord said, Because the daughters of Zion are haughty ... therefore the Lord will smite...." (3:16 ff.)

Callousness and self-indulgence make the religious observances a mockery. Even when the people do not relapse into idolatry and do worship God, their worship is unacceptable. God says: "I delight not in the blood of bullocks.... It is an offering of abomination to Me." (1:11-13) "When ye make many prayers, I will not hear. Your hands are full of blood." (1:20) "When ye come to appear before Me, who hath required this, at your hand to trample My courts?" (1:12) Such ritual, lacking foundation in moral and righteous living, is a mockery, a ceremonial learned by rote which does not reach the heart of the worshiper nor can be pleasing to God: "With their mouth and with their lips do they honor Me, but have removed their heart far from Me, and their fear of Me is a commandment of men learned by rote." (29:13)

There is only one way in which worship can become meaningful, when it is based upon the earnest effort to live according to the moral mandate of the Holy God: "Put away the evil of your doings from before Mine eyes. Learn to do well; seek justice, relieve the oppressed." (1:16-17)

But although Isaiah is confident of the rightness of his message, he is not confident of its immediate efficacy. The habits of evil are too deeply ingrained and the profits of oppression too precious to be given up. The people will remain deaf to the stern preachment calling for justice. He feels that their insensitivity was foretold by God: "Make the heart of this people fat. Make their ears heavy and shut their eyes" (6:10) and he himself says scornfully to the leaders whom he is denouncing: "Stupefy yourselves and be stupid! . . . Ye that are drunken but not [only] with wine." (29:9)

He knows that his preaching will not penetrate into their conscience. God's recreant children must be cleansed in some other way. Only a national calamity will shock them sufficiently to change their lives. So Isaiah becomes a prophet of doom and says that the vineyard of the Lord shall now be laid waste: "I will tell you what I will do to my vineyard. I will break down the fence thereof and it shall be trodden down." (5:5) The invading armies of Assyria will be God's instrument to punish His people. Yet God's training of these His children will not be entirely wasted. A remnant will survive and rebuild the land in accordance with God's law of righteousness: "A remnant shall return . . . unto God the mighty." (10:21) A new society will be built, "a foundation." (28:16) "Justice the measuring line and righteousness the plummet." (28:17) "Zion shall be redeemed with justice." (1:27)

But in the meantime the tiny state of Judah is surrounded by enemies. Until the time for the fulfillment of God's stern purpose comes, the nation must somehow endure and live through these dangerous times. Therefore Isaiah, besides his ultimate vision of a remnant restoring an era of righteousness, has a definite international policy for the dangerous present. This policy is the subject of his advice to king and people. When Pekah of the northern people allied himself to Rezin, king of Damascus, to destroy Jerusalem, the advice of Isaiah to King Ahaz was, "Keep calm and be quiet. Fear not, neither let thy heart be faint." (7:3) And so again: "In quietness and confidence shall be your strength." (30:15) Isaiah was opposed to all alliances with one or the other of the foreign powers and called upon the king and the court to rely upon the working out of God's plan, when "Zion shall be redeemed with justice." (1:27)

1

A COMPLETE SERMON, beginning with rebuke and ending with consolation, the first chapter is Isaiah's analysis of the relationship of Israel to God revealing the essential prophetic ideas. God's children have rebelled against Him (Verse 2); their sin is social injustice, chiefly the perversion of justice. (Verses 21, 22) Because of injustice, their worship has become meaningless. (Verses 11-15) Suffering has therefore come to the once holy city; the whole country is now devastated by the invader. Jerusalem is isolated and lonely. (Verses 7, 8) The people and their leaders have as yet failed to learn a lesson from their suffering and have not yet repented. Therefore learn to do justice, says the prophet; God will help you cleanse the city of evil. Zion "shall be redeemed with justice." "They that forsake the Lord shall be consumed."

1. The vision of Isaiah the son of Amoz, which he saw concerning Judah and Jerusalem, in the days of Uzziah, Jotham, Ahaz, and Hezekiah, kings of Judah.

Isaiah 1

1 : 1 *The vision of Isaiah the son of Amoz.* This opening verse of the book presented difficulties to almost every traditional commentator. Rashi comments on the words, "concerning Judah and Jerusalem." Since Isaiah also preached sermons against many other nations this can hardly be the heading for the entire book.

15

Isaiah

1

2. Hear, O heavens, and give ear, O earth,
    For the LORD hath spoken:
    Children I have reared, and brought up,
    And they have rebelled against Me.
3. The ox knoweth his owner,
    And the ass his master's crib;
    But Israel doth not know,

In fact, he says (and modern scholars agree) that this actually is not the opening chapter of the book. The opening chapter is Chapter 6, in which Isaiah describes the beginning of his career as a prophet. But Rashi then says, following the talmudic statement, that the chapters are not necessarily given in order. ("There is no earlier and later in Scripture," Pesachim 6b.) Ibn Ezra explains (and Elijah of Vilna agrees) that the heading simply means that the greater part of his prophecies concern Judah and Jerusalem. The Malbim says that Isaiah preached his sermon first in the time of the King Uzziah but repeated it in the reigns of the other kings who followed Uzziah.

Uzziah, Jotham, Ahaz, and Hezekiah. As to this list of four kings, Rashi quotes the Talmud (Pesachim 87b) that every prophet survived four kings. The statement is based upon this verse in Isaiah.

1 : 2 *Hear, O heavens, and give ear, O earth.* Rashi calls attention to the fact that Moses in Deuteronomy 24:2 reverses the order of the verbs and says, "Give ear, O heavens, and hear, O earth." He refers to the fact that the rabbis have made many homiletic explanations of this difference. But Ibn Ezra calmly says that there is really no substantial difference between "give ear" and "listen."

Children I have reared . . . they have rebelled. The traditional Aramaic translation, the Targum, is always concerned with explaining away any word or phrase in the biblical text which attributes human form or human emotions to God. Therefore he translates "children I have reared" as follows: "I have called them (i.e., instead of reared) My beloved children, yet they rebelled against Me." Kimchi gives an historical proof for the correctness of Isaiah's indictment by calling attention to the report in II Chronicles 27:2 and 28:1 ff., where a factual description is given of the corruption and idolatry of the people of Israel

My people doth not consider.
4. Ah sinful nation,
   A people laden with iniquity,
   A seed of evil-doers,
   Children that deal corruptly;
   They have forsaken the LORD,
   They have contemned the Holy One of Israel,
   They are turned away backward.

Isaiah

1

during the reigns of the kings mentioned in Verse 1 of this chapter.

For the Lord hath spoken. Ibn Ezra says that this phrase means that the prophet is telling the people, "What I am saying to you is not my own invention, but God it is Who has spoken to me and speaks these words to me." (See also Altschuler, *Mezudas David*.)

1 : 3 *The ox knoweth his owner and the ass his master's crib.* Rashi: These animals obey without complaint. Kimchi: These domestic animals know well who is kind to them. They do their work and return to their crib. Ibn Ezra says Isaiah mentions the two animals who are in constant contact with man and says that the people who know these animals must realize that in their own characters they are inferior to the cattle. Samuel Krauss says that these animals are mentioned because they are the ones that were known best in ancient Palestine.

My people doth not consider. The Hebrew simply says, "My people does not know." Therefore Rashi finds it necessary to say, "My people does not wish to know; it does not try to understand." The Gaon of Vilna said that the people may not know anything of God's promise of a future life but at least they ought to know what even the animals know—the benefits of goodness in this world.

1 : 4 *Ah sinful nation.* The Targum paraphrases, "Alas, the people that once was called a holy nation is now called sinful."

A seed of evil-doers. The obvious meaning of this verse is unacceptable to the commentators, for why should the fathers be called corrupt? Are they not called in Isaiah 61:9 "the seed blessed by the Lord"? Therefore both Rashi and Kimchi say that this is not meant to be a deprecation of their parents. Krauss says that the phrase, "seed of evil-doers," is simply parallel to the

Isaiah
1

5. On what part will ye be yet stricken,
   Seeing ye stray away more and more?
   The whole head is sick,
   And the whole heart faint;
6. From the sole of the foot even unto the head
   There is no soundness in it;
   But wounds, and bruises, and festering sores:
   They have not been pressed, neither bound up,
   Neither mollified with oil.
7. Your country is desolate;
   Your cities are burned with fire;

following phrase, "children that deal corruptly." In other words, it does not mean children of evil parents but the children who do evil. But Ibn Ezra says simply that they and also their fathers were indeed wicked.

Turned away backward. The Malbim says it is not merely that they have abandoned God; they could have done that and merely remained irreligious. But they did worse; they abandoned God and turned back to the old idolatries.

The Holy One of Israel. Luzzato (quoted by Krauss) says that this description of God is a favorite one of Isaiah. It is used thirty times in the book.

1 : 5 *On what part will ye be yet stricken?* The Hebrew permits the translation, "Why should you be stricken further?" It is to this translation that most of the traditional commentators react. Rashi says it means, "What is the use of smiting you further? You have already been greatly afflicted and yet you have not learned a lesson." Kimchi likewise says, "Do not ask why you are smitten. Did not Moses already explain that because of your sins 'God will smite you with madness and blindness' "? (Deuteronomy 28:28) The Targum takes the word "yet" ("od") to go with the following phrase and translates the verse as follows: "You do not ask why you are smitten, but [od] you continue to do evil." Ibn Ezra's explanation comes closer to our English translation. He takes the verse to mean, "What is the use of smiting you further? The more you are smitten, the more you will revolt. Logically you should repent, but you do not."

1 : 6 *From the sole of the foot even unto the head.* Kimchi

Your land, strangers devour it in your presence,
And it is desolate, as overthrown by floods.
8. And the daughter of Zion is left
As a booth in a vineyard,
As a lodge in a garden of cucumbers,
As a besieged city.
9. Except the LORD of hosts
Had left unto us a very small remnant,
We should have been as Sodom,
We should have been like unto Gomorrah.

Isaiah

1

again, as in the preceding verse, recalls that the anathema given in the Torah, describing how God will punish them, uses virtually the same languge as Isaiah uses here: "The Lord will smite thee from the sole of thy foot unto the crown of thy head." (Deuteronomy 28:25) Elijah of Vilna quotes the Zohar in which the various levels of leadership in a community are compared to the various parts of the human body; the chief of the community with the head and, finally, the police officers with the feet. Therefore, he says, the prophet here in saying "from the sole of the foot..." "there is no soundness" can mean that the entire establishment of the community, from top to bottom, is corrupt.

1:7 *Your land ... is desolate, as overthrown by floods.* Kimchi again shows a parallel with an anathema in the Torah, this time in Leviticus 26:33: "And your land shall be desolate."

1:8 *A booth in a vineyard.* The Targum gives an explanation which most of the commentators follow. The booths in the vineyard are empty after the harvest has been gathered. Rashi then says, "The city will thus be empty and the people gone away to exile." Both Kimchi and Ibn Ezra emphasize not the emptiness of the harvest booth after the harvest but its loneliness. The Assyrians, says Kimchi, in the time of King Hezekiah, destroyed every city in the land except Jerusalem. Therefore, both commentators say, "The city stood lonely like an abandoned harvest booth with no other houses near it."

1:9 *Except the Lord ... had left unto us a small remnant.* Ibn Ezra explains that here the people of Israel is speaking. Rashi following the Targum says, "God in His kindness, and not for our merit, has left us a remnant."

Isaiah
1

10. Hear the word of the LORD,
    Ye rulers of Sodom;
    Give ear unto the law of our God,
    Ye people of Gomorrah.
11. To what purpose is the multitude of your sacrifices unto Me?
    Saith the LORD;
    I am full of the burnt-offerings of rams,
    And the fat of fed beasts;
    And I delight not in the blood
    Of bullocks, or of lambs, or of he-goats.
12. When ye come to appear before Me,
    Who hath required this at your hand,
    To trample My courts?
13. Bring no more vain oblations;
    It is an offering of abomination unto Me;
    New moon and sabbath, the holding of convocations—

1:10 *Ye rulers of Sodom ... people of Gomorrah.* The people in the preceding verse feared that they might have been left completely desolate like the cities of Sodom and Gomorrah. Therefore, here, the prophet actually calls them the people of those evil cities. Ibn Ezra says the prophet by calling them people of Sodom means to say, "If you were completely overthrown as those two cities were, you would have well deserved it, since you act like the people of those two cities."

1:11 *To what purpose is the multitude of your sacrifices unto Me?* Rashi reminds us of the verse, "The sacrifices of the wicked are an abomination." (Proverbs 21:27) Kimchi says, "I commanded you to bring sacrifices only that you may express your thanks unto Me, and not sin; but now that you are sinful, I despise the sacrifices." So the Malbim says, "It is the law of Moses that sacrifices cannot atone for any sin unless they are accompanied with repentance and sincere regret." Ibn Ezra paraphrases the dialogue between God and the people as follows: "Why should I leave you here any longer to inhabit the land? Is it for the sake of the sacrifices that you might bring? I do not need them." Krauss calls attention to the fact that it is a classic

I cannot endure iniquity along with the solemn assembly.
14. Your new moons and your appointed seasons
My soul hateth;
They are a burden unto Me;
I am weary to bear them.
15. And when ye spread forth your hands,
I will hide Mine eyes from you;
Yea, when ye make many prayers,
I will not hear;
Your hands are full of blood.
16. Wash you, make you clean,
Put away the evil of your doings
From before Mine eyes,
Cease to do evil;

Isaiah 1

prophetic theme that sacrifices without sincerity and righteousness are an abomination. (See I Samuel 15:27, Hosea 6:7, Amos 5:21, Jeremiah 7:21, Micah 6:7.)

1:12 *To trample My courts?* Kimchi refers to the fact that they were required to come to the Temple courts on the three pilgrimage festivals: "Three times in the year shall all thy males appear before the Lord God. (Exodus 34:23) But now you have sinned, your presence brings only shame." He also calls attention to the fact that the prophet uses the word "courts." This refers to the outer court, where the people were permitted to come. The inner section of the Temple, the Hechal, was only for the priests. The Malbim stresses the word "trample" and says, "Since you are not fulfilling My commandments, all you are doing on your pilgrimage is just trampling the sacred court."

1:15 *And when ye spread forth your hands.* The Targum refers this verse to the priests who spread their hands in blessing the people and translates the verse as follows: "When the priests spread their hands to bless you, I will remove the Divine Presence from you; and, when you yourself pray, I will not receive your prayers. Your hands are full of the blood of the innocent." Kimchi calls to mind the talmudic rule (Berachot 32b) that is based upon this verse, namely, that no priest who has committed murder shall be permitted to bless the people.

Isaiah 1

17. Learn to do well;
    Seek justice, relieve the oppressed,
    Judge the fatherless, plead for the widow.
18. Come now, and let us reason together,
    Saith the LORD;
    Though your sins be as scarlet,
    They shall be as white as snow;
    Though they be red like crimson,
    They shall be as wool.
19. If ye be willing and obedient,
    Ye shall eat the good of the land;
20. But if ye refuse and rebel,
    Ye shall be devoured with the sword;
    For the mouth of the LORD hath spoken.
21. How is the faithful city
    Become a harlot!

1 : 18 *Come now, and let us reason together.* The Targum translated, "When you return to My law, you will plead before Me and I will answer you, that your sins will be forgiven." Rashi says, "God says, 'Even if you have sinned, I will give you hope of repentance.'" Kimchi says, "Come let us reason" depicts a case heard in court. "God will tell of His kindness and of your ingratitude. Then you will repent; and though your sins be as scarlet..." Ibn Ezra does not think that it is God speaking here but it is the prophet and the people who are included in the word "us," because the prophet as well as the people must repent, since Moses said, "God will forgive *our* sins." (Exodus 34:9) Ibn Ezra also calls attention to the fact that Isaiah's promise that "the scarlet sins will become whiter than snow" is the opposite of what Jeremiah said: "For though thou wash thee and take much soap, yet thine iniquity is marked before me." (2:22)

1 : 19 *Ye shall eat the good of the land.* Ibn Ezra: This is in contrast to the condition in Verse 7, "Your land, strangers devour it." So, also, Kimchi.

1 : 20 *Ye shall be devoured with the sword ... the Lord hath spoken.* Since this is in the past tense, Rashi tells where God had spoken and said, "devoured with the sword." He calls attention to the anathema in Leviticus 26:25: "And I shall bring the sword against you." Ibn Ezra and Kimchi say that the words

> She that was full of justice,
> Righteousness lodged in her,
> But now murderers.
> 22. Thy silver is become dross,
> Thy wine mixed with water.
> 23. Thy princes are rebellious,
> And companions of thieves;
> Every one loveth bribes,
> And followeth after rewards;
> They judge not the fatherless,
> Neither doth the cause of the widow come unto them.
> 24. Therefore saith the Lord, the LORD of hosts,
> The Mighty One of Israel:
> Ah, I will ease Me of Mine adversaries,
> And avenge Me of Mine enemies;

Isaiah
1

"God hath spoken" simply mean that they can be certain the words will be fulfilled.

1 : 21 *Become a harlot!* Krauss calls attention to the parallel thought in the Prophet Hosea, who compares Israel's apostasy from God to harlotry.

Righteousness lodged in her. The word "lodged" means "overnight." Rashi says that in every trial involving capital punishment the case was always postponed overnight, in the hope that, before the court reconvened in the morning, some new defense might perhaps be found for the accused. Kimchi, however, does not take the word as meaning specifically, "overnight," but takes it to mean "permanence"; thus the prophet says, "Once righteousness was a permanent and unswerving element in the city of Jerusalem."

1 : 22 *Silver is become dross.* Both Rashi and Kimchi take this to mean cheating in business. The coins are debased and commodities are inferior. But Ibn Ezra connects this with the next verse, "Thy princes love bribes," and takes the phrase to mean, "Thy silver is used to debase morality."

1 : 24 *I will ease Me of Mine adversaries.* The Targum and all the commentators say it means that God will, as it were, feel relieved when He will have punished the evil men. The Malbim comments on the words, "Mine adversaries," and says, "Those

Isaiah 1

25. And I will turn My hand upon thee,
And purge away thy dross as with lye,
And will take away all thine alloy;
26. And I will restore thy judges as at the first,
And thy counsellors as at the beginning;
Afterward thou shalt be called The city of righteousness,
The faithful city.
27. Zion shall be redeemed with justice,
And they that return of her with righteousness.
28. But the destruction of the transgressors and the sinners shall be together,
And they that forsake the LORD shall be consumed.

who are hostile to their fellow man are considered by God as hostile to Him."

1 : 26 *I will restore thy judges as at the first.* The Targum says, "I will appoint righteous judges, as in the past, and you will become a righteous city again." Kimchi, as he frequently does, ascribes this verse to the messianic times when there will be no wickedness left on earth. Ibn Ezra, who avoids special mention of messianic times, says more prosaically, "When the evil influence of the Northern Kingdom will cease to corrupt you, I will appoint righteous judges, 'as at first,' i.e., as in the days of David and Solomon."

1 : 27 *Zion shall be redeemed with justice and they that return of her with righteousness.* "They that return" is interpreted in two ways. Rashi and Ibn Ezra say it means, "They who return to God," i.e., the penitents. Kimchi and later Malbim say it

29. For they shall be ashamed of the terebinths which ye have desired,
    And ye shall be confounded for the gardens that ye have chosen.
30. For ye shall be as a terebinth whose leaf fadeth,
    And as a garden that hath no water.
31. And the strong shall be as tow,
    And his work as a spark;
    And they shall both burn together,
    And none shall quench them.

Isaiah
1

means, when the exiles return, the city will be a righteous city and Zion will be redeemed.

1 : 28 *The destruction of the transgressors.* The evil-doers will be destroyed. The metaphor of wickedness burnt up like stubble is repeated in the Prophet Malachi: "All that work wickedness shall be stubble." (3:19)

1 : 29 *Gardens that ye have chosen.* The next three verses describe the destruction of the wicked, although Kimchi says "they shall burn" in Verse 31 refers not to the destruction of the wicked but to the burning up of the idols; in spite of the idol-maker who seeks for indestructible wood, as in Isaiah 40:20: "He chooseth a tree that will not rot." Ibn Ezra gives the same explanation.

In general in these three verses describing the destruction of evil, Kimchi, as mentioned above (as he frequently does), says that this cannot refer to the period after the Exile nor specifically to the cessation of idolatry (because idolatry virtually ceased in Israel after the Exile), but it refers to the complete cessation of wickedness everywhere in the messianic days.

2

CHAPTER 2 BEGINS with the same magnificent vision found also in Micah that in "the end of days" wars will cease and the world will be at peace, "beating their swords into plowshares." This great vision is considered by most modern scholars as not original with Isaiah. According to Eissfeldt (p. 318) it is postexilic, but some scholars believe that it was written earlier. Their argument is that since it is virtually the same passage as is found in Micah (4:1–4) both prophets took it from some earlier source. (So, also, Krauss.) At all events, the chapter begins with a radiant vision.

The rest of the chapter denounces the people for the second sin of which they are guilty; the first, as mentioned in the earlier chapter, is the social injustice due to the perversion of the law. Here the sin is idolatry. Time and again the kings, the priests, and the common people have reverted from the worship of God to idolatry, its superstitions, and corruptions. The prophet denounces this (Verse 8) and the chapter ends with the coming of God's day of retribution with the people hiding in terror for the punishment that is bound to come. In the popular mind "the Day of the Lord" was a day to be anticipated with hope, as the day when the Lord will deliver Israel from its enemies. The Prophet Amos (5:18) was the first to give this popular term a new and an ominous meaning. He said: "Woe unto you that desire the day of the Lord! Wherefore would ye have the day of the Lord? It is darkness, and not light." Isaiah uses the term here in the same ominous sense.

1. The word that Isaiah the son of Amoz saw concerning Judah and Jerusalem.
2. And it shall come to pass in the end of days,
   That the mountain of the LORD's house shall be established as the top of the mountains,
   And shall be exalted above the hills;
   And all nations shall flow unto it.
3. And many peoples shall go and say:
   'Come ye, and let us go up to the mountain of the LORD,
   To the house of the God of Jacob;
   And He will teach us of His ways,
   And we will walk in His paths.'
   For out of Zion shall go forth the law,
   And the word of the LORD from Jerusalem.
4. And He shall judge between the nations,
   And shall decide for many peoples;
   And they shall beat their swords into plowshares,
   And their spears into pruning-hooks;
   Nation shall not lift up sword against nation,
   Neither shall they learn war any more.

Isaiah 2

2 : 1-4 *The end of days . . . mountain of the Lord's house . . . spears into pruning-hooks.* Kimchi makes the general comment that the prophet, having denounced the people, begins now to give them his consolation. As for the phrase, "end of days," Kimchi (as is his usual preference) says that this means the messianic times, when all evils shall cease. Ibn Ezra agrees with Kimchi because here the passage cannot mean the return from the Exile, an explanation which he usually prefers for such predictions; because, he says, as we learn from Josephus (he uses the family name "Ben Gurion" for Josephus) wars had not ceased during the period after the return from Babylon. Therefore this description of a warless world must refer to messianic days. Rashi explains the phrase, "the mountain shall be established as the top of the mountains," as meaning that Mount Moriah where the Temple will stand will be honored by all the world; and Kimchi adds, "More than all the other mountains upon which the nations had built their idolatrous temples."

Isaiah 2

5. O house of Jacob, come ye, and let us walk
   In the light of the Lord.
6. For Thou hast forsaken Thy people the house of Jacob;
   For they are replenished from the east,
   And with soothsayers like the Philistines,
   And they please themselves in the brood of aliens.
7. Their land also is full of silver and gold,
   Neither is there any end of their treasures;
   Their land also is full of horses,
   Neither is there any end of their chariots.
8. Their land also is full of idols;
   Every one worshippeth the work of his own hands,
   That which his own fingers have made.
9. And man boweth down,
   And man lowereth himself;
   And Thou canst not bear with them.
10. Enter into the rock,
    And hide thee in the dust,

2 : 5 *O house of Jacob . . . let us walk.* Rashi says that this is what the other nations will say to Israel: "Come with us to the mountain of the Lord." But Kimchi and Ibn Ezra agree that it is the prophet who is saying this to Israel. Kimchi says the prophet means: Since all the nations will come to worship God, you should be the first to do so. Ibn Ezra calls attention to the plural, "Let us go," and says that the prophet includes himself among those who need to repent as Moses said of himself, together with the people: "Forgive our iniquities." (Exodus 34:9)

2 : 6 *Thou hast forsaken Thy people . . . they are replenished . . . with soothsayers . . . aliens.* Most of the commentators take this to mean simply that God has forsaken His people Israel because of its superstitions and witchcraft; but the Malbim emphasizes the words of the text, "They please themselves in the brood of aliens," that is to say, they have union with pagan women, and the children, following the status of the mother, are therefore pagan. Hence, he says, that the text refers not to God but to the people and means: "Thou, O Jacob, hast abandoned thy people."

From before the terror of the Lord,
And from the glory of His majesty.
11. The lofty looks of man shall be brought low,
And the haughtiness of men shall be bowed down,
And the Lord alone shall be exalted in that day.
12. For the Lord of hosts hath a day
Upon all that is proud and lofty,
And upon all that is lifted up, and it shall be brought low;
13. And upon all the cedars of Lebanon
That are high and lifted up,
And upon all the oaks of Bashan;
14. And upon all the high mountains,
And upon all the hills that are lifted up;
15. And upon every lofty tower,
And upon every fortified wall;
16. And upon all the ships of Tarshish,
And upon all delightful imagery.
17. And the loftiness of man shall be bowed down,
And the haughtiness of men shall be brought low;
And the Lord alone shall be exalted in that day.
18. And the idols shall utterly pass away.

Isaiah 2

2:9 *Thou canst not bear with them.* The usual translation is that God cannot forgive them or endure them. But Krauss quotes Ehrlich, who says that the Hebrew verb here means, "They cannot be lifted up again."

2:10 *Enter into the rock.* This is what the people will say to each other in those days of punishment, "Let us hide." (Kimchi and Ibn Ezra)

2:11 *Lofty looks.* Haughty pride. The idea is expressed also in Psalm 101:5: "Haughty of eye and proud of heart."

2:14 *The high mountains.* Rashi explains that God's punishment will be directed against those who live on the high mountains. Malbim elaborates on this explanation and says it refers to those rich and powerful who build their houses on mountaintops and imagine they are secure.

2:18 *Idols shall utterly pass away.* Kimchi, with his usual messianism, says, "Although the people among whom we live (i.e., Christians and Moslems) are not idolators, there is still idol

Isaiah 2

19. And men shall go into the caves of the rocks,
    And into the holes of the earth,
    From before the terror of the Lord
    And from the glory of His majesty,
    When He ariseth to shake mightily the earth.
20. In that day a man shall cast away
    His idols of silver, and his idols of gold,
    Which they made for themselves to worship,
    To the moles and to the bats;
21. To go into the clefts of the rocks,
    And into the crevices of the crags,
    From before the terror of the Lord,
    And from the glory of His majesty,
    When He ariseth to shake mightily the earth.
22. Cease ye from man, in whose nostrils is a breath;
    For how little is he to be accounted!

worship in the Orient. In Messiah's time, all the idol worship will cease."

2 : 19 *Men shall go into the caves.* On the day of judgment men shall seek to hide.

2 : 22 *Cease ye from man.* Krauss calls attention to the fact that in the ancient Greek translation, the Septuagint, this verse is not found. Besides it has no clear connection with the rest of the passage. Therefore it is a later addition to the words of the prophet.

However, the traditional commentators, with the verse before them, endeavor to establish connection between this verse and the passage which speaks of the destruction of idolatry. Rashi says it means, "Do not listen to the idolators." Kimchi in his usual messianic mood says it means, "Cease being afraid of man; there will come a day when there will be no more violence." Ibn Ezra explains it as follows: Cease appealing to mortal man. God's decree cannot be changed.

3

THE SIN denounced here is, again, social injustice: "Ye grind the face of the poor." (Verse 15) The money exacted unjustly from the poor enables the upper classes to live in ostentatious luxury. The end of the chapter describes in detail all the ornaments of the pampered rich women of Jerusalem. As punishment for this the whole social order will be upturned, the young will behave insolently to the aged (Verse 3), responsibility and moral leadership will cease. (Verse 7)

> 1. For, behold, the LORD, the LORD of hosts,
> Doth take away from Jerusalem and from Judah
> Stay and staff,
> Every stay of bread, and every stay of water;
> 2. The mighty man, and the man of war;
> The judge, and the prophet,
> And the diviner, and the elder;

Isaiah 3

3:1 *The Lord ... doth take away ... stay and staff.* Verses 1 to 5 are a list of punishments that God will send. Rashi, quoting the Talmud (Chagigah 14a), says that these curses mount up to a climax, the worst of all of them being: "The child shall behave insolently against the aged." (Verse 5) The contempt and the hostility of the young generation against the older is deemed by the prophet and the Talmud to be the worst curse that can come to a society.

31

Isaiah 3

3. The captain of fifty, and the man of rank,
   And the counsellor, and the cunning charmer, and the skilful enchanter.
4. And I will give children to be their princes,
   And babes shall rule over them.
5. And the people shall oppress one another,
   Every man his fellow, and every man his neighbour;
   The child shall behave insolently against the aged,
   And the base against the honourable.
6. For a man shall take hold of his brother of the house of his father:
   'Thou hast a mantle,
   Be thou our ruler,
   And let this ruin be under thy hand.'

3 : 3 *The skilful enchanter.* Ibn Ezra suggests that this may refer not only to a magician but to a clever orator, as we would say today, a spellbinder.

3 : 4 *And babes shall rule over them.* The word translated "babes" (taalulim) is variously interpreted by the commentators. The Targum says, "You will be governed by weaklings." Rashi takes the word to mean "mockers." The people will have so little respect for their leaders that there will be a general air of cynicism. Kimchi says it means the young since, as stated in the previous verses, the older leaders will all be killed in war and famine. The Malbim agrees that it means young but indicates that the word itself implies impulsiveness. In other words, "You will be governed by the young, who themselves will be motivated by wild impulses." Krauss offers a similar explanation: "You will be governed by youth, who will rule you with violence."

3 : 5 *The people shall oppress one another.* Kimchi elaborates and says that the people will scorn and fight each other; there will be no mutual respect.

3 : 6 *Thou hast a mantle.* Rashi bases his comment on the Talmud (Sabbath 119b) in which knowledge of the law is compared to a garment, and therefore he says the verse means, "You have learning, so become our ruler." Kimchi says it means, "You look respectable; be our ruler." Ibn Ezra says, "We do not want anything from you; keep your clothes, just rule us."

7. In that day shall he swear, saying:
   'I will not be a healer;
   For in my house is neither bread nor a mantle;
   Ye shall not make me ruler of a people.'
8. For Jerusalem is ruined,
   And Judah is fallen;
   Because their tongue and their doings are against the LORD,
   To provoke the eyes of His glory.
9. The show of their countenance doth witness against them;
   And they declare their sin as Sodom, they hide it not.
   Woe unto their soul!

Isaiah 3

Let this ruin be under thy hand. The Hebrew word here means literally "let this stumbling." Rashi says, "The people say to the man whom they have picked up on the street to be their ruler: 'Guide us in those commandments which we do not understand and which we stumble over.'" Kimchi says, "Be our ruler because we are all stumbling and quarreling with each other." Ibn Ezra says that this stumbling simply means, "Rule thou over Jerusalem," because the same verb is used of Jerusalem in Verse 8, "for Jerusalem stumbles." In our translation the words are, "Jerusalem is ruined," but the Hebrew reads, "Jerusalem has stumbled."

3 : 7 *In my house is neither bread nor a mantle.* Kimchi says that this is the proof of poverty, that, even in the house of the respectable, there is a lack of decent clothing.

3 : 8 *Provoke the eyes of His glory.* Ibn Ezra: They provoke God publicly.

3 : 9 *The show of their countenance.* The Hebrew literally is "the recognition of their countenance." Therefore Rashi says that the meaning of the verse is connected with Deuteronomy 16:19, which in our translation says, "Thou shalt not respect persons," but in Hebrew is "Thou shalt not recognize faces in judgment." Therefore Rashi says the prophet means that their perversion of justice, their recognizing of faces, testifies against them. Kimchi connects this phrase with "They declare their sin" in the next line and says that the verse means, "Their face

Isaiah
3

For they have wrought evil unto themselves.
10. Say ye of the righteous, that it shall be well with him;
For they shall eat the fruit of their doings.
11. Woe unto the wicked! it shall be ill with him;
For the work of his hands shall be done to him.
12. As for My people, a babe is their master,
And women rule over them.
O My people, they that lead thee cause thee to err,
And destroy the way of thy paths.
13. The LORD standeth up to plead,
And standeth to judge the peoples.
14. The LORD will enter into judgment
With the elders of His people, and the princes thereof:
'It is ye that have eaten up the vineyard;
The spoil of the poor is in your houses;
15. What mean ye that ye crush My people,
And grind the face of the poor?'
Saith the LORD, the God of hosts.
16. Moreover the LORD said:
Because the daughters of Zion are haughty,
And walk with stretched-forth necks
And wanton eyes,

betrays their sin and their mouth openly declares it." (So, too, Ibn Ezra, Malbim, and Krauss.)

3:10-11 *Say ye of the righteous ... woe unto the wicked!* Since these verses interrupt the sequence, Krauss agrees with modern scholars that they are a later insertion but they can also be described as having some connection with the preceding verses which speak of perverting justice. They condemn the righteous and vindicate the wicked; and the prophet therefore calls upon them to depart from this sin but to vindicate the righteous and condemn the wicked.

3:12 *A babe is their master and women rule over them.* The same word here is used for "babe" as in Verse 4, and the commentators translate it as either a symbol of weak rulers or of mockers and cynics. Kimchi adds that, because of their sexuality,

Walking and mincing as they go,
And making a tinkling with their feet;
17. Therefore the LORD will smite with a scab
The crown of the head of the daughters of Zion,
And the LORD will lay bare their secret parts.
18. In that day the LORD will take away the bravery of their anklets, and the fillets, and the crescents; 19. the pendants, and the bracelets, and the veils; 20. the headtires, and the armlets, and the sashes, and the corselets, and the amulets; 21. the rings, and the nosejewels; 22. the aprons, and the mantelets, and the cloaks, and the girdles; 23. and the gauze robes, and the fine linen, and the turbans, and the mantles.
24. And it shall come to pass, that
Instead of sweet spices there shall be rottenness;
And instead of a girdle rags;
And instead of curled hair baldness;
And instead of a stomacher a girding of sackcloth;
Branding instead of beauty.
25. Thy men shall fall by the sword,
And thy mighty in the war.
26. And her gates shall lament and mourn;
And utterly bereft she shall sit upon the ground.

Isaiah
3

the men will fall under the domination of women. Krauss calls attention to the fact that the word for "women" (nashim) can also be read as "creditors," and that all the ancient translations indicate that one of the misfortunes that will come to them is that they will be always in the hands of their creditors.

3 : 16-26 *Daughters of Zion are haughty.* Rashi connects this passage with Verse 12, "The women shall rule over them." They will be ruled by vain and haughty and wanton women. The detailed description of all the various ornaments that the women wore are, as Krauss indicates, typical of the wealthy in the capital city. Isaiah's detailed knowledge of these various ornaments is a further indication that he was part of the upper circles of society.

4

CHAPTER 4 IS A CONTINUATION of the thought in Chapter 3. But perhaps the first verse, describing the desperation of the women left after the men have been killed in war or captured, really belongs to the end of the preceding chapter describing the punishment of the luxury-loving daughters of Zion. If this verse were put with the preceding chapter, the rest of Chapter 4 would be a unit, describing a favorite thought of Isaiah, symbolized by his naming his son, "A remnant shall return," namely, that "them that are escaped" (Verse 2) will establish a decent society which God will protect "like a sheltering cloud."

Isaiah 4

1. And seven women shall take hold of one man in that day, saying: 'We will eat our own bread, and wear our own apparel; only let us be called by thy name; take thou away our reproach.'

4 : 1 *And seven women.* Rashi explains that owing to the wars there will be many widows who will seek husbands. (So, too, Krauss.) Kimchi and Ibn Ezra comment on the number "seven." Kimchi says merely that seven is a round number as, for example, "sevenfold for your sins" (Leviticus 26:21) or, "seven times will the righteous fall and rise again." (Proverbs 24:16) Ibn Ezra explains that seven is a convenient number because of the seven days of the week.

2. In that day shall the growth of the LORD be beautiful and glorious,
And the fruit of the land excellent and comely
For them that are escaped of Israel.
3. And it shall come to pass, that he that is left in Zion, and he that remaineth in Jerusalem, shall be called holy, even every one that is written unto life in Jerusalem; 4. when the LORD shall have washed away the filth of the daughters of Zion, and shall have purged the blood of Jerusalem from the midst thereof, by the spirit of judgment, and by the spirit of destruction. 5. And the LORD will create over the whole habitation of mount Zion, and over her assemblies, a cloud and smoke by day, and the shining of a flaming fire by night; for over all the glory shall be a canopy. 6. And there shall be a pavilion for a shadow in the day-time from the heat, and for a refuge and for a covert from storm and from rain.

Isaiah
4

4:2 *Growth of the Lord ... beautiful.* The Targum explains that the Messiah will be a source of joy; and those who will be saved will glory in the presence of those who fulfill the Torah. Rashi connects this with the previous chapter as follows: After God will remove the self-beautifying ornaments of the wanton woman (with which the last chapter ends) the remaining righteous and scholars will be honored as beautiful. Ehrlich also relates this to the ornaments denounced in the previous chapter but interprets the connection as follows: After the women of Zion will be deprived of their luxuries and will become humble, they will appreciate the simple blessings of home and field.

The fruit of the land. Rashi says this refers to the children of the righteous. Kimchi, as he usually does, says it is the Messiah, the son of David; and Ibn Ezra, who prefers an historical explanation, says it means that by the defeat of Sennacherib, Hezekiah and the people of Jerusalem will be saved.

4:3 *Even every one that is written unto life.* All the commentators are reminded of the "Book of Life," so Kimchi says that the righteous will be blessed with longevity. So, too, Krauss. But Rashi says that even those who will have died before the

37

restoration will have eternal life (as the Targum says) and will see God's consolation of Jerusalem.

4:5 *A cloud ... by day ... a canopy.* Kimchi says that originally there was a cloud of glory over the Tabernacle in the wilderness and over the Temple, but, now in the restoration, God will send a protecting cloud over the homes of the sages and the righteous. Ehrlich says that this verse does not mean a symbolic protective booth made by God for Israel. It is simply an ordinary house. The women cured of luxury will be content with the quiet happiness of home.

5

CHAPTER 5 is a sermon built upon a symbol, fully developed—Israel is God's vineyard which He had carefully tended, but it produced bad wine. The sin that this symbolizes is, first of all, social injustice (Verse 7), unfair distribution of wealth (Verse 8), and self-indulgent luxury. (Verse 11) For this God will break down the defense of the vineyard and will call nations from afar (Verse 26) that will destroy. The sermon ends gloomily with "darkness and distress." (Verse 30)

Isaiah 5

1. Let me sing of my well-beloved,
   A song of my beloved touching his vineyard.
   My well-beloved had a vineyard
   In a very fruitful hill;

5 : 1 *Let me sing of my well-beloved, a song of my beloved.* There is some lack of clarity here as to who is speaking. Who is the "beloved"? Both Kimchi and Malbim give the same explanation and say that the "I" is the prophet, the beloved is the Lord, and the vineyard is the symbol for Israel. So Kimchi: "The prophet says, 'I shall sing of God and the vineyard, which is Israel, just as Solomon's Song of Songs is a song of God's love for Israel.'" And the Malbim puts it this way: "I will sing God's own song about His vineyard."

In a very fruitful hill.   Ibn Ezra says that the phrase is not

39

Isaiah 5

2. And he digged it, and cleared it of stones,
   And planted it with the choicest vine,
   And built a tower in the midst of it,
   And also hewed out a vat therein;
   And he looked that it should bring forth grapes,
   And it brought forth wild grapes.
3. And now, O inhabitants of Jerusalem and men of Judah,
   Judge, I pray you, betwixt me and my vineyard.
4. What could have been done more to my vineyard,
   That I have not done in it?
   Wherefore, when I looked that it should bring forth grapes,
   Brought it forth wild grapes?
5. And now come, I will tell you
   What I will do to my vineyard:
   I will take away the hedge thereof,
   And it shall be eaten up;
   I will break down the fence thereof,
   And it shall be trodden down;
6. And I will lay it waste:
   It shall not be pruned nor hoed,
   But there shall come up briers and thorns;
   I will also command the clouds
   That they rain no rain upon it.
7. For the vineyard of the LORD of hosts is the house of Israel,
   And the men of Judah the plant of His delight;
   And He looked for justice, but behold violence;
   For righteousness, but behold a cry.
8. Woe unto them that join house to house,
   That lay field to field,

to be translated but is the proper name of a very fertile vineyard near Jerusalem (Karen ben Shemen). Krauss says that it simply means a very fertile hilltop, as our translation has it.

5 : 7 *He looked for justice, but behold violence.* It is almost impossible to convey in English the striking assonance of the words here. "Mishpat" is contrasted with "mispach," and "tzedakah" is contrasted with "tzeakah."

Till there be no room, and ye be made to dwell
Alone in the midst of the land!
9. In mine ears said the LORD of hosts:
Of a truth many houses shall be desolate,
Even great and fair, without inhabitant.
10. For ten acres of vineyard shall yield one bath,
And the seed of a homer shall yield an ephah.
11. Woe unto them that rise up early in the morning,
That they may follow strong drink;
That tarry late into the night,
Till wine inflame them!
12. And the harp and the psaltery, the tabret and the pipe,
And wine, are in their feasts;
But they regard not the work of the LORD,
Neither have they considered the operation of His hands.
13. Therefore My people are gone into captivity,
For want of knowledge;
And their honourable men are famished,
And their multitude are parched with thirst.
14. Therefore the nether-world hath enlarged her desire,
And opened her mouth without measure;
And down goeth their glory, and their tumult, and their uproar,
And he that rejoiceth among them.
15. And man is bowed down,
And man is humbled,
And the eyes of the lofty are humbled;
16. But the LORD of hosts is exalted through justice,
And God the Holy One is sanctified through righteousness.

Isaiah
5

5 : 14 *The nether-world.* Krauss explains that this simply means a sort of cave leading under the earth. It does not mean the later concept of hell as a place of torture but merely the abode of the dead, underground.

He that rejoiceth. Who is it that rejoiceth? Kimchi says the verse refers to the destruction of the enemies who rejoice against us; but it may also mean, he says, those in Jerusalem who were rejoicing in their prosperity.

Isaiah

5

17. Then shall the lambs feed as in their pasture,
    And the waste places of the fat ones shall wanderers eat.
18. Woe unto them that draw iniquity with cords of vanity,
    And sin as it were with a cart rope,
19. That say: 'Let Him make speed, let Him hasten His work,
    That we may see it;
    And let the counsel of the Holy One of Israel draw nigh and come,
    That we may know it!'
20. Woe unto them that call evil good,
    And good evil;
    That change darkness into light,
    And light into darkness;
    That change bitter into sweet,
    And sweet into bitter!
21. Woe unto them that are wise in their own eyes,
    And prudent in their own sight!
22. Woe unto them that are mighty to drink wine,
    And men of strength to mingle strong drink;
23. That justify the wicked for a reward,
    And take away the righteousness of the righteous from him!
24. Therefore as the tongue of fire devoureth the stubble,
    And as the chaff is consumed in the flame,

5 : 17 *The waste places of the fat ones shall wanderers eat.* It is not quite clear who are the fat ones and who are the wanderers. Both the Targum and Rashi say it means that the righteous will enjoy the possessions of the wicked (i.e., "the fat ones"). But Krauss calls attention to the fact that most modern commentators omit the word "gorim" (which Targum and Rashi translate as "the righteous"). This simplifies the verse which then means, "and in the waste places the fat lambs shall eat." Ehrlich says, "This verse interrupts the thought." Modern commentators suggest that it follow Verse 10, where it would continue the description of the devastation.

42

So their root shall be as rottenness,
And their blossom shall go up as dust;
Because they have rejected the law of the LORD of hosts,
And contemned the word of the Holy One of Israel.

25. Therefore is the anger of the LORD kindled against His people,
And He hath stretched forth His hand against them, and hath smitten them,
And the hills did tremble,
And their carcasses were as refuse in the midst of the streets.
For all this His anger is not turned away,
But His hand is stretched out still.

26. And He will lift up an ensign to the nations from far,
And will hiss unto them from the end of the earth;
And, behold, they shall come with speed swiftly;

27. None shall be weary nor stumble among them;
None shall slumber nor sleep;
Neither shall the girdle of their loins be loosed,
Nor the latchet of their shoes be broken;

28. Whose arrows are sharp,
And all their bows bent;
Their horses' hoofs shall be counted like flint,
And their wheels like a whirlwind;

29. Their roaring shall be like a lion,
They shall roar like young lions, yea, they shall roar,

Isaiah 5

5 : 18 *Cords of vanity . . . cart rope.* Rashi contrasts these two nouns and uses them to describe the growth of the habits of evil self-indulgence. At first we pull temptation to us with a thin string like a spider web which we can easily break if we wish, but, if we do not, it becomes as strong as a cart rope in which we are helplessly bound (based upon the Talmud, Sukah 52a).

5 : 19 *Let Him make speed.* Who is it that speaks these words? Kimchi and Ibn Ezra, and later Malbim, agree that it is the mockers who say it, and Kimchi explains the verse as follows: "When I send them prophets to warn them of God's impending punishment, they mock skeptically and say, 'Let Him hurry up. Let us see Him do it.'"

Isaiah 5

And lay hold of the prey, and carry it away safe,
And there shall be none to deliver.
30. And they shall roar against them in that day
Like the roaring of the sea;
And if one look unto the land,
Behold darkness and distress,
And the light is darkened in the skies thereof.

6

CHAPTER 6 is Isaiah's consecration as a prophet. He sees a scene in which God is like a King on a throne and His court surrounding Him. He is asked by one of the angels, "Will you be God's messenger?" and he replies without hesitation, "Yes, here am I; send me." But God warns him that the people will not listen and will stubbornly hold on to their sinfulness until the country is laid waste. The last phrase of the chapter voices the hope that there will be some life and regeneration even after the tree of their life is cut down.

Isaiah 6

1. In the year that king Uzziah died I saw the LORD sitting upon a throne high and lifted up, and His train filled the temple. 2. Above Him stood the seraphim; each one had six wings: with twain he covered his face, and with twain he covered his feet, and with twain he did fly. 3. And one called unto another, and said:
Holy, holy, holy, is the LORD of hosts;
The whole earth is full of His glory.

6 : 1 *In the year that king Uzziah died.* Rashi here repeats what he said at the beginning of the book, that this chapter is really the opening chapter of the book. Most modern scholars agree, since this is Isaiah's description of the beginning of his

Isaiah 6

4. And the posts of the door were moved at the voice of them that called, and the house was filled with smoke. 5. Then said I:
Woe is me! for I am undone;
Because I am a man of unclean lips,
And I dwell in the midst of a people of unclean lips;
For mine eyes have seen the King,
The LORD of hosts.
6. Then flew unto me one of the seraphim, with a

prophecy. Rashi gives an additional argument to those that he gave at the beginning of the book: In the first chapter, Verse 8, Isaiah says that Zion is alone like a booth in a harvest field. This clearly refers to the time when the Ten Tribes were exiled by Sennacherib and Zion and Jerusalem were left alone, isolated like a harvest booth. But this occurred much later than the time of king Uzziah mentioned at the beginning of this Chapter 6.

The Targum is evidently concerned with a question which later commentators also asked: How did Isaiah, when he wrote this chapter, or preached this sermon, know that king Uzziah was going to die that year? So, the Targum answers, that the heading of the chapter means: In the year in which king Uzziah was smitten with leprosy; therefore the prophet knew that he would die soon. (See II Kings 15:5, "And the Lord smote the king so that he was a leper unto the day of his death.") The Talmud, Nedarim 64b, says that four types of people are considered to be virtually dead: the blind, the poor, the childless, and the leper. Krauss gives the same explanation as the Targum.

6 : 2 *Above Him stood the seraphim.* To Ibn Ezra the picture here is symbolic and is borrowed from human experience. The poet is visualizing the pomp and ceremony of a king's audience chamber.

6 : 3 *Holy, holy, holy.* This phrase, which has become a central part of the liturgy in Judaism and also in Christianity, "Trishagion," is elaborated by the Targum which explains that the threefold use of the word "holy" means holy in heaven, holy on earth, holy to eternity. The Targum's elaboration was itself also embodied in the liturgy and forms part of certain forms of the "Kedushah."

glowing stone in his hand, which he had taken with
the tongs from off the altar; 7. and he touched
my mouth with it, and said:
Lo, this hath touched thy lips;
And thine iniquity is taken away,
And thy sin expiated.

8. And I heard the voice of the LORD, saying:
Whom shall I send,
And who will go for us?
Then I said: 'Here am I; send me.'

Isaiah 6

6 : 4 *And the posts of the door were moved.* The Temple doors shook at the voice of the angel. So Rashi explains and adds, "This was the earthquake which occurred in the reign of king Uzziah; this earthquake in Uzziah's reign is referred to in Amos (1:1): 'In the reign of king Uzziah, two years before the earthquake,' and also in Zechariah (14:5): 'The earthquake in the days of Uzziah the king.'" In other words, Rashi says it was not only the doors of the Temple, where Isaiah saw the vision which shook at the voice of the angel, but the whole area felt the earthquake.

6 : 5 *For mine eyes have seen the King.* The Targum, as it always does, softens the anthropomorphic description of God and says, "Mine eyes have seen the glory of the Shechinah (the Presence) of the Lord," and Ibn Ezra says, "It is only in the prophetic vision that he saw Him."

6 : 6 *One of the seraphim, with a glowing stone.* This means one of the coals from the fire on the altar. Here the Targum again paraphrases: "One of the servers flew toward me and had in his *mouth* a word (instead of "in his hand a coal") which he had received from the Holy Presence. Malbim has this comment of the Targum in mind when he says, "God's word which the angel brought was like a fire." Ibn Ezra says, "The glowing coal was taken from the altar where the fire is always holy."

6 : 7 *He touched my mouth with it.* The Targum continues its paraphrase consistently and, instead of speaking of a coal touching the lips of the prophet, it says, "I have placed My word in thy mouth and your sins will be forgiven."

6 : 8 *Here am I; send me.* Ibn Ezra says that this verse is definite proof that this was Isaiah's first prophecy.

Isaiah 6

9. And He said: 'Go, and tell this people:
   Hear ye indeed, but understand not;
   And see ye indeed, but perceive not.
10. Make the heart of this people fat,
    And make their ears heavy,
    And shut their eyes;
    Lest they, seeing with their eyes,
    And hearing with their ears,
    And understanding with their heart,
    Return, and be healed.'
11. Then said I: 'Lord, how long?'

6:9 *Hear ye ... but understand not.* There are two possible interpretations of this verse. The first is that they would hear the prophet's message but, as in the past, they would refuse to listen. In other words, the text is a prediction, descriptive of what will happen. The second interpretation is that the text is imperative: Listen, but you will not understand. Since the punishment of the people has already been deserved, God will not permit them easy repentance but will treat them as He did Pharaoh when "He hardened the heart of Pharaoh" (Exodus 9:12) and also as God did to Sichon, king of the Amorites: "God hardened his spirit." (Deuteronomy 2:30) Ibn Ezra has the same explanation and says, "Some say that God does not accept the repentance of the sinner to cancel his sentence after the punishment has already been decreed."

6:10 *Make the heart of this people fat, and ... their ears heavy.* This confirms the second explanation of the above verse, that the people had done so much evil that they had forfeited for the present the opportunity for repentance.

6:13 *Whose stock remaineth ... so the holy seed.* In this de-

And He answered:
'Until cities be waste without inhabitant,
And houses without man,
And the land become utterly waste,
12. And the LORD have removed men far away,
And the forsaken places be many in the midst of the land.
13. And if there be yet a tenth in it, it shall again be eaten up; as a terebinth, and as an oak, whose stock remaineth, when they cast their leaves, so the holy seed shall be the stock thereof.'

Isaiah 6

scription of the destruction that will come to the land for its sins, the only mitigation is the final phrase, "the stock" (or the stump) of the tree and the "holy seed." So all the commentators, Rashi, the Targum, Kimchi, and Ibn Ezra agree that the meaning of the verse is that, though the tree (i.e., the community and the state) will be chopped down, the righteous (i.e., the holy seed) will find, or represent, enough vitality in the very stump of the tree to revive the life of the people.

Krauss points out the fact that the three last words, "the holy seed," in the stump, are not found in the ancient Greek translation, the Septuagint. He concludes that these words were a marginal and consolatory note by some later writer and that note crept into the text. Whoever this ancient annotator was, the consolatory words which he added express the deep feeling of the people of Israel. All the traditional commentators emphasize this footnote (if footnote it is). Like that annotator, they insist that no blows struck against the people of Israel will ever destroy it and Israel will always find the power to begin new growth and new life.

7

THIS CHAPTER deals with the invasion of Judea by Pekah, king of Northern Israel, allied with Rezin of Damascus, king of Aram (Syria). Isaiah appears before king Ahaz and assures him that the enemies themselves will be destroyed. The sign of deliverance is that a young woman will bear a child to be called Immanuel, a symbolic name for God's help. The chapter ends as a number of chapters end, with a description of coming devastation.

Isaiah 7

1. And it came to pass in the days of Ahaz the son of Jotham, the son of Uzziah, king of Judah, that Rezin the king of Aram, and Pekah the son of Remaliah, the king of Israel, went up to Jerusalem to war against it; but could not prevail against it. 2. And it was told the house of David, saying: 'Aram is confederate with Ephraim.' And his heart was moved, and the heart of his people, as the trees of the forest are moved with the wind.

7 : 1 *In the days of Ahaz ... Rezin ... king of Aram, and Pekah ... king of Israel, went up to Jerusalem to war against it.* The events told in this chapter and in the beginning of Chapter 8 are described more fully in the Second Book of Kings, Chapter 16, Verses 5 ff. There we are told that Ahaz, king of Judah, sent to Tiglath Pilezer, king of Assyria, and asked for assistance and

Isaiah 7

3. Then said the Lord unto Isaiah: 'Go forth now to meet Ahaz, thou, and ªShear-jashub thy son, at the end of the conduit of the upper pool, in the highway of the fullers' field; 4. and say unto him: Keep calm, and be quiet; fear not, neither let thy heart be faint, because of these two tails of smoking firebrands, for the fierce anger of Rezin and Aram, and of the son of Remaliah. 5. Because Aram hath counselled evil against thee, Ephraim also, and the son of Remaliah, saying: 6. Let us go up against Judah, and vex it, and let us make a breach therein for us, and set up a king in the midst of it, even the son of Tabeel; 7. thus saith the Lord God: It shall not stand, neither shall it come to pass.

that the king of Assyria, having received the treasures which Ahaz sent him, marched against Syria and captured Damascus and killed Rezin, king of Syria. Rashi, influenced by the Midrash (Genesis Rabah 63:1), asks, "Why should it be necessary to mention Jotham, the father of Ahaz, and Uzziah, his grandfather? It is because Jotham and Uzziah were righteous men, but Ahaz himself was a wicked man and an idolator. He did not deserve to be saved when Rezin and Pekah attacked Jerusalem, but, for the sake of his righteous forebears, God saved him." Hence they are mentioned; they are crucial to the events which occurred. Kimchi, likewise, refers to this Midrash.

7 : 3 *Isaiah: 'Go forth . . . to meet Ahaz, thou, and Shear-jashub thy son.'* At God's command Isaiah had given each of his two sons a symbolic name. This son, now accompanying him to the presence of the king, was named "A remnant will return." (Shear-jashub) The second son was called "Looting, spoiling are rapidly on the way." (Mahar shalal chash baz) However the Targum says that it was not his son, although Scripture calls him his son, but it was his beloved disciple. This idea is found in the Midrash. (Genesis Rabah 42:3)

7 : 4 *Say unto him: Keep calm.* Krauss calls attention to the fact that Isaiah could approach into the king's presence without anybody stopping him and asking him to identify himself. This

---
ª That is, *A remnant shall return.*

Isaiah 7

8. For the head of Aram is Damascus,
And the head of Damascus is Rezin;
And within threescore and five years
Shall Ephraim be broken, that it be not a people;
9. And the head of Ephraim is Samaria,
And the head of Samaria is Remaliah's son.
If ye will not have faith, surely ye shall not be established.
10. And the Lord spoke again unto Ahaz, saying: 11. 'Ask thee a sign of the Lord thy God: ask it either in the depth, or in the height above.' 12. But Ahaz said: 'I will not ask, neither will I try the Lord.' 13. And he said: 'Hear ye now, O house of David:

---

confirms the tradition that he was (very likely) related to the royal family. Certainly he was well known in the palace.

Tails of smoking firebrands. Both Ibn Ezra and Kimchi explain the metaphor: Those two kings (of Israel and Syria) have little power left. Their fire is dying out like the stump of a torch. They can no longer burn and destroy. They can only now emit an ill-smelling smoke.

7:6 *The son of Tabeel.* There have been various attempts to fix the identity of this person. (See Krauss.) The Targum says this is not even a name but it means, "We will put on the throne whoever seems good (tov) in our eyes" (i.e., "whom we please"). Ibn Ezra also says there are many theories as to his identity and he himself prefers to say that Tabeel must have been some prince of Israel or of Aram.

7:9 *If ye will not have faith ... ye shall not be established.*
Most of the commentators say that the verse means faith in the words of the prophet. And Malbim varies this explanation slightly and says in dialogue form: "Do you not believe me? (You do not) because you have no faith."

7:10 *Ask thee a sign of the Lord thy God.* Rashi: "Isaiah says to the king, 'Since you do not believe that my message is true, then ask for a sign directly from God.'" This explanation of Rashi's goes well with the next verse, when Ahaz says, "I will ask not a sign from God."

7:13 *For you to weary men, that ye will weary my God also?*
Both the Targum and Rashi explain this as follows: Is it not bad

Is it a small thing for you to weary men, that ye will weary my God also? 14. Therefore the LORD Himself shall give you a sign: behold, the young woman shall conceive, and bear a son, and shall call his name ᵇImmanuel. 15. Curd and honey shall he eat, when he knoweth to refuse the evil, and choose the good. 16. Yea, before the child shall know to refuse the evil, and choose the good, the land whose two kings thou hast a horror of shall be forsaken. 17. The LORD shall bring upon thee, and upon thy people, and upon thy father's house, days that have not come, from the day that Ephraim departed from Judah; even the king of Assyria.'

Isaiah 7

enough that you weary the prophets (by ignoring them)? Will you now weary God with your wickedness? The Malbim's explanation is akin to this. He also takes "men" to mean the prophets and says, "Do you think that God is as weary (and therefore ineffective) as you imagine the prophets are?" Ibn Ezra gives a somewhat different explanation: "You, O king, use your power to wear men down until they can no longer resist your will; do you think you can weary God also?"

7 : 14 *The young woman shall conceive, and bear a son.* Rashi says the young woman is the young wife of the prophet. Kimchi says the child was the son of king Ahaz and adds that the word "alma" does not mean "virgin" but "young woman." Ibn Ezra is more definite. He asks, "How can the Christians say that this child is Jesus who was born many years later? Nor can this be a reference to the birth of Hezekiah, a son of Ahaz, because Hezekiah was twenty-five years old when he became king, and his father Ahaz reigned only sixteen years, so Hezekiah could not have been born during his father's reign." Evidently Ibn Ezra accepts the explanation that this was a child of the prophet.

7 : 16 *Before the child shall know to refuse the evil, and choose the good.* That is, before the child will grow up, both Syria and the Northern Kingdom will be destroyed.

7 : 17 *The Lord shall bring upon thee ... the king of Assyria.* As for you who bribed the king of Assyria with the treasures of the Temple, he will turn against you and conquer the land.

ᵇ That is, *God is with us.*

Isaiah 7

18. And it shall come to pass in that day,
That the Lord shall hiss for the fly
That is in the uttermost part of the rivers of Egypt,
And for the bee that is in the land of Assyria.
19. And they shall come, and shall rest all of them
In the rugged valleys, and in the holes of the rocks,
And upon all thorns, and upon all brambles.
20. In that day shall the Lord shave with a razor that is hired in the parts beyond the River, even with the king of Assyria, the head and the hair of the feet; and it shall also sweep away the beard.
21. And it shall come to pass in that day, that a man shall rear a young cow, and two sheep; 22. and

7 : 18-20 *The fly ... Egypt ... the bee ... Assyria ... a razor that is hired ... Assyria.* Rashi explains that the armies of Egypt, which are as numerous as the flies, will join the Assyrians and make war against you. "The razor that is hired" is explained simply by the Targum as a sharp sword, but Krauss explains more clearly that Assyria was called "the razor that was hired" because Ahaz bought Assyria's assistance with his gift of gold and silver.

The last verses of the chapter (21-25) are not very clear, and because of their lack of clarity they affect the interpretation of Verses 19 and 20. The traditional commentators take the Verses 21-25 to be a description of the prosperity that will come and therefore in Verse 20 the "hired razor" will be the sharp

it shall come to pass, for the abundance of milk that they shall give, he shall eat curd; for curd and honey shall every one eat that is left in the midst of the land.

23. And it shall come to pass in that day, that every place, where there were a thousand vines at a thousand silverlings, shall even be for briers and thorns. 24. With arrows and with bow shall one come thither, because all the land shall become briers and thorns. 25. And all the hills that were digged with the mattock, thou shalt not come thither for fear of briers and thorns, but it shall be for the sending forth of oxen, and for the treading of sheep.

Isaiah 7

sword that will destroy the Assyrians, and therefore it refers, according to the traditional commentators, to the coming destruction of Sennacherib before the walls of Jerusalem. But Krauss, following modern scholars, takes these closing verses to describe the desolation of the land of Judah, and therefore the "hired razor" is not the destruction of Sennacherib but the destruction by Sennacherib of the land of Judah. The fact is that the closing verses remain vague. Verses 21 and 22 seem like a description of prosperity (that might come after the destruction of the Assyrians) and therefore fit better into the traditional interpretation. The last three verses (23-25) are a picture of desolation (i.e., wrought by the Assyrians) and fit better with the modern interpretation.

8

AT LEAST the first part of this chapter continues the events discussed in Chapter 7. Here the prophet for the third time gives a baby boy a symbolic and prophetic name. The first boy thus named was "A remnant shall return." (Isaiah 7:3) The second is the child to be called Immanuel, and this third boy, now, who is called "The spoil speedeth, the prey hasteth." And again, Isaiah predicts the coming of the Assyrian armies who will destroy the Northern Kingdom, and he says that the prophecies, which are not listened to now, should be at least taught to the disciples (Verse 16); for the time will come when the people will abandon their present superstitions (Verse 19) and, in their time of trouble, will return to God; but for the meantime there is devastation, afflicting first the Northern Kingdom (Verse 23), the lands of Zebulun and Naphtali.

The preceding prophecy (Chapter 7) continues up to Verse 18.

Isaiah 8

1. And the LORD said unto me: 'Take thee a great tablet, and write upon it in common script: The spoil speedeth, the prey hasteth; 2. and I will take unto Me faithful witnesses to record, Uriah the

8:1 *In common script.* The Targum and Rashi take this phrase to mean in writing that could be easily understood by the average man. But Kimchi says that it means that Isaiah should not take this command (to inscribe a tablet) to mean merely another

priest, and Zechariah the son of Jeberechiah.' 3. And I went unto the prophetess; and she conceived, and bore a son. Then said the LORD unto me: 'Call his name ªMaher-shalal-hash-baz. 4. For before the child shall have knowledge to cry: My father, and: My mother, the riches of Damascus and the spoil of Samaria shall be carried away before the king of Assyria.'

Isaiah
8

prophetic metaphor but that he should actually write it down so that people may read it. Malbim takes this to mean not writing but pictures, showing men in battle. This sort of picture any man will be able to understand even if he is unlettered. Malbim evidently had in mind the many ancient Egyptian battle scenes. Ehrlich takes this phrase to mean letters as tall as a man.

The spoil speedeth, the prey hasteth. This will be the symbolic name which he will give to his second son. The two phrases, according to Kimchi, are merely for the sake of emphasis. But Rashi says that the first phrase predicts the destruction of the Northern Kingdom by the Assyrians and the second, the later destruction of Judea by the Babylonians.

8 : 2 *I will take ... witnesses ... Uriah the priest, and Zechariah.* The Targum comments upon these two names and says that just as the curses mentioned by Uriah will be fulfilled so the consolations mentioned by Zechariah (the prophet) will also some day be fulfilled.

The tradition upon which this imaginative explanation is based is found fully in the Talmud (Makot 24a, 24b) where we are told that Rabbi Akiba and his colleagues were walking near the ruins of the Temple on Mount Moriah. He saw a fox prowling around the ruins of the Temple. He did not weep, as his companions did, but he laughed. When asked why he had laughed, he cited the fact that Uriah said: "Jerusalem shall be a heap of ruins" (Micah 3:12, Jeremiah 26:20) but Zechariah said: "Old men and women shall yet dwell in safety in Jerusalem." (8:4) So, Akiba said, I am confident that just as Uriah's dire prediction has been fulfilled so Zechariah's hopeful one also will be fulfilled.

ª That is, *The spoil speedeth, the prey hasteth.*

Isaiah 8

5. And the Lord spoke unto me yet again, saying:
6. Forasmuch as this people hath refused
   The waters of Shiloah that go softly,
   And rejoiceth with Rezin and Remaliah's son;
7. Now therefore, behold, the Lord bringeth up upon them
   The waters of the River, mighty and many,
   Even the king of Assyria and all his glory;
   And he shall come up over all his channels,
   And go over all his banks;
8. And he shall sweep through Judah
   Overflowing as he passeth through
   He shall reach even to the neck;
   And the stretching out of his wings
   Shall fill the breadth of thy land, O Immanuel.

Rashi, Kimchi, and Ibn Ezra all refer to the same tradition.

8 : 3   *She conceived, and bore a son.*   Rashi said that Isaiah, at God's command, gave this child the symbolic name, "Mahar shalal" etc., but this was the same son (mentioned in the previous chapter, Verse 14) whom his mother called Immanuel.

8 : 4   *Before the child shall have knowledge.*   Kimchi notes that this thought is similar to the prophecy with regard to the child Immanuel in the preceding chapter.

8 : 6   *As this people hath refused the waters of Shiloah.*   The Targum paraphrases it as follows: Since this people have despised the kingdom of David who had spoken to them gently, I will bring upon them the tempestuous waters of the mighty river (Assyria). So, too, Rashi and Ibn Ezra and Kimchi. Malbim adds that David had been crowned beside the quiet stream of Shiloah as a symbol or prophecy that his kingdom would move along gently (he would govern with a gentle hand).

8 : 8   *O Immanuel.*   This exclamation seems not connected with the rest of the verse, but the commentators try to connect it in various ways. The Targum says that Immanuel means "Judah," so the phrase reads, "Thy lands, Immanuel" (i.e., Judah). Rashi says that Immanuel was the name of a subdivision of the kingdom of Judah. Eliezer of Beaugency says also that it means Judah and explains that just as the Prophet Hosea names his son symbolically "Jezreel," and then called the whole people of

9. Make an uproar, O ye peoples, and ye shall be broken in pieces;
And give ear, all ye of far countries;
Gird yourselves, and ye shall be broken in pieces;
Gird yourselves, and ye shall be broken in pieces.
10. Take counsel together, and it shall be brought to nought;
Speak the word, and it shall not stand;
For God is with us.
11. For the Lord spoke thus to me with a strong hand, admonishing me that I should not walk in the way of this people, saying: 12. 'Say ye not: A conspiracy, concerning all whereof this people do say: A

Isaiah 8

Israel "Jezreel," so the prophet named the child Immanuel and here extends this name to the entire people. However both Kimchi and Ibn Ezra take the exclamation literally and say it means what the name means, "We will be redeemed because God is with us."

8 : 9-10 *Make an uproar, O ye peoples . . . take counsel together . . . it shall be . . . nought.* The Hebrew word permits the possible meaning of "alliance" instead of "uproar." So the Targum and Rashi both say, "Make a confederation, O ye peoples, but you will still be broken." Kimchi takes that word to mean "be broken up." In other words, you may make your confederation but Assyria will break it up. So, also, Ibn Ezra. This seems to be addressed to the multinational army mobilized by the Assyrian kings and the prophet says that this army will fail because "God is with us." Ibn Ezra adds: These closing words explain the prophetic purpose of giving the child the name of Immanuel.

8 : 11 *The Lord spoke . . . to me with a strong hand.* The Targum avoiding the anthropomorphic word "hand" says, "The Lord spoke to me through the strength of the prophecy." Rashi also says it means that the prophecy grew strong within me, and he cites the verse in Ezckiel 3:14: "And the hand of the Lord was strong upon me." So, too, Ibn Ezra. Kimchi, however, takes the word "strong" to mean, "God's strong hand which will deliver."

8 : 12 *Say ye not: A conspiracy.* Do not join in the conspiracy

59

Isaiah 8

conspiracy; neither fear ye their fear, nor account it dreadful. 13. The Lord of hosts, Him shall ye sanctify; and let Him be your fear, and let Him be your dread. 14. And He shall be for a sanctuary; but for a stone of stumbling and for a rock of offence to both the houses of Israel, for a gin and for a snare to the inhabitants of Jerusalem. 15. And many among them shall stumble, and fall, and be broken, and be snared, and be taken.'

16. 'Bind up the testimony, seal the instruction among My disciples.' 17. And I will wait for the Lord, that hideth His face from the house of Jacob, and

with those who wish to surrender to the Assyrians. This is Rashi's explanation. (So, too, Ibn Ezra.)

8 : 14 *He shall be for a sanctuary.* This phrase seems to be an interruption and Krauss agrees with other modern critics that the word is a mistaken echo of the word "snare" later in the chapter (i.e., "migdash," an echo of the later word "mokesh"). But the traditional commentators contrast the word "sanctuary" with the words "stone of stumbling." God will be a sanctuary or a stronghold to the people, but a stumbling-block to Assyria. Ibn Ezra makes a similar contrast but explains it differently, applying both words to the king of Assyria. He takes the verse to mean: Those who believe that the king of Assyria will be a sanctuary will find out that he is only a stumbling-block to them.

8 : 16 *Bind up the testimony, seal the instruction.* God tells the prophet: Seal up the prophecy, stop revealing it to those who do not listen to it. Rashi gives the reverse explanation: Seal up means inscribe the teaching permanently on the hearts of the disciples. Kimchi divides the passage and uses part of both explanations. He says: Stop prophesying to those who do not listen but place it in the hearts of your disciples.

8 : 17-18 *The Lord, that hideth His face . . . Behold, I and the children.* The Targum paraphrases as follows: Though God said He would hide His face from us, I pray to Him; as long as I and my children are present, they are a testimony that if Israel repents it will be delivered. Rashi takes the words "my children" to mean here "my beloved disciples" in whose heart I have sealed God's testimony. Kimchi says it means: I named my children

I will look for Him. 18. Behold, I and the children whom the LORD hath given me shall be for signs and for wonders in Israel from the LORD of hosts, who dwelleth in mount Zion. 19. And when they shall say unto you: 'Seek unto the ghosts and the familiar spirits, that chirp and that mutter; should not a people seek unto their God? on behalf of the living unto the dead 20. for instruction and for testimony?' —Surely they will speak according to this word, wherein there is no light.—21. And they shall pass

Isaiah 8

at God's command Who dwelleth on Mount Zion, and He will yet save us.

8 : 19-20 Modern scholars say that this prophecy of Isaiah ended with Verse 18. From Verse 19 on is by another hand. The Midrash (Leviticus Rabah 15:2) says the same thing, namely, that the next two verses are not by Isaiah but by Beeri, who is identified as the father of the Prophet Hosea. The Midrash says that since Beeri's prophecy was so brief, two verses, it would have been lost. Therefore it was appended here to the prophecy of Isaiah. According to this midrash, Beeri was exiled to Assyria by God's intent so that he could guide his fellow exiles. Hence these verses which warn the people, exiled to the pagan environment of Assyria, against falling into the prevailing idolatry and superstition. The Verses 19 and 20 therefore must be understood as a dialogue between the Assyrian pagans and the Jewish captives. Therefore the Targum amplifies the biblical words, "when they shall say," by adding, "the people among whom you dwell." The words in Verse 19, "Should not a people seek unto their God," are according to Rashi the answer, that is, the refusal of the Jewish captives to follow these superstitions suggested to them. Kimchi takes the words, "Should not a people seek unto their God" as referring not to God but to the various gods of the people, and he says the answer of the Judeans to their captives is this: "Of course you Assyrians should worship your own god, but this consulting of ghosts is ridiculous." In Verse 20 the opening words, "for instruction and testimony," go with the preceding verse and complete it.

8 : 21 *They shall pass this way.* Since Verses 19 and 20 are an interruption, the thought here continues that of Verse 18. It

Isaiah 8

this way that are sore bestead and hungry; and it shall come to pass that, when they shall be hungry, they shall fret themselves, and curse by their king and by their God, and, whether they turn their faces upward, 22. or look unto the earth, behold distress and darkness, the gloom of anguish, and outspread thick darkness. 23. For is there no gloom to her that was stedfast? Now the former hath lightly afflicted the land of Zebulun and the land of Naphtali, but the latter hath dealt a more grievous blow by the way of the sea, beyond the Jordan, in the district of the nations.

describes the imminent devastation of the land and the people wandering about the ruined country. So Rashi says that this refers to the devastated Northern Kingdom. The wandering remnants of the people will now curse their king and their idols and turn again to God. Kimchi and Ibn Ezra make a similar explanation but apply it not to the devastation of the Northern Kingdom but to that of Judea.

8 : 22 *Look unto the earth, behold distress.* Rashi explains it as follows: The people will still think of seeking earthly help, alliances with Egypt, etc., but all this will only increase their distress.

8 : 23 *No gloom to her that was stedfast?* Rashi applies this opening phrase to Assyria. That strong or steadfast nation will not lose its vigor and its strength. First it has conquered the Northern Kingdom and now it will turn against Judea. But Kimchi and Ibn Ezra apply the phrase to the people of Judea. The Southern Kingdom still feels confident in spite of the destruction which Assyria has wrought in the Northern Kingdom.

9

A LITTLE BOY is born who symbolizes the future. Again it is Isaiah's favorite symbol. In Chapter 9 the boy is a sign of coming quiet and peace in the land. The reference is very likely to Hezekiah, son of Ahaz, who would prove to be a righteous king. (Verse 6: "Upon the throne of David, to establish justice.") The Northern Kingdom imagines it will survive its troubles and go on to greater prosperity, but the enemies "devour Israel with open mouth." (Verse 11) Yet the people of Israel learns no lesson, practices no justice. It will be destroyed by famine and invasion.

> 1. The people that walked in darkness
>   Have seen a great light;
>   They that dwelt in the land of the shadow of death,
>   Upon them hath the light shined.

Isaiah 9

9:1 *The people that walked in darkness.* Having spoken in the last chapter of the suffering that is coming, and having described it as "distress and darkness, gloom and anguish," (8:22) the prophet continues the symbol as he now utters his words of consolation using the metaphor of light.

Both Rashi and Kimchi refer this verse specifically to the dark days of the siege of Jerusalem by Sennacherib, and then to the sense of radiance that dispelled the gloom when the siege was lifted.

Isaiah 9

2. Thou hast multiplied the nation,
   Thou hast increased their joy;
   They joy before Thee according to the joy in harvest,
   As men rejoice when they divide the spoil.
3. For the yoke of his burden,
   And the staff of his shoulder,
   The rod of his oppressor,
   Thou hast broken as in the day of Midian.
4. For every boot stamped with fierceness,
   And every cloak rolled in blood,
   Shall even be for burning, for fuel of fire.
5. For a child is born unto us,
   A son is given unto us;
   And the government is upon his shoulder;
   And his name is called
   ªPele-joez-el-gibbor-
   Abi-ad-sar-shalom;
6. That the government may be increased,
   And of peace there be no end,
   Upon the throne of David, and upon his kingdom,
   To establish it, and to uphold it
   Through justice and through righteousness
   From henceforth even for ever.

9 : 3 *The . . . oppressor . . . broken as in the day of Midian.* Rashi: This refers to the great victory by Gideon over the Midianites. (Judges, Chapter 7) Kimchi amplified this by reminding us that this victory over Midian was the defeat of a great host by a handful of three hundred men.

9 : 5 *For a child is born unto us.* The traditional commentators all agree that this is the child Hezekiah born to king Ahaz. Hezekiah as a righteous king will restore the kingdom.

His name is called Pele-joez . . . ('wonderful in counsel . . . Eternal Father, Prince of peace'). This is another example of a symbolic name analogous to those given to the two sons of the prophet. The commentators feel the need of explaining the name, especially since it seems, at first glance, that one of the names

---

ª That is, *Wonderful in counsel is God the Mighty, the Everlasting Father, the Ruler of peace.*

The zeal of the LORD of hosts doth perform this.
7. The LORD sent a word into Jacob,
And it hath lighted upon Israel.
8. And all the people shall know,
Even Ephraim and the inhabitant of Samaria,
That say in pride and in arrogancy of heart:
9. 'The bricks are fallen, but we will build with hewn stones;
The sycamores are cut down, but cedars will we put in their place.'
10. Therefore the LORD doth set upon high the adversaries of Rezin against him,
And spur his enemies;
11. The Arameans on the east, and the Philistines on the west;
And they devour Israel with open mouth.
For all this His anger is not turned away,
But His hand is stretched out still.
12. Yet the people turneth not unto Him that smiteth them,
Neither do they seek the LORD of hosts.
13. Therefore the LORD doth cut off from Israel head and tail,
Palm-branch and rush, in one day.
14. The elder and the man of rank, he is the head;

Isaiah
9

of the little child is "Eternal Father." They all follow the example of the Targum who says that these epithets, except the last one, apply to God who is naming the child. Therefore it is to be read, "God the Mighty, the Eternal Father, calls his name 'Prince of peace.'" However, Ibn Ezra does not object to the term "Avi Ad" (Eternal Father) being applied to the child. He says it means: He who will be the father, the source of the perpetuation of the kingdom, namely, Hezekiah. This explanation would fit with Verse 6 which speaks of the child on the throne of David to establish it forever.

9 : 13 *Head and tail.* As Rashi explains this to mean the king and the other officers.

Palm-branch and rush. Kimchi explains this as meaning both the strong and the weak will be destroyed.

Isaiah 9

And the prophet that teacheth lies, he is the tail.
15. For they that lead this people cause them to err;
And they that are led of them are destroyed.
16. Therefore the LORD shall have no joy in their young men,
Neither shall He have compassion on their fatherless and widows;
For every one is ungodly and an evil-doer,
And every mouth speaketh wantonness.
For all this His anger is not turned away,
But His hand is stretched out still.
17. For wickedness burneth as the fire;
It devoureth the briers and thorns;
Yea, it kindleth in the thickets of the forest,
And they roll upward in thick clouds of smoke.
18. Through the wrath of the LORD of hosts is the land burnt up;
The people also are as the fuel of fire;
No man spareth his brother.
19. And one snatcheth on the right hand, and is hungry;
And he eateth on the left hand, and is not satisfied;
They eat every man the flesh of his own arm:
20. Manasseh, Ephraim; and Ephraim, Manasseh;
And they together are against Judah.
For all this His anger is not turned away,
But His hand is stretched out still.

9 : 19 *Snatcheth to the right ... eateth on the left.* The anarchy will be widespread; the people will snatch food from each other. (Rashi)

The flesh of his own arm. The Targum translates the word "his own arm" to mean: Each will consume the food of the neighbor who lives at his side. So, too, Rashi. Ibn Ezra takes the words "his own arm" figuratively: The whole nation is to be considered as one body, yet its members are now consuming each other. This idea is carried out by the next verse; Manasseh and Ephraim are both part of the kingdom of Israel, but they are hostile to each other. Then after quarreling, they both unite to join in battle against Judah.

10

THE PROPHET begins with a denunciation of social oppression by the leaders of the community. God says He is sending for Assyria to be His instrument of punishment, "the rod of Mine anger." (Verse 5) But Assyria itself, having performed its God-given task, will not think of itself humbly as merely an instrument but act pridefully as a conqueror and so will itself be punished. (Verse 25) Assyria is like the axe that boasts that it is superior to the axeman. (Verse 15) From the destruction "a remnant of Israel shall return" to reconstitute a nation. (Verse 21) The rest of the chapter describes the onward march of the Assyrian army and the devastation it will wreak.

1. Woe unto them that decree unrighteous decrees,
   And to the writers that write iniquity;
2. To turn aside the needy from judgment,
   And to take away the right of the poor of My people,
   That widows may be their spoil,
   And that they may make the fatherless their prey!
3. And what will ye do in the day of visitation,
   And in the ruin which shall come from far?
   To whom will ye flee for help?
   And where will ye leave your glory?

Isaiah 10

10 : 1-3   The classic prophetic denunciation of social injustice.

Isaiah 10

4. They can do nought except crouch under the captives,
   And fall under the slain.
   For all this His anger is not turned away,
   But His hand is stretched out still.
5. O Asshur, the rod of Mine anger,
   In whose hand as a staff is Mine indignation!
6. I do send him against an ungodly nation,
   And against the people of My wrath do I give him a charge,
   To take the spoil, and to take the prey,
   And to tread them down like the mire of the streets.
7. Howbeit he meaneth not so,
   Neither doth his heart think so;
   But it is in his heart to destroy,
   And to cut off nations not a few.
8. For he saith:
   'Are not my princes all of them kings?
9. Is not Calno as Carchemish?
   Is not Hamath as Arpad?
   Is not Samaria as Damascus?
10. As my hand hath reached the kingdoms of the idols,

10 : 3-4 When God will send the invader against you (Assyria) where will you find refuge? You will be either captured or slain.
For all this His anger. This section ends with the same solemn refrain of God's continued wrath which ended each of three groups of punishment in Chapter 9, Verses 11, 16, 20. This seems to indicate that this is part of the same sermon. It continues from Chapter 9 to at least this point.

10 : 5 *O Asshur, the rod of Mine anger.* The prophet now addresses Assyria whom He will send as the instrument of divine punishment against Israel and Judah.

10 : 7 *Howbeit he meaneth not so.* But Assyria does not realize that it is merely an instrument fulfilling an ordained purpose. It believes that it is marching by its own will for its own victory and spoils.

10 : 8-14 The boastful speech of Assyria, vaunting its power and success.

Whose graven images did exceed them of Jerusalem and of Samaria;
11. Shall I not, as I have done unto Samaria and her idols,
So do to Jerusalem and her idols?'
12. Wherefore it shall come to pass, that when the Lord hath performed His whole work upon mount Zion and on Jerusalem, I will punish the fruit of the arrogant heart of the king of Assyria, and the glory of his haughty looks. 13. For he hath said:
By the strength of my hand I have done it,
And by my wisdom, for I am prudent;
In that I have removed the bounds of the peoples,
And have robbed their treasures,
And have brought down as one mighty the inhabitants;
14. And my hand hath found as a nest the riches of the peoples;
And as one gathereth eggs that are forsaken,
Have I gathered all the earth;
And there was none that moved the wing,
Or that opened the mouth, or chirped.

Isaiah 10

Is not Calno as Carchemish? Have I not conquered, says Assyria, Calno and Carchemish and all the other cities including Samaria and Damascus, and have I not overcome and destroyed their gods? Thus will I now do to the gods of Jerusalem.

When the Lord hath performed His whole work upon mount Zion. This verse is an interlude in the boastful speech of Assyria. Rashi explains it as follows: When God's unknowing messenger, Assyria, had finished God's work in Judea and conquered all the cities except Jerusalem, then Jerusalem will repent and then God will punish Assyria for its pride.

10: 13-14 These verses complete the boastful speech of Assyria. He said that he had gathered all the wealth of the conquered people; without effort, as easily as one gathers eggs that are abandoned in the nest, and not a single bird dared even twitter against him.

69

Isaiah 10

15. Should the axe boast itself against him that heweth therewith?
    Should the saw magnify itself against him that moveth it?
    As if a rod should move them that lift it up,
    Or as if a staff should lift up him that is not wood.
16. Therefore will the Lord, the LORD of hosts,
    Send among his fat ones leanness;
    And under his glory there shall be kindled
    A burning like the burning of fire.
17. And the light of Israel shall be for a fire,
    And his Holy One for a flame;
    And it shall burn and devour his thorns
    And his briers in one day.
18. And the glory of his forest and of his fruitful field,
    He will consume both soul and body;
    And it shall be as when a sick man wasteth away.
19. And the remnant of the trees of his forest shall be few,
    That a child may write them down.
20. And it shall come to pass in that day,
    That the remnant of Israel,

10 : 15 Begins God's answer which reminds Assyria (which was described as merely the rod of God's anger) that an axe should not boast that it is superior to the axeman, "lift up him that is not wood." Does the staff imagine that it controls the motions of the living man? Thus Rashi: It is not the staff that lifts; it is the man.

10 : 16-19 *Therefore will the Lord ... the burning of fire.* The same metaphor of fire, that was used in the preceding chapter to predict the destruction of Israel, is now used in predicting the destruction of Assyria. As in the preceding chapter, the fire will burn the great trees (the strong) and even the weeds (the weak).

A child may write them down. There will be so few trees left that even a little child could count them and record them.

10 : 20 *The remnant of Israel ... shall stay upon the Lord.* After the destruction of Assyria what is left of Israel will no longer depend upon the Assyrian officers for their protection but will learn again to rely upon God in truth.

And they that are escaped of the house of Jacob,
Shall no more again stay upon him that smote them;
But shall stay upon the LORD, the Holy One of Israel, in truth.
21. ᵃA remnant shall return, even the remnant of Jacob, Unto God the Mighty.
22. For though thy people, O Israel, be as the sand of the sea,
Only a remnant of them shall return;
An extermination is determined, overflowing with righteousness.
23. For an extermination wholly determined
Shall the Lord, the GOD of hosts, make in the midst of all the earth.
24. Therefore thus saith the Lord, the GOD of hosts: O My people that dwellest in Zion, be not afraid of Asshur, though he smite thee with the rod, and lift up his staff against thee, after the manner of Egypt. 25. For yet a very little while, and the indignation shall be accomplished, and Mine anger shall be to their destruction. 26. And the LORD of hosts shall stir up against him a scourge, as in the slaughter of

10 : 21 *A remnant shall return.* Thus fulfilling the prophecy indicated in the name given by Isaiah to his older son.

10 : 22 *Extermination ... overflowing with righteousness.* The word for "overflowing" can also be translated "to wash away" as by the torrent of a river. Therefore Rashi explains this verse to mean that although the extermination was decreed nevertheless the righteousness of the returning remnant will wash it away like an overflowing river. However Kimchi takes the phrase more literally and says it means that it was right that the extermination should be decreed; and that this verse refers specifically to the Ten Lost Tribes.

10 : 24 *Asshur ... smite thee with the rod ... after the manner of Egypt.* Both Rashi and Kimchi explain this to mean that Assyria ruled them as harshly as the Egyptians did, who "appointed taskmasters to afflict them with their burdens." (Exodus 1:11)

ᵃ Heb. *shear jashub.*

Isaiah 10

Midian at the Rock of Oreb; and as His rod was over the sea, so shall He lift it up after the manner of Egypt. 27. And it shall come to pass in that day, that

His burden shall depart from off thy shoulder,
And his yoke from off thy neck,
And the yoke shall be destroyed by reason of fatness.

28. He is come to Aiath,
He is passed through Migron;
At Michmas he layeth up his baggage;

29. They are gone over the pass;
They have taken up their lodging at Geba;
Ramah trembleth;
Gibeath-shaul is fled.

10 : 27 *His burden shall depart from off thy shoulder.* He continues the metaphor comparing Assyrian oppression with the burdens imposed by Egypt.

The yoke shall be destroyed by reason of fatness. Here Rashi cites the rabbinical statement (Sanhedrin 94b) that the "fatness" which shall destroy the yoke of Assyria means oil, the oil which the pious Hezekiah used to kindle light in synagogues and schools. But Ibn Ezra explains the phrase literally: The

30. Cry thou with a shrill voice, O daughter of Gallim!
Hearken, O Laish! O thou poor Anathoth!
31. Madmenah is in mad flight;
The inhabitants of Gebim flee to cover.
32. This very day shall he halt at Nob,
Shaking his hand at the mount of the daughter of Zion,
The hill of Jerusalem.
33. Behold, the Lord, the LORD of hosts,
Shall lop the boughs with terror;
And the high ones of stature shall be hewn down,
And the lofty shall be laid low.
34. And He shall cut down the thickets of the forest with iron,
And Lebanon shall fall by a mighty one.

Isaiah
10

Assyrian yoke will be broken because Judah will grow strong and fat.

Verses 33 and 34 conclude the prophecy with the same metaphor of destruction which was used in Chapter 9 (Verses 13, 14), the chopping down of the forest. There it was used in describing the destruction of the Northern Kingdom of Israel. Here it describes the future destruction of Assyria.

11

AGAIN A VISION of the great future in which a child born of David's house will usher in a period of universal peace among men and even in the animal world. At that time the scattered exiles of Israel will come and live in unity. It will be a second redemption of Israel, the first being the exodus from Egypt.

Isaiah 1. And there shall come forth a shoot out of the stock
11 of Jesse,
And a twig shall grow forth out of his roots.

11 : 1 *A shoot out of the stock of Jesse.* This is one of the three messianic passages in this early part of the Book of Isaiah. The first is in Chapter 2, Verses 2-4: "And it shall come to pass at the end of days"; the second is in Chapter 9, Verses 1-8: "For a child is born unto us"; and this is the third. These messianic passages present a difficulty to those critical scholars who are, as many of them are, Christian theologians. The three passages mentioned are especially precious to the Christian Church which sees in them the prophecy of the coming of the founder of their faith. For this reason the commentators are strongly inclined to retain these passages as genuine prophecies of Isaiah. On the other hand, these are consolatory passages embodying a great promise to the people of Israel, and these critics have a tendency to consider such promises as being the addition of a later writer who is moved to mitigate the severities of Isaiah's promise. Eissfeldt (p. 317) says: "The return to a homeland, teeming with marvelous

2. And the spirit of the LORD shall rest upon him,
   The spirit of wisdom and understanding,
   The spirit of counsel and might,
   The spirit of knowledge and of the fear of the LORD.

Isaiah 11

fruitfulness, under the rule of a righteous king. It is generally recognized that these passages do not derive from Isaiah."

As a result of these opposing moods in the modern critics, these three messianic passages are constantly debated. Generally, only the second is considered to be by Isaiah. But Ehrlich believes, contrary to most modern commentators, that it is much older than Isaiah. Whether the passage is Isaiah's or not, it is well integrated into the thought of the prophet. In the tenth chapter, especially Verses 18 and 19, the metaphor used for the destruction of Assyria is that the trees of the forest will be chopped down. Also in the end of the sixth chapter, in the punishment for sinful Israel, the same metaphor is used, and, there in 6:13, it speaks of only a stump remaining and the holy seed inherent in the stump which will sprout again. If in 6:13 the phrase of "the holy seed" is indeed a later addition, as some critics say, then the later author who wrote this messianic passage in chapter 11 used the same metaphor and speaks of a sprout coming out of the stump of the tree of the house of Jesse. Ibn Ezra, Rashi, and the Malbim, and Krauss recognize this passage as not foretelling the reign of the good Hezekiah but as being messianic. The Targum makes this quite clear in its paraphrase. It reads the verse as follows: "A king will come from among the sons of Jesse and a Messiah from his children." Kimchi somehow merges the two possibilities as to Hezekiah and the Messiah and understands the verse as follows: That the sermon was preached in the days of Hezekiah when the miracle of the destruction of the Assyrian army besieging Jerusalem took place; and he says that what Isaiah told his people was this: Do not wonder at the miracle of the destruction of the Assyrian army; God will bring about a greater miracle, namely, the coming of the Messiah.

11:2 *The spirit of the Lord.* The Targum says this means the spirit of prophecy; and Kimchi says the spirit of the Lord refers to the succeeding words, as if to say the spirit of the Lord which is the spirit of wisdom, understanding, etc.

Wisdom and understanding. These are the same qualities given to the Messiah in Chapter 9, Verse 5. Ibn Ezra calls at-

75

Isaiah 11

3. And his delight shall be in the fear of the LORD;
   And he shall not judge after the sight of his eyes,
   Neither decide after the hearing of his ears;
4. But with righteousness shall he judge the poor,
   And decide with equity for the meek of the land;
   And he shall smite the land with the rod of his mouth,
   And with the breath of his lips shall he slay the wicked.
5. And righteousness shall be the girdle of his loins,
   And faithfulness the girdle of his reins.
6. And the wolf shall dwell with the lamb,
   And the leopard shall lie down with the kid;
   And the calf and the young lion and the fatling together;
   And a little child shall lead them.
7. And the cow and the bear shall feed;
   Their young ones shall lie down together;
   And the lion shall eat straw like the ox.

tention to the fact that Joshua too was endowed with the "spirit of understanding." (Deuteronomy 34:9)

11 : 3 *His delight shall be ... he shall not judge after the sight of his eyes ... his ears.* The word translated here "his delight" Rashi takes to come from the word "ruach" (spirit) meaning he will be infused with the spirit of the Lord. Ibn Ezra, however, takes this word in connection with the rest of the verse: He shall not judge by his eyes and his ears. He takes the word here translated "delight" as connected with the noun "reach" (smell) and he says the eye or the ear can be deceived but the nose can never be deceived. In other words, the Messiah will not judge by appearances or sounds but will be able instantly to scent out wickedness.

11 : 4 *Smite the land with the rod of his mouth.* The Targum says that he will strike down the wicked to the ground. (So, too, Rashi.) Kimchi, emphasizing the words "the rod of his mouth," said the Messiah will utter a curse against the wicked and they shall perish.

11 : 5 *Righteousness ... the girdle of his loins.* The Targum takes this symbolically and says it means that he will surround

76

8. And the sucking child shall play on the hole of the asp,
And the weaned child shall put his hand on the basilisk's den.
9. They shall not hurt nor destroy
In all My holy mountain;
For the earth shall be full of the knowledge of the LORD,
As the waters cover the sea.
10. And it shall come to pass in that day,
That the root of Jesse, that standeth for an ensign of the peoples,
Unto him shall the nations seek;
And his resting-place shall be glorious.
11. And it shall come to pass in that day,
That the Lord will set His hand again the second time
To recover the remnant of His people,
That shall remain from Assyria, and from Egypt,

Isaiah
11

himself with faithful servants (as a man wraps himself in a cloak). (So does Rashi.)

11 : 6-8 *The wolf shall dwell with the lamb . . . the lion shall eat straw like the ox.* There will be peace in the animal kingdom which now is "red in beak and claw." The carnivorous animals will cease to be carnivorous (shall eat straw) and will no longer need to kill for their food.

11 : 9 *They shall not hurt . . . earth shall be full of the knowledge of the Lord.* Ibn Ezra comments: He who knows the Lord will never destroy. He will always build and improve.

11 : 11 *The Lord will set His hand . . . the second time . . . To recover the remnant of His people.* In the messianic day there will be a complete ingathering of the children of Israel scattered all over the world. The commentators say that this messianic ingathering is called "the second time," because the first time was the redemption from Egypt. But this explanation creates a difficulty. Were they not also redeemed from Babylon after the captivity? Then should not the prophet have called the messianic ingathering "the third time"? Rashi explains that the prophet could not count the return from Babylon as the second deliver-

77

Isaiah 11

And from Pathros, and from Cush, and from Elam,
And from Shinar, and from Hamath, and from the islands of the sea.

12. And He will set up an ensign for the nations,
And will assemble the dispersed of Israel,
And gather together the scattered of Judah
From the four corners of the earth.

13. The envy also of Ephraim shall depart,
And they that harass Judah shall be cut off;
Ephraim shall not envy Judah,
And Judah shall not vex Ephraim.

14. And they shall fly down upon the shoulder of the Philistines on the west;
Together shall they spoil the children of the east;

ance because after they had returned they were still under the rule of a foreign king, Cyrus. Kimchi explains that from Babylon only the tribes of Judah and Benjamin returned; and Ibn Ezra adds that not even all of Judah returned from Babylon. The complete ingathering will not come before Messiah's time.

11 : 13 *Ephraim shall not envy Judah.* The old hostility between the Northern Kingdom and the southern will cease in the time of the Messiah. The same thought is given in Ezekiel (37: 11) when he symbolically takes a stick representing Judah and a stick representing Ephraim and holds them together in his hands.

11 : 14 *Fly down upon the shoulder of the Philistines.* The next two verses describing conquest are out of harmony with the spirit of peace that is described as reigning in messianic times. The phrase "the shoulder of the Philistines" is taken by the

> They shall put forth their hand upon Edom and Moab;
> And the children of Ammon shall obey them.
> 15. And the LORD will utterly destroy the tongue of the Egyptian sea;
> And with His scorching wind will He shake His hand over the River.
> And will smite it into seven streams,
> And cause men to march over dryshod.
> 16. And there shall be a highway for the remnant of His people,
> That shall remain from Assyria;
> Like as there was for Israel
> In the day that he came up out of the land of Egypt.

Targum and Rashi to refer to the union between Ephraim and Judah who will fight their enemies, "shoulder to shoulder."

11 : 15 *Destroy the tongue of the Egyptian sea.* The Targum explains this to mean that God will dry up the sea, and Rashi adds so that those who are exiled in Egypt can return. This explanation of Rashi clearly has in mind "the second time" of redemption, Egypt being the first. In the first redemption they crossed the sea dry shod. So the miracle will be repeated.

11 : 16 *There shall be a highway.* The same thought is expressed in Chapter 40, Verse 3. God will have a highway built for the return of the exiles.

The text would read more smoothly if the second half of Verse 16 were the first half. Thus it would read (15, 16): And cause men to march over dry shod as Israel did in the day that he came up out of the land of Egypt.

12

THIS CHAPTER is a psalm, and it is the psalm which the people will be singing at the time of the messianic deliverance. Two other psalms in Isaiah are Chapter 25 beginning, "O Lord, Thou art my God," and Chapter 26 beginning, "In that day shall this song be sung."

Isaiah 12

1. And in that day thou shalt say:
   'I will give thanks unto Thee, O LORD;
   For though Thou wast angry with me,
   Thine anger is turned away, and Thou comfortest me.
2. Behold, God is my salvation;
   I will trust, and will not be afraid;
   For GOD the LORD is my strength and song;
   And He is become my salvation.'

3. Therefore with joy shall ye draw water
   Out of the wells of salvation.
4. And in that day shall ye say:
   'Give thanks unto the LORD, proclaim His name,
   Declare His doings among the peoples,
   Make mention that His name is exalted.
5. Sing unto the LORD; for He hath done gloriously;
   This is made known in all the earth.
6. Cry aloud and shout, thou inhabitant of Zion;
   For great is the Holy One of Israel in the midst of thee.'

Isaiah 12

12 : 1 *I will give thanks ... though Thou wast angry.* The Targum says, "I sing because although when I had sinned You were angry with me, yet, when I returned to Your law, You showed me mercy." Rashi: "I sing because my exile was an atonement for my sins." The thought expressed by Rashi is analogous to that in Psalm 119:71: "It is good for me that I have been afflicted for thus have I learned Thy precepts." Kimchi says, "The reason for my singing is that You did not let me remain in the exile, as I had deserved."

12 : 3 *With joy ... Out of the wells of salvation.* Both the Targum and Rashi make use of a favorite rabbinic metaphor in which the Torah and study are compared to water. The Targum translates the verse, "You will receive new learning in joy from the noblest of the righteous." And Rashi says: God's redemption will broaden their minds and the deeper meanings of the Torah will become clear to them, those which in Babylon were forgotten because of their troubles. Ehrlich notes: The great victories were celebrated at the feast of Sukot. Part of the Sukot ceremony is the water libation. The phrase here, "waters of joy," refers to this.

13

THIS IS the first of a series of dirges, prophesying the downfall of various nations. These dirges continue through Chapter 23. Many scholars consider Chapters 13 through 23 as a separate booklet of denunciations appended to the collection of the prophecies of Isaiah. This first one is a "burden" against Babylon. He describes how the powerful Babylonians who had conquered Assyria will now be overcome by a new enemy, the Medes and the Persians. (Verse 17) The end of the chapter is similar to other descriptions of devastation in the book, in which the city becomes a wilderness and only desert animals live among its ruins.

Isaiah 13 1. The burden of Babylon, which Isaiah the son of Amoz did see.

13 : 1 *The burden of Babylon, which Isaiah the son of Amoz did see.* The word "burden" is used in the prophetic literature for a prophecy predicting doom against a foreign nation. Jeremiah (23:33, 34) calls upon his people not to use the word any more. This burden, or dire prophecy, is the first of a succession of "burdens" preached against various nations, Babylon, Moab, Tyre, Egypt, Ethiopia, Damascus, and others. Krauss says that Isaiah lived in the time of the Assyrian ascendancy and could hardly have predicted the fall of Babylon, a nation which had not yet become prominent. Eissfeldt calls attention to the fact that

Isaiah 13

2. Set ye up an ensign upon the high mountain,
   Lift up the voice unto them,
   Wave the hand, that they may go
   Into the gates of the nobles.
3. I have commanded My consecrated ones,
   Yea, I have called My mighty ones for Mine anger,
   Even My proudly exulting ones.
4. Hark, a tumult in the mountains,
   Like as of a great people!
   Hark, the uproar of the kingdoms
   Of the nations gathered together!
   The LORD of hosts mustereth
   The host of the battle.
5. They come from a far country,
   From the end of heaven,
   Even the LORD, and the weapons of His indignation,
   To destroy the whole earth.
6. Howl ye; for the day of the LORD is at hand;
   As destruction from the Almighty shall it come.
7. Therefore shall all hands be slack,

the prophecy here mentions the Medes who appeared 538 B.C.E., a century and a half after Isaiah's time. But Ibn Ezra believes that Isaiah predicts the fall of Babylon because in his time the Babylonians had begun to conquer Assyria.

13 : 2 *Lift up the voice ... Wave the hand.* Rashi says that the voice was lifted up for those of the invaders who were near, and the hand waved as a signal to those who were further away.

13 : 3 *My consecrated ones ... I have called.* God calls the Medes and the Persians "His" because it is He who summons them to carry out His purposes against Babylon, as in Chapter 10, Verse 5 He calls upon Assyria to be the rod of "Mine anger" to carry out His purposes against Israel.

13 : 5 *From a far country.* Ibn Ezra calls attention to the fact that the Medes came from far away. (Elam)

13 : 6 *As destruction from the Almighty.* Both Kimchi and Ibn Ezra explain this as a destruction having come from God, one from which one cannot escape. Perhaps this expression is the origin of our modern phrase for natural catastrophe, "act of God."

Isaiah 13

And every heart of man shall melt.
8. And they shall be affrighted;
Pangs and throes shall take hold of them;
They shall be in pain as a woman in travail;
They shall look aghast one at another;
Their faces shall be faces of flame.
9. Behold, the day of the LORD cometh,
Cruel, and full of wrath and fierce anger;
To make the earth a desolation,
And to destroy the sinners thereof out of it.
10. For the stars of heaven and the constellations thereof
Shall not give their light;
The sun shall be darkened in his going forth,
And the moon shall not cause her light to shine.
11. And I will visit upon the world their evil,
And upon the wicked their iniquity;
And I will cause the arrogancy of the proud to cease,
And will lay low the haughtiness of the tyrants.
12. I will make man more rare than fine gold,
Even man than the pure gold of Ophir.
13. Therefore I will make the heavens to tremble,
And the earth shall be shaken out of her place,

13 : 8 *Their faces shall be faces of flame.* Rashi says that means their faces (i.e., of the Babylonians) will be yellow with fear. Kimchi says, red with shame. And Ibn Ezra, stressing the root of the word which means "fire" or "flame," says that it means the face burned with intense pain.

13 : 10 *Stars . . . and constellations.* The word translated here as "constellations" is "kesil" which literally means a fool. In Job (9:9) and Amos (5:8) this constellation which has always been visualized as a man is translated Orion (i.e., the heavenly hunter). The Targum translates it as "giants." Our translation, because the word is used here for the only time in Scripture in the plural, calls it "constellations." But Krauss explains the plural and retains the usual translation of "Orion" by saying that it means Orion and its accompanying stars (i.e., the Dog Stars, Sirius and Procyon).

13 : 12 *I will make man more rare than fine gold.* Ibn Ezra

> For the wrath of the LORD of hosts,
> And for the day of His fierce anger.
>
> 14. And it shall come to pass, that as the chased gazelle,
> And as sheep that no man gathereth,
> They shall turn every man to his own people,
> And shall flee every man to his own land.
> 15. Every one that is found shall be thrust through;
> And every one that is caught shall fall by the sword.
> 16. Their babes also shall be dashed in pieces before their eyes;
> Their houses shall be spoiled,
> And their wives ravished.
> 17. Behold, I will stir up the Medes against them,
> Who shall not regard silver,
> And as for gold, they shall not delight in it.
> 18. And their bows shall dash the young men in pieces;
> And they shall have no pity on the fruit of the womb;
> Their eye shall not spare children.
> 19. And Babylon, the glory of kingdoms,
> The beauty of the Chaldeans' pride,
> Shall be as when God overthrew Sodom and Gomorrah.

Isaiah 13

gives the plain meaning of this verse that the men will be killed out and so men will be rare among the survivors. Kimchi connects this verse with Verse 17 which says that the invading Medes and Persians have no use for gold and silver; and, he says, men will be more rare than gold means that the Medes and Persians will scorn to accept money ransom but will spare nobody. However, Rashi gives an imaginative interpretation. In the Book of Daniel in Chapter 5, at the end of the chapter, it is Daniel who interprets the handwriting on the wall to mean that the Medes and the Persians will soon conquer Babylon. Therefore it is he who is referred to in this verse. He is called "the man more precious than gold" because the Babylonian king, Belshazzar, "clothed Daniel with purple and put a chain of gold around his neck."

13 : 19 *Babylon ... shall be as ... Sodom and Gomorrah.* This same symbol of complete destruction is used in Chapter 1, Verse

Isaiah 13

20. It shall never be inhabited,
    Neither shall it be dwelt in from generation to generation;
    Neither shall the Arabian pitch tent there;
    Neither shall the shepherds make their fold there.
21. But wild-cats shall lie there;
    And their houses shall be full of ferrets;
    And ostriches shall dwell there,
    And satyrs shall dance there.
22. And jackals shall howl in their castles,
    And wild-dogs in the pleasant palaces;
    And her time is near to come,
    And her days shall not be prolonged.

9 when the children of Judah say, "If God had not left us a remnant, we would have been like Sodom and Gomorrah," i.e., completely destroyed.

13 : 21-22 *Wild-cats . . . jackals . . . wild-dogs.* Babylon will be so completely destroyed that it will become a desert and a desolation and wild animals will wander through its ruins. The same description of Babylon turned into a wilderness is used by Jeremiah (50:39) and he also speaks of jackals and wild-cats.

14

THE FIRST PART of the chapter up to Verse 23 continues the "burden" against Babylon, and it describes how the proud king of Babylon will be received by shouts of derision when he descends into the nether-world. Babylon is described as if it were the bright morning star fallen into darkness like a meteor in the skies.

Verse 24 to Verse 27 is a short "burden" against Assyria; and Verse 28 to the end is a short "burden" against the Philistines.

1. For the LORD will have compassion on Jacob, and will yet choose Israel, and set them in their own land; and the stranger shall join himself with them, and they shall cleave to the house of Jacob. 2. And the peoples shall take them, and bring them to their place; and the house of Israel shall possess them in

Isaiah 14

14:1 *The Lord will have compassion on Jacob.* The first three verses constitute a prose interlude in the midst of the dirge, and it is for the purpose of explaining why Babylon will be destroyed. The reason is that since they captured Judah and subjected the people to servitude Babylon must now be destroyed that the people of Israel may go free.

14:2 *Peoples shall take them, and bring them to their place.* Babylonians or other captive people will accompany the Jews on their return to their homeland. The same idea is expressed in

Isaiah 14

the land of the LORD for servants and for handmaids; and they shall take them captive, whose captives they were; and they shall rule over their oppressors. 3. And it shall come to pass in the day that the LORD shall give thee rest from thy travail, and from thy trouble, and from the hard service wherein thou wast made to serve, 4. that thou shalt take up this parable against the king of Babylon, and say:
How hath the oppressor ceased!
The exactress of gold ceased!
5. The LORD hath broken the staff of the wicked,
The sceptre of the rulers,
6. That smote the peoples in wrath
With an incessant stroke,
That ruled the nations in anger,
With a persecution that none restrained.
7. The whole earth is at rest, and is quiet;
They break forth into singing.
8. Yea, the cypresses rejoice at thee,
And the cedars of Lebanon:

Isaiah 60, and for that reason some scholars consider that this dirge or this explanatory prose interlude is by the same author as Isaiah 60.

Israel shall possess them . . . for servants. Ibn Ezra explains this by saying that during the liberation from Babylon people of various races will note the great honor that the Persian king Cyrus is doing to the people of Israel, and so they will want to join them on their return home and to work for them and be their servants.

14:8 *The cypresses rejoice . . . No feller is come up against us.* The various destructions described by Isaiah always involve destruction of the forests. Therefore, now that he described the land at peace, he pictured the forests themselves as feeling secure. The cypresses and the cedars rejoice and say, "No destroyer is coming to fell us down."

14:9 *The nether-world . . . is moved . . . to meet thee.* The nether-world in Scripture is not a place of torment and punishment as it became in the imagination of later generations but is a subterranean dwelling place where the dead are, something like

'Since thou art laid down,
No feller is come up against us.'
9. The nether-world from beneath is moved for thee
To meet thee at thy coming;
The shades are stirred up for thee,
Even all the chief ones of the earth;
All the kings of the nations
Are raised up from their thrones.
10. All they do answer
And say unto thee:
'Art thou also become weak as we?
Art thou become like unto us?
11. Thy pomp is brought down to the nether-world,
And the noise of thy psalteries;
The maggot is spread under thee,
And the worms cover thee.'
12. How art thou fallen from heaven,
O day-star, son of the morning!
How art thou cut down to the ground,
That didst cast lots over the nations!

Isaiah

14

the Greek concept of Hades. While the biblical writers do not think of this too often to describe it in detail, the author of this chapter visualizes those shades who were kings on earth now seated on thrones in the nether-world, "The kings of the nations are raised up from their thrones." The poet describes in the next few verses how the kings in the nether-world greet Babylon with taunts and mockeries, with the general theme, "Now you who were so boastful and strong are as weak and helpless as we are."

14 : 12 *Fallen from heaven.* Among the taunts of the kings in the nether-world is that Babylon has fallen like a star from the heavens. This is a picture of the sudden plunging and extinguishing of a meteor. The phrase, "day-star, son of the morning," refers to that very bright morning star, Lucifer the light-carrier. Out of this metaphor of Babylon, like the bright morning star flashing and extinguishing like a meteor, arose the later legend in which Lucifer the morning star became a name for Satan, that Satan rebelled against God and was hurled down to the nether-world as punishment; so in Luke 10:18, "I saw Satan cast down from heaven." The legend of Satan cast down for his rebellion

Isaiah 14

13. And thou saidst in thy heart:
    'I will ascend into heaven,
    Above the stars of God
    Will I exalt my throne;
    And I will sit upon the mount of meeting,
    In the uttermost parts of the north;
14. I will ascend above the heights of the clouds;
    I will be like the Most High.'
15. Yet thou shalt be brought down to the nether-world,
    To the uttermost parts of the pit.
16. They that saw thee do narrowly look upon thee,
    They gaze earnestly at thee:
    'Is this the man that made the earth to tremble,
    That did shake kingdoms;
17. That made the world as a wilderness,
    And destroyed the cities thereof;
    That opened not the house of his prisoners?'
18. All the kings of the nations,
    All of them, sleep in glory,
    Every one in his own house.
19. But thou art cast forth away from thy grave
    Like an abhorred offshoot,
    In the raiment of the slain, that are thrust through with the sword,
    That go down to the pavement of the pit,
    As a carcass trodden under foot.

against God is reinforced further in the taunting of the kings when they described Babylon's boastful pride, "I will ascend into heaven; above the stars of God will I exalt my throne."

Thou didst cast lots over the nations! The words "cast lots" in this translation can mean also to weaken or defeat. Both Kimchi and Ibn Ezra take it that way. But Rashi, based on the statement in the Talmud, Sabbath 149b, takes the verse to mean "cast lots," as in our translation.

14 : 18 *Kings of the nations . . . sleep in glory.* The kings would build beautiful mausoleums or other imposing graves for themselves.

14 : 19 *Thou art cast forth . . . from thy grave.* Ibn Ezra cites the tradition that Nebuchadnezzar, king of Babylon, was dragged

Isaiah 14

20. Thou shalt not be joined with them in burial,
    Because thou hast destroyed thy land,
    Thou hast slain thy people;
    The seed of evil-doers shall not
    Be named for ever.
21. Prepare ye slaughter for his children
    For the iniquity of their fathers;
    That they rise not up, and possess the earth,
    And fill the face of the world with cities.
22. And I will rise up against them, saith the LORD of hosts, and cut off from Babylon name and remnant, and offshoot and offspring, saith the LORD. 23. I will also make it a possession for the bittern, and pools of water; and I will sweep it with the besom of destruction, saith the LORD of hosts.
24. The LORD of hosts hath sworn, saying:
    Surely as I have thought, so shall it come to pass;
    And as I have purposed, so shall it stand,
25. That I will break Asshur in My land,
    And upon My mountains tread him under foot;
    Then shall his yoke depart from off them,
    And his burden depart from off their shoulder.
26. This is the purpose that is purposed upon the whole earth;
    And this is the hand that is stretched out upon all the nations.

out of his grave and cast about, as the verse says, as a "carcass trodden under foot."

14 : 25 *That I will break Asshur in My land.* This seems to be an interruption of a dirge against Babylon but it really is not, though our English translation does not quite make the connection clear. Rashi's comment clarified the meaning: "God says to Babylon, 'From what I have done to Asshur, you can be certain of what I will now do to you.'" In other words, it is addressed to Babylon and so is consistent with the rest of the dirge.

14 : 26 *This is the purpose ... upon the whole earth.* Rashi and Ibn Ezra both explain this to mean: "As I did to Asshur, so I will do to Babylon and so I will do to all oppressors among the nations."

Isaiah 14

27. For the LORD of hosts hath purposed,
    And who shall disannul it?
    And His hand is stretched out,
    And who shall turn it back?
28. In the year that king Ahaz died was this burden.
29. Rejoice not, O Philistia, all of thee,
    Because the rod that smote thee is broken:
    For out of the serpent's root shall come forth a basilisk,
    And his fruit shall be a flying serpent.
30. And the first-born of the poor shall feed,
    And the needy shall lie down in safety;

14:28 *In the year that Ahaz died.* Although part of this chapter, this is another subject. It is a "burden" or a dirge against the Philistines. The dating of this "burden" is relevant to its meaning; during the reign of the evil king Ahaz, the Philistines invaded Judea and devastated the land. (II Chronicles 28:18) So Rashi explains, "Now that the wicked king (Ahaz) is dead, and his righteous son Hezekiah is coming to the throne, God will grant us the strength to defeat the Philistines."

14:29 *Rejoice not, O Philistia ... out of the serpent's root ... a basilisk.* Rashi and the Targum both indicate that this means Hezekiah. The Philistines are told, "Do not rejoice that your enemy Ahaz is dead. His son will be of even greater danger to you."

And I will kill thy root with famine,
And thy remnant shall be slain.
31. Howl, O gate; cry, O city;
Melt away, O Philistia, all of thee;
For there cometh a smoke out of the north,
And there is no straggler in his ranks.
32. What then shall one answer the messengers of the nation?
That the Lord hath founded Zion,
And in her shall the afflicted of His people take refuge.

Isaiah 14

14 : 30 *The poor shall feed . . . I will kill thy root with famine.* Those whom you have impoverished will now have food, and you yourself will be tried by famine.

14 : 31 *O Philistia . . . a smoke out of the north.* Rashi and Kimchi take this to refer to Hezekiah, who will march down from the north, i.e., Jerusalem to Gaza, the chief city of the Philistines.

14 : 32 *What shall one answer the messengers . . . ?* Rashi takes "messengers" to be the subject of the verb "answer." He takes this verse to mean that when the messengers go forth from Jerusalem and are asked what happened they will answer, "The Lord hath founded Zion." Ibn Ezra understands it as follows: What will the nations of the world say when asked? They will say the Lord hath founded Zion.

15

Isaiah 15

THE "BURDEN" here is against Moab. The prophet describes the destruction of each of the cities of Moab as they are being destroyed.

> 1. The burden of Moab.
> For in the night that Ar of Moab is laid waste,
> He is brought to ruin;
> For in the night that Kir of Moab is laid waste,
> He is brought to ruin.

15 : 1 *The burden of Moab.* This dirge against Moab continues through Chapter 16. Most scholars agree that it is not by Isaiah. Krauss believes that the sermon is older than Isaiah and was embodied in the book as appropriate in this section of dirges. (See also Eissfeldt, p. 320.) The basis for this belief is very likely Verse 13 of Chapter 16, "This is the word that the Lord spoke concerning Moab in times past, but now the Lord hath spoken: 'Within three years,'" etc. In other words, this older dirge is quoted here, now, because the time has come for its fulfillment. Krauss suggests that this dirge against Moab was written in the time of the king Jereboam the Second, who invaded and conquered Moab; and this conquest had been prophesied by the Prophet Jonah, the son of Amittai. (See II Kings 14:25.) It is therefore speculated that this dirge against Moab was the one

Isaiah 15

2. He is gone up to Baith, and to Dibon,
   To the high places, to weep;
   Upon Nebo, and upon Medeba, Moab howleth;
   On all their heads is baldness,
   Every beard is shaven.
3. In their streets they gird themselves with sackcloth;
   On their housetops, and in their broad places,
   Every one howleth, weeping profusely.
4. And Heshbon crieth out, and Elealeh;
   Their voice is heard even unto Jahaz;
   Therefore the armed men of Moab cry aloud;
   His soul is faint within him.
5. My heart crieth out for Moab;
   Her fugitives reach unto Zoar,
   A heifer of three years old;
   For by the ascent of Luhith
   With weeping they go up;
   For in the way of Horonaim
   They raise up a cry of destruction.
6. For the Waters of Nimrim shall be desolate;
   For the grass is withered away, the herbage faileth,
   There is no green thing.
7. Therefore the abundance they have gotten,
   And that which they have laid up,
   Shall they carry away to the brook of the willows.
8. For the cry is gone round about
   The borders of Moab;
   The howling thereof unto Eglaim,

---

prophesied by Jonah, as stated in the Book of Kings. It consists chiefly of a list of the various cities, one by one, as they were conquered in succession.

15 : 2 *To the high places, to weep.* The Temples were on the high places.

Baldness ... beard shaven. The hair was cut off or plucked out as a mark of mourning.

15 : 5 *A heifer of three years old.* Rashi and Krauss explain that a three-year-old heifer is then at its best in health and beauty. So Moab at its most prosperous period was to be destroyed.

15 : 7 *Carry away to the brook of the willows.* Ibn Ezra ex-

Isaiah 15

And the howling thereof unto Beerelim.
9. For the waters of Dimon are full of blood;
For I will bring yet more upon Dimon,
A lion upon him that escapeth of Moab,
And upon the remnant of the land.

plains the invaders will carry away the loot to the brook where their boats are waiting to receive them.

16

CHAPTER 16 continues the dirge for Moab. It begins with a gift sent by the fugitive Moabites to the king of Judah, asking that he give refuge to the Moabite fugitives. A fuller version of this "burden" is found in Jeremiah, Chapter 48.

> 1. Send ye the lambs for the ruler of the land
> From the crags that are toward the wilderness,
> Unto the mount of the daughter of Zion.

Isaiah 16

16 : 1 *Send ye the lambs ... unto ... the daughter of Zion.* Rashi reads this as connected with the account in II Kings 3:4 where Mesha, king of Moab, sent the wool of a hundred thousand lambs to the king of Israel, and therefore what the prophet is saying now is: "Let your present ruler send a similar tribute to Jerusalem." Kimchi further explains that this prophecy was uttered after the Assyrians destroyed the Northern Kingdom to whom the Moabite tribute was originally sent. Therefore it should be sent to Jerusalem, to king Hezekiah who, being a righteous king, will deal mercifully with you. The general relevance of this verse, "send ... lambs," in the dirge of doom is that the Moabites, fleeing from destruction, gathered as we are told in Verse 2 like flying birds at the brook of Arnon, which is the border of Israel. Ibn Ezra translates the noun instead of "lambs" as "a swift camel"

Isaiah 16

2. For it shall be that, as wandering birds,
   As a scattered nest,
   So shall the daughters of Moab be
   At the fords of Arnon.
3. 'Give counsel, execute justice;
   Make thy shadow as the night in the midst of the noonday;
   Hide the outcasts; betray not the fugitive.
4. Let mine outcasts dwell with thee,
   As for Moab, be thou a covert to him from the face of the spoiler.'
   For the extortion is at an end, spoiling ceaseth,
   They that trampled down are consumed out of the land;
5. And a throne is established through mercy,
   And there sitteth thereon in truth, in the tent of David,
   One that judgeth, and seeketh justice, and is ready in righteousness.
6. We have heard of the pride of Moab;
   He is very proud;

which is called "the king of the desert" and he reads the sentence, "Send the swift camel, the king of the desert, to Zion to ask for refuge."

From the crags. The word translated here as "crags" means simply "rock" and is in the singular. Krauss says this is the Rock City or Petra, which may have been the capital of Moab in those days.

16 : 2 *The fords of Arnon.* This is the border. The refugees are gathered "like birds" at the border waiting for a chance to fly over to safety in Judah.

16 : 4 *Let mine outcasts dwell with thee.* Moab asks for refuge and says in Verse 3: Protect us as a cloud against the heat of the noon-day sun. But Verse 4 says: "Moab be thou a covert" which could imply that the refugees are going the other way, from Israel to Moab. This is how Rashi and Ibn Ezra take the verse. But the text is clearly difficult and confusing. The whole dirge is against Moab, so we would expect that it is the Moabites who will be the refugees. In fact, the reading is corrected by Krauss

> Even of his haughtiness, and his pride, and his arrogancy,
> His ill-founded boastings.
> 7. Therefore shall Moab wail for Moab,
> Every one shall wail;
> For the sweet cakes of Kir-hareseth shall ye mourn,
> Sorely stricken.
> 8. For the fields of Heshbon languish,
> And the vine of Sibmah,
> Whose choice plants did overcome
> The lords of nations;
> They reached even unto Jazer,
> They wandered into the wilderness;
> Her branches were spread abroad,
> They passed over the sea.
> 9. Therefore I will weep with the weeping of Jazer
> For the vine of Sibmah;
> I will water thee with my tears,
> O Heshbon, and Elealeh;
> For upon thy summer fruits and upon thy harvest
> The battle shout is fallen.

Isaiah 16

on the basis of the ancient versions and reads: "Let the outcasts of Moab dwell with thee." This fits the sequence much better and is in harmony with Verse 5: "There sitteth in the tent of David one that seeketh righteousness." There is a just king now in Jerusalem (Hezekiah) and the Moabite refugees can expect mercy from him.

16 : 6 *The pride of Moab.* After mentioning the episode of a swift messenger sent to Jerusalem asking for refuge, the dirge continues, speaking of the pride of Moab and its impending misfortune.

16 : 7 *Sweet cakes of Kir.* The word translated here "sweet cakes" can also be translated "the walls" or the "fortifications." So do Rashi, Kimchi, and Ibn Ezra take it. But Ibn Ezra prefers to translate it, "the sweet wine of Kir." Jeremiah reads: "The men of Kir." (48:31)

16 : 8 *Choice plants did overcome the lords of nations.* Ibn Ezra reverses the phrase and says the chief of the nations (i.e., Assyria) destroyed the choice plants (i.e., of Moab).

Isaiah 16

10. And gladness and joy are taken away
    Out of the fruitful field;
    And in the vineyards there shall be no singing,
    Neither shall there be shouting;
    No treader shall tread out wine in the presses;
    I have made the vintage shout to cease.
11. Wherefore my heart moaneth like a harp for Moab,
    And mine inward parts for Kirheres.
12. And it shall come to pass, when it is seen that Moab hath wearied himself upon the high place, that he shall come to his sanctuary to pray; but he shall not prevail.
13. This is the word that the LORD spoke concerning Moab in time past.
14. But now the LORD hath spoken, saying: 'Within three years, as the years of a hireling, and the glory of Moab shall wax contemptible for all his great multitude; and the remnant shall be very small and without strength.'

16 : 12 *Moab hath wearied himself.* In final desperation the Moabites will abandon all their minor shrines and deities and gather at the great shrine in final appeal.

16 : 13 *This is the word ... spoken ... in time past.* It is on the basis of this verse that some scholars conclude that this dirge against Moab is an older prophecy which is embodied here in Isaiah.

16 : 14 *But now the Lord hath spoken ... 'Within three years, as the years of a hireling.'* The reason for putting this ancient prophecy here is that now the Lord says the old dirge will be fulfilled within three years. "The years of a hireling" mean that a man hired out for a certain time counts the days and does not stay a day longer than he has to. Therefore it means in three short years will the prophecy of doom be fulfilled.

17

CHAPTER 17 is the "burden" against Damascus. Aram (Syria) whose capital is Damascus joined the Northern Kingdom of Israel in the attempt to capture Jerusalem (referred to in Chapters 7 and 8). Now Damascus will itself be destroyed by the Assyrians. The result of this conquest will be that the people of the Northern Kingdom, now that their great ally is gone, will begin to abandon the idols which they worshiped (Verse 8) and will return to God. From Verse 9 to the end, the chapter describes the desolation of the land in the path of the onrushing Assyrian armies.

1. The burden of Damascus.
   Behold, Damascus is taken away from being a city,
   And it shall be a ruinous heap.
2. The cities of Aroer are forsaken;
   They shall be for flocks,

Isaiah 17

17 : 1 *The burden of Damascus.* Actually this "burden" or dirge is directed against the Northern Kingdom of Israel as well as against Damascus, but the editor who wrote this heading felt impelled to omit the name of Israel from it. The two kingdoms, Aram and Northern Israel, conspired against Judah and tried to capture Jerusalem. (See Chapters 7 and 8, where Isaiah preaches on this event.) Therefore most scholars are inclined to believe that this particular dirge, dealing with the same theme,

Isaiah 17

Which shall lie down, and none shall make them afraid.

3. The fortress also shall cease from Ephraim,
And the kingdom from Damascus;
And the remnant of Aram shall be as the glory of the children of Israel,
Saith the LORD of hosts.

4. And it shall come to pass in that day,
That the glory of Jacob shall be made thin,
And the fatness of his flesh shall wax lean.

5. And it shall be as when the harvestman gathereth the standing corn,
And reapeth the ears with his arm;
Yea, it shall be as when one gleaneth ears
In the valley of Rephaim.

6. Yet there shall be left therein gleanings,
As at the beating of an olive-tree,
Two or three berries
In the top of the uppermost bough,
Four or five in the branches of the fruitful tree,
Saith the LORD, the God of Israel.

7. In that day shall a man regard his Maker,
And his eyes shall look to the Holy One of Israel.

8. And he shall not regard the altars,
The work of his hands,
Neither shall he look to that which his fingers have made,
Either the Asherim, or the sun-images.

---

is by Isaiah himself. In the war against Aram and the Northern Kingdom, waged by Assyria, both capitals, Damascus and Samaria, were destroyed and both nations conquered.

17 : 3 *The fortress ... from Ephraim ... the kingdom from Damascus.* This makes it clear that the dirge is directed against both of them. Nevertheless, in the rest of the dirge Damascus is not mentioned further.

17 : 5 *Gleaneth ... in the valley of Rephaim.* Ibn Ezra says (and so does Ehrlich) that Rephaim is a rocky valley where the harvests are always scanty. The Northern Kingdom of Israel after the conquest by Assyria will be virtually starving.

9. In that day shall his strong cities be as the forsaken places, which were forsaken from before the children of Israel, after the manner of woods and lofty forests; and it shall be a desolation.
10. For thou hast forgotten the God of thy salvation,
And thou hast not been mindful of the Rock of thy stronghold;
Therefore thou didst plant plants of pleasantness,
And didst set it with slips of a stranger;
11. In the day of thy planting thou didst make it to grow,
And in the morning thou didst make thy seed to blossom—
A heap of boughs in the day of grief
And of desperate pain.
12. Ah, the uproar of many peoples,
That roar like the roaring of the seas;
And the rushing of nations, that rush
Like the rushing of mighty waters!
13. The nations shall rush like the rushing of many waters;
But He shall rebuke them, and they shall flee far off,
And shall be chased as the chaff of the mountains before the wind,
And like the whirling dust before the storm.

Isaiah 17

17 : 7 *In that day shall a man regard his Maker.* After the defeat of the nation, the chastened people will abandon its idols and return to God.

17 : 9 *In that day . . . shall strong cities be . . . forsaken.* This prose interlude introduces the resumption of the earlier theme of the dirge which speaks of Israel's idolatry and the inevitable invasion.

17 : 12 *The uproar of many peoples.* This refers to the multinational armies of the Assyrians.

17 : 13 *But He shall rebuke them.* Kimchi says that this is a prediction of the destruction of the army of Sennacherib before Jerusalem. In other words, the Assyrians will now conquer Samaria and Damascus but soon they will perish before the walls of Jerusalem.

Isaiah 17

14. At eventide behold terror;
And before the morning they are not.
This is the portion of them that spoil us,
And the lot of them that rob us.

17 : 14 *At eventide ... terror ... before the morning they are not.* According to the account in the Second Book of Kings it was during the night, before dawn, that the Assyrian army perished: "That night the angel of the Lord smote the camp of the Assyrians and in the morning they were dead." (19:35)

18

CHAPTERS 18 AND 19 deal with the "burdens" against Ethiopia and Egypt. Ethiopia is the concern of the prophet because the kings of Judah tried to arrange a multinational alliance against Assyria, the cornerstone of which was to be Egypt which at that time was virtually one with Ethiopia, since there was an Ethiopian dynasty in control of Egypt. The Ethiopians are described as "tall and of glossy skin" and it is predicted that some day they will do homage to the Lord of hosts and Zion. (18:7)

Isaiah 18

1. Ah, land of the buzzing of wings,
   Which is beyond the rivers of Ethiopia;

18:1 *Land of the buzzing of wings.* The Targum translates this as follows: Woe to the land to which ships come from a distant country with their sails spread like eagle's wings, beyond the rivers of India. Even though the word "Kush" which the Targum translates here as "India" is translated nowadays as Ethiopia, in ancient times Ethiopia and India were considered as the same country. Rashi explains the words "buzzing of wings" by the fact that in the East the birds gather in great numbers in the warm lands. In other words, Rashi evidently knew that in the subequatorial countries the birds gather for their winter stay. Ibn Ezra takes the word for "buzzing" from the root "tzel" (shadow), a land shadowed by wings; whereas Krauss takes it to

Isaiah 18

2. That sendeth ambassadors by the sea,
Even in vessels of papyrus upon the waters!
Go, ye swift messengers,
To a nation tall and of glossy skin,
To a people terrible from their beginning onward;
A nation that is sturdy and treadeth down,
Whose land the rivers divide!

3. All ye inhabitants of the world, and ye dwellers on the earth,
When an ensign is lifted up on the mountains, see ye;
And when the horn is blown, hear ye.

4. For thus hath the LORD said unto me:
I will hold Me still, and I will look on in My dwelling-place,
Like clear heat in sunshine,
Like a cloud of dew in the heat of harvest.

mean buzzing of flies, a land which produces armies as numerous as flies.

18 : 2 *Vessels of papyrus.* Kimchi cites Saadia who was an Egyptian and certainly knew much about the Nile country. Saadia said it means papyrus boats which regularly traveled up and down the Nile.

A nation . . . sturdy and treadeth down. The word translated here "sturdy" seems to mean literally "line by line." Rashi, therefore, takes this phrase to mean a nation which for its sins, one by one ("line by line"), will be punished (trodden down). Ibn Ezra has a somewhat related translation. He says it means an illiterate people that has to be taught things "line by line," and, being illiterate, the people is downtrodden.

18 : 3 *When the horn is blown, hear ye.* Both Rashi and Kimchi take this to mean the horn that is sounded at the time of the Messiah. They connect this with Ethiopia as follows: In messianic times, messengers will be sent to Ethiopia so that the exiles may return to the land of Israel.

5. For before the harvest, when the blossom is over,
   And the bud becometh a ripening grape,
   He will cut off the sprigs with pruning-hooks,
   And the shoots will He take away and lop off.
6. They shall be left together unto the ravenous birds of the mountains,
   And to the beasts of the earth;
   And the ravenous birds shall summer upon them,
   And all the beasts of the earth shall winter upon them.
7. In that time shall a present be brought unto the Lord of hosts of a people tall and of glossy skin, and from a people terrible from their beginning onward; a nation that is sturdy and treadeth down, whose land the rivers divide, to the place of the name of the Lord of hosts, the mount Zion.

Isaiah 18

18 : 4 *My dwelling-place, like clear heat.* The Targum which is the source of Rashi and Kimchi's messianic explanation renders this verse to mean, "I will give Israel a secure dwelling-place and will shield them like a cloud in the heat of the day."

18 : 5 *He will cut off the sprigs.* Both Rashi and Kimchi, consistent with their messianic explanation, say that the destruction referred to will take place in the great wars of Gog and Magog, which will take place just before the coming of the Messiah. (See Ezekiel, Chapters 38, 39.) But Ibn Ezra says that this means that God will destroy the Assyrians before their plans of conquest are ripe.

18 : 7 *A present . . . unto the Lord of hosts.* Kimchi says that this means that all nations shall bring offerings unto the Lord, as is mentioned in Isaiah 66:20. Krauss, following the modern understanding that the word "Kush" means Ethiopia, says that a portion of the Ethiopian people will convert to Judaism (as actually has occurred with the Falashas).

19

THE "BURDEN" of Egypt occupies all of Chapter 19. It describes calamities that will come to Egypt, the calamities symbolized by the subsidence of the life-giving River Nile and the consequent drought. From Verse 16 on, Egypt is described as being humbled by its misfortunes and, like Ethiopia, doing homage to the Lord of hosts. Then as if in summary of the preceding "burdens" the chapter ends with the idea that Assyria and Egypt, together with Israel, will be brothers in the worship of God.

Isaiah 19

1. The burden of Egypt.
Behold, the LORD rideth upon a swift cloud,
And cometh unto Egypt;
And the idols of Egypt shall be moved at His presence,
And the heart of Egypt shall melt within it.
2. And I will spur Egypt against Egypt;

19:1 *The Lord rideth upon a swift cloud.* This Metaphor is used also in Psalm 104:3: "Who makest the clouds Thy chariot." Rashi and Ibn Ezra say that this swift cloud simply means that this is not a prophecy for some distant time but one that will be swiftly fulfilled. The Targum, always watchful to avoid human terms used for God, reads the phrase, "God appears in His cloud of glory."

Isaiah 19

And they shall fight every one against his brother,
And every one against his neighbour;
City against city, and kingdom against kingdom.

3. And the spirit of Egypt shall be made empty within it;
And I will make void the counsel thereof;
And they shall seek unto the idols, and to the whisperers,
And to the ghosts, and to the familiar spirits.
4. And I will give over the Egyptians
Into the hand of a cruel lord;
And a fierce king shall rule over them,
Saith the Lord, the LORD of hosts.
5. And the waters shall fail from the sea,
And the river shall be drained dry.
6. And the rivers shall become foul;
The streams of Egypt shall be minished and dried up;
The reeds and flags shall wither.
7. The mosses by the Nile, by the brink of the Nile,
And all that is sown by the Nile,
Shall become dry, be driven away, and be no more.
8. The fishers also shall lament,
And all they that cast angle into the Nile shall mourn,
And they that spread nets upon the waters shall languish.
9. Moreover they that work in combed flax,
And they that weave cotton, shall be ashamed.
10. And her foundations shall be crushed,
All they that make dams shall be grieved in soul.

---

19 : 4 *Egyptians into the hand of a cruel lord.* Since it is difficult to date the chapter precisely, the commentators differ as to who is referred to as the cruel master. Some say the Persians who did conquer the land in the time of Cambyses, and some say it was an earlier conquest.

19 : 5-10 *The waters shall fail . . . the river . . . drained.* Egypt lives by the flooding of the Nile annually to water the land. Therefore a year or a series of years of low water in which the Nile does not rise sufficiently is a national calamity. When the

Isaiah 19

11. The princes of Zoan are utter fools;
    The wisest counsellors of Pharaoh are a senseless counsel;
    How can ye say unto Pharaoh: 'I am the son of the wise,
    The son of ancient kings'?
12. Where are they, then, thy wise men?
    And let them tell thee now;
    And let them know what the LORD of hosts
    Hath purposed concerning Egypt.
13. The princes of Zoan are become fools,
    The princes of Noph are deceived;
    They have caused Egypt to go astray,
    That are the corner-stone of her tribes.
14. The LORD hath mingled within her
    A spirit of dizziness;
    And they have caused Egypt to stagger in every work thereof,
    As a drunken man staggereth in his vomit.
15. Neither shall there be for Egypt any work,
    Which head or tail, palm-branch or rush, may do.

Nile floods the country, the farmers build dams in their fields to keep the Nile water from flowing back to the river too soon. Therefore in Verse 10, "They that make dams shall be grieved in soul." So parched will the country be that even the natural vegetation by the riverside will be dried up (Verse 6: "The reeds and flags shall wither") and even the fish in the river will die because of the low water. (Verse 8: "The fishers also shall lament.")

19:11 *The princes of Zoan are ... fools.* Zoan is another name for Egypt. The verse can mean either that none of the plans made to save the country will succeed and, therefore, the counselors will be frustrated and look foolish; or it may mean that the people will scorn the counselors as fools because of their ineffectiveness.

19:15 *Which head or tail, or branch may do.* The Targum takes this to mean there will not be any king or government left to accomplish anything in Egypt. Ibn Ezra takes this to mean that not even the plants will remain alive.

16. In that day shall Egypt be like unto women; and it shall tremble and fear because of the shaking of the hand of the LORD of hosts, which He shaketh over it. 17. And the land of Judah shall become a terror unto Egypt, whensoever one maketh mention thereof to it; it shall be afraid, because of the purpose of the LORD of hosts, which He purposeth against it.

18. In that day there shall be five cities in the land of Egypt that speak the language of Canaan, and swear to the LORD of hosts; one shall be called The city of destruction.

19. In that day shall there be an altar to the LORD in the midst of the land of Egypt, and a pillar at the border thereof to the LORD. 20. And it shall be for a sign and for a witness unto the LORD of hosts in the land of Egypt; for they shall cry unto the LORD because of the oppressors, and He will send them a saviour, and a defender, who will deliver them. 21. And the LORD shall make Himself known to Egypt, and the Egyptians shall know the LORD in that day; yea, they shall worship with sacrifice and offering, and shall vow a vow unto the LORD, and shall per-

Isaiah
19

19 : 17 *Judah shall become a terror unto Egypt.* Rashi and Kimchi say that this means that when Egypt will hear of God's miraculous deliverance of Judah from Sennacherib they will turn to the worship of God; and Kimchi adds that it will be for this reason that they will turn to God. Therefore Isaiah 45:14: "Egypt and Ethiopia . . . shall make supplication unto Thee: Surely God is in thee . . . (they shall say) there is no other God." It is upon the interpretation of this verse in Chapter 45 that Kimchi bases the vision of the conversion of Egypt to God, spoken of in Verses 18 ff.

19 : 18 *Egypt that speak the language of Canaan.* Ibn Ezra comments that this indicates that the Canaanites spoke the holy tongue.

City of destruction. Ibn Ezra says that the word for destruction "heres" is an error for "cheres" which means the sun and is the name of a town. So does Krauss: It means the City of the Sun or Heliopolis.

III

Isaiah 19

form it. 22. And the LORD will smite Egypt, smiting and healing; and they shall return unto the LORD, and He will be entreated of them, and will heal them. 23. In that day shall there be a highway out of Egypt to Assyria, and the Assyrian shall come into Egypt, and the Egyptian into Assyria; and the Egyptians shall worship with the Assyrians. 24. In that day shall Israel be the third with Egypt and with Assyria, a blessing in the midst of the earth; 25. for that the LORD of hosts hath blessed him, saying: 'Blessed be Egypt My people and Assyria the work of My hands, and Israel Mine inheritance.'

19 : 22 *Smiting and healing.* The punishment that will eventually lead to healing.

19 : 23 *The Egyptians shall worship with the Assyrians.* The Hebrew word for "with" ("et") can also be translated as the mark of the objective case and can mean Egypt will serve the Assyrians. Therefore Ibn Ezra says that some Egyptians will be captured by the Assyrians and then they will make peace. But Kimchi simply says that the word "et" here is used in the sense "im," meaning "with." Therefore it means, as our translation gives it, Egypt will worship God together with the Assyrians.

19 : 25 *Blessed be Egypt My people and Assyria ... and Israel.*
The Targum confines the blessing to Israel and paraphrases the verse, "Blessed be My people Israel who are slaves in Egypt and for whom I did miracles against the Assyrians." But Kimchi renders the text as in our translation. And so does Ibn Ezra: "God has blessed all three nations."

20

THIS IS NOT a prophecy but a record of an historical event. There is another insertion of an historical chronicle in the Book of Isaiah, namely, Chapters 36 to 39. The account here deals with the destruction by the Assyrians of the Philistine metropolis, Ashdod. The small states of Palestine and Syria had made an alliance, counting on the help of Egypt and Ethiopia to overthrow Assyria. The Assyrian army, however, after a long siege, captured Ashdod and the alliance collapsed. (See Eissfeldt, p. 305.)

> 1. In the year that Tartan came unto Ashdod, when Sargon the king of Assyria sent him, and he fought against Ashdod and took it; 2. at that time the LORD spoke by Isaiah the son of Amoz, saying: 'Go, and loose the sackcloth from off thy loins, and put thy shoe from off thy foot.' And he did so, walking naked and barefoot.

20 : 2 *Isaiah . . . loose the sackcloth.* Kimchi explains that Isaiah was wearing sackcloth at the time as a symbol of mourning for the exile of the Ten Tribes by Assyria which had recently occurred.

Walking naked and barefoot. Both Kimchi and Ibn Ezra say that this cannot possibly be taken literally. The Prophet Isaiah would not be walking around naked. Ibn Ezra says in his

Isaiah 20

3. And the LORD said: 'Like as My servant Isaiah hath walked naked and barefoot to be for three years a sign and a wonder upon Egypt and upon Ethiopia, 4. so shall the king of Assyria lead away the captives of Egypt, and the exiles of Ethiopia, young and old, naked and barefoot, and with buttocks uncovered, to the shame of Egypt. 5. And they shall be dismayed and ashamed, because of Ethiopia their expectation, and of Egypt their glory. 6. And the inhabitant of this coast-land shall say in that day: Behold, such is our expectation, whither we fled for help to be delivered from the king of Assyria; and how shall we escape?'

comment to this verse, "See my comment to Hosea 1:1." There he gives the same comment that we find here with Kimchi, namely, that this was merely a prophetic vision; Isaiah saw himself as walking naked. As analogies to this imaginary picture of the prophet, Kimchi says, "One cannot take as literal that God told Hosea to marry a prostitute, or that He told Ezekiel to shave his head and beard or eat bread cooked over burning dung. All these were visions (self-visualizations) not actual occurrences."

20 : 3 *Isaiah ... naked and barefoot ... a sign ... upon Egypt.*
Krauss calls attention to the fact that the siege of Ashdod lasted for three years before the Assyrians could capture the city. The fact that Ashdod was finally captured after three years was a sign to Egypt and Ethiopia that now the road was open for their conquest by the Assyrian armies.

20 : 5-6 *They shall be dismayed.* This clearly means that those who formed the alliance against Assyria, counting on the help of Egypt and Ethiopia, now are dismayed, knowing that those two great powers will be helpless to assist them. Ibn Ezra takes literally the words "whither we fled for help" to mean that those Israelites who fled into Egypt for safety are not secure any more.

21

THERE ARE three "burdens" in this chapter. The first, "the wilderness of the sea," refers to Babylon. It speaks of the Elamites and the Medes (Verse 2) who will march against Babylon. The princes of Babylon will rise from their banquet table and go to the walls. But Babylon will fall. (Verse 9: "Fallen is Babylon.") The second "burden" is against Duma, which may mean Edom. (Verses 11, 12) It consists of a poetic but cryptic dialogue. The man asks the watchman how long the night will last. The watchman answers, "Dawn will come, but then there will be another night." The chapter ends with the third "burden," and it is against Arabia for refusing to give refuge to fugitives from war.

> 1. The burden of the wilderness of the sea.
> As whirlwinds in the South sweeping on,
> It cometh from the wilderness, from a dreadful land.

Isaiah 21

21 : 1 *The burden of the wilderness of the sea.* It is clear that this burden is in reference to the fall of Babylon. (See Verse 9, "Fallen, fallen is Babylon.") But the phrase in the heading, "wilderness of the sea," or "desert of the sea," is difficult to understand. Eissfeldt (pp. 321, 2) says it means the desert road which leads to the Persian Gulf. Ibn Ezra takes the word "yam" here translated as "sea" to mean "west." Therefore to him the heading is "desert of the west," and it means the deserts west of Babylon through which the Persian invaders will come.

Isaiah 21

2. A grievous vision is declared unto me:
    'The treacherous dealer dealeth treacherously, and the spoiler spoileth.
    Go up, O Elam! besiege, O Media!
    All the sighing thereof have I made to cease.'
3. Therefore are my loins filled with convulsion;
    Pangs have taken hold upon me, as the pangs of a woman in travail; I am bent so that I cannot hear;
    I am affrighted so that I cannot see.
4. My heart is bewildered, terror hath overwhelmed me;
    The twilight that I longed for hath been turned for me into trembling.
5. They prepare the table, they light the lamps, they eat, they drink—
    'Rise up, ye princes, anoint the shield.'

It cometh from the wilderness. Ibn Ezra: This refers to the armies of the Medes and the Persians marching against Babylon.

21 : 2 *The treacherous . . . dealeth treacherously.* Rashi and Kimchi take the verb here translated "dealeth" as passive rather than active. In this they follow the Targum. The verse then means, "The treacherous one is being dealt with treacherously and (as the verse continues) the spoiler is being despoiled." They therefore understand the verse as follows: Babylon, which dealt so treacherously with other nations and despoiled them, will now get the same treatment from Persia.

All the sighing . . . have I made to cease. Rashi, following the Targum, says it means, "God says by destroying Babylon all the sighing of the oppressed will now cease."

21 : 3-5 *Pangs have taken hold upon me . . . prepare the table . . . eat . . . drink—'rise up, princes.'* Ibn Ezra gives a most original interpretation of these verses. He begins by saying that it is impossible to accept the interpretation that the prophet Isaiah says that he is suffering these pangs of sorrow. On the contrary, the prophet must have rejoiced at the fall of Babylon or at predicting it. This whole passage, says Ibn Ezra, is spoken by Belshazzar, the last king of Babylon, who gave a banquet to his nobles and they drank out of the sacred vessels taken from the Temple in Jerusalem. Then came the writing on the wall and

6. For thus hath the Lord said unto me:
   Go, set a watchman;
   Let him declare what he seeth!
7. And when he seeth a troop, horsemen by pairs,
   A troop of asses, a troop of camels,
   He shall hearken diligently with much heed.
8. And he cried as a lion: 'Upon the watch-tower,
      O Lord,
   I stand continually in the day-time,
   And I am set in my ward all the nights.'
9. And, behold, there came a troop of men, horsemen
      by pairs.
   And he spoke and said:
   'Fallen, fallen is Babylon;
   And all the graven images of her gods are broken
      unto the ground.'

Isaiah 21

Daniel's prophecy that the city would be destroyed. So it is at the banquet where "they eat, they drink," that the Babylonian king cries out, "Pangs have taken hold of me."

21:5 *Light lamps ... anoint the shield.* Here Rashi, too, refers this verse to Belshazzar's feast. In the midst of the banquet the news comes that the Persians are at the gate and the princes must rise from the table to mobilize the defense. He explains the words, "anoint the shield," that the shields were oiled so that the spears would slip off their surfaces.

21:6 *Go, set a watchman.* Kimchi says that the prophet is addressing Babylon, warning it to set a watchman; the watchman will see (Verse 7) troop, horsemen, camels, etc. But Rashi calls attention to Chapter 2, Verse 1 of the prophecy of Habakkuk in which the prophet says, "I stand as a watchman." According to Rashi, Habakkuk was the disciple of Isaiah and it was Habakkuk whom Isaiah set up as a watchman.

21:8 *He cried as a lion.* Rashi continues here his identification of Isaiah's disciple watchman with Habakkuk. He says that if the word "aryeh" ("lion") is added up by the value of the Hebrew letters ("gematria," i.e., aleph for 1, resh for 200, yod for ten, and heh for five) the total comes to 216. So the "gematria" for the name Habakkuk totals 216. And this again is a reference to Habakkuk.

Isaiah 21

10. O thou my threshing, and the winnowing of my floor,
That which I have heard from the LORD of hosts,
The God of Israel, have I declared unto you.
11. The burden of Dumah.
One calleth unto me out of Seir:
'Watchman, what of the night?
Watchman, what of the night?'
12. The watchman said:
'The morning cometh, and also the night—
If ye will inquire, inquire ye; return, come.'
13. The burden upon Arabia.
In the thickets in Arabia shall ye lodge, O ye caravans of Dedanites.
14. Unto him that is thirsty bring ye water!

21 : 10 *O thou my threshing.* Rashi takes this to mean Israel: O Israel, the crop that I have carefully nurtured. But Kimchi and Ibn Ezra take this to mean Babylon, which will be threshed out as wheat on the threshing floor.

21 : 11 *The burden of Dumah.* Another "burden," this time against Seir or Edom, but the name "Dumah" is not identified. Some modern commentators guess that Dumah should be emended to Edom, but Rashi simply says that Dumah is Edom.

Watchman, what of the night? Rashi says Israel addresses these words to God, "O Guardian of Israel, how long will this oppression last?" The Targum has these words addressed by God to the prophet, "O watchman, tell the people of Israel what the future will bring." Ibn Ezra notes that the question is asked more than once. It is like a man going from one watchman to another and repeating his question. But he cites Saadia who says that the

The inhabitants of the land of Tema did meet the fugitive with his bread.

15. For they fled away from the swords, from the drawn sword,
And from the bent bow, and from the grievousness of war.

16. For thus hath the Lord said unto me: 'Within a year, according to the years of a hireling, and all the glory of Kedar shall fail; 17. and the residue of the number of the archers, the mighty men of the children of Kedar, shall be diminished; for the LORD, the God of Israel, hath spoken it.'

Isaiah 21

double question means that the questioner asks, "How much of the night has passed and how much yet remains?"

21 : 12 *The morning cometh . . . also the night . . . inquire . . . return.* The Targum takes "morning" and "night" as symbolic words and "return" as meaning "repent," and takes the verse to mean: "There will be reward for the righteous (i.e., a dawn) and punishment for the wicked (i.e., night); if you repent, do so while you have yet time." Rashi takes it to mean, "If you wish to bring the redemption, then return and repent." But Kimchi takes the verse more literally and says it means, "There will be relief but there will be trouble again. You will inquire many times and get the same answer: There will be many nights of oppression."

21 : 13 *Burden upon Arabia.* This dirge against Arabia is a plea to the Arabians, the desert people, to be hospitable to the fugitives fleeing from war. The desert people (Arabians, Dedanites, children of Kedar) will be punished for letting the fugitives die of thirst.

22

A "BURDEN" for the Valley of Vision. The Valley of Vision refers to Judah and Jerusalem. The chapter describes the siege of the city, with the people in the early days of the siege still hilarious and pleasure-seeking: "Let us eat and drink, for tomorrow we shall die!" (Verse 13) But after the siege has lasted for a while, Isaiah is sent to the official Shebna to tell him that he will be exiled and that Eliakim will take his place.

Isaiah 22

1. The burden concerning the Valley of Vision. What aileth thee now, that thou art wholly gone up to the housetops,

22 : 1 *The Valley of Vision.* All the commentators agree that the Valley of Vision is Jerusalem and this is a "burden," a dirge depicting the dangers which are impending for the Holy City. Krauss dates this at the time when Sennacherib had destroyed all the other Judean cities and now was besieging Jerusalem. However, Rashi declares that this chapter refers to the time, a century later, when the Babylonians were besieging the city. The reason for this latter dating is that Verse 3 says, "All thy rulers are fled," and it was in the siege by the Babylonians that king Zedekiah tried to flee the city.

Gone up to the housetops. The people during the siege climbed to the roofs of their houses to see the enemy. Rashi, Kimchi, and Ibn Ezra give the same interpretation.

2. Thou that art full of uproar, a tumultuous city, a joyous town?
Thy slain are not slain with the sword, nor dead in battle.
3. All thy rulers are fled together,
Without the bow they are bound;
All that are found of thee are bound together, they are fled afar off.
4. Therefore said I: 'Look away from me, I will weep bitterly;
Strain not to comfort me, for the destruction of the daughter of my people.'
5. For it is a day of trouble, and of trampling, and of perplexity,
From the Lord, the GOD of hosts, in the Valley of Vision;
Kir shouting, and Shoa at the mount.

Isaiah 22

22:2 *A tumultuous city, a joyous town.* Rashi explains it as meaning that only yesterday, before the enemy had come, Jerusalem was a tumultuous, joyous town.

Not slain with the sword. Rashi, Ibn Ezra, and Kimchi explain this to mean that now that the city is besieged its people will die, not by the sword but by famine.

22:3 *All thy rulers are fled.* It is because of this verse that Rashi says the prophecy was made during the siege by the Babylonians, as described in II Kings 25.

Without the bow they are bound. Ibn Ezra translates this as follows: Because of the bow (i.e., when they saw the bows of the enemy archers) they surrendered and were bound as captives. Kimchi says that they were captured by the archers when they tried to flee the besieged city. He agrees with Rashi that this refers to the Babylonian siege when Zedekiah tried to flee.

22:5 *Kir shouting...Shoa at the mount.* Krauss cites various scholars who translate "Kir" and "Shoa" as "nations" (as in this translation) but he agrees with the traditional commentators that Kir means a city wall (which now is breached) and Shoa (a "shout") means the shouting of the invaders. The likelihood that this translation as given here is the more correct, namely, that Kir is the name of a nation, is increased by the fact that in

Isaiah 22

6. And Elam bore the quiver, with troops of men, even horsemen;
   And Kir uncovered the shield.
7. And it came to pass, when thy choicest valleys were full of chariots,
   And the horsemen set themselves in array at the gate,
8. And the covering of Judah was laid bare,
   that thou didst look in that day to the armour in the house of the forest. 9. And ye saw the breaches of the city of David, that they were many; and ye gathered together the waters of the lower pool. 10. And ye numbered the houses of Jerusalem, and ye broke down the houses to fortify the wall; 11. ye made also a basin between the two walls for the water of the old pool—
   But ye looked not unto Him that had done this,
   Neither had ye respect unto Him that fashioned it long ago.
12. And in that day did the Lord, the GOD of hosts, call
    To weeping, and to lamentation, and to baldness, and to girding with sackcloth;
13. And behold joy and gladness,
    Slaying oxen and killing sheep,
    Eating flesh and drinking wine—
    'Let us eat and drink, for to-morrow we shall die!'
14. And the LORD of hosts revealed Himself in mine ears:

---

the next sentence Kir is mentioned as a parallel to Elam, which certainly is the name of a people.

22 : 8 *The covering of Judah was laid bare.* The walls were breached, the enemy could look right into the city. Rashi says that the "covering of Judah" specifically means the Temple which covered and protected the people of Israel.

The house of the forest. Rashi calls attention to I Kings, Chapter 7 where Solomon's own palace was called "the house of the forest," and there we are told that Solomon deposited various armor. This would fit to the reference in this verse, "armor in the house of the forest."

Surely this iniquity shall not be expiated by you till ye die,
Saith the Lord, the GOD of hosts.

15. Thus saith the Lord, the GOD of hosts:
Go, get thee unto this steward,
Even unto Shebna, who is over the house:

16. What hast thou here, and whom hast thou here,
That thou hast hewed thee out here a sepulchre,
Thou that hewest thee out a sepulchre on high,
And gravest a habitation for thyself in the rock?

17. Behold, the LORD will hurl thee up and down with a man's throw;
Yea, He will wind thee round and round;

18. He will violently roll and toss thee
Like a ball into a large country;
There shalt thou die, and there shall be the chariots of thy glory,
Thou shame of thy lord's house.

19. And I will thrust thee from thy post,
And from thy station shalt thou be pulled down.

20. And it shall come to pass in that day,
That I will call my servant Eliakim the son of Hilkiah;

21. And I will clothe him with thy robe,
And bind him with thy girdle,
And I will commit thy government into his hand;
And he shall be a father to the inhabitants of Jerusalem, and to the house of Judah.

Isaiah 22

22 : 9 *Ye gathered . . . the waters of the lower pool.* The Targum says that the people gathered at the waters to man the breaches of the walls.

22 : 11 *Ye looked not unto Him that had done this.* The words "done this" are not clear. Rashi explains it to mean, "Ye looked not to God who had protected you hitherto."

22 : 12 *The Lord . . . God . . . did call to weeping.* Rashi and Kimchi both say that God himself, as it were, weeps for you, but you feast and revel. (Verse 13: "Let us eat and drink . . .")

22 : 20 *My servant Eliakim.* From Verse 15 through the end of the chapter, Isaiah is called upon to denounce the officer

Isaiah 22

22. And the key of the house of David will I lay upon his shoulder;
And he shall open, and none shall shut;
And he shall shut, and none shall open.
23. And I will fasten him as a peg in a sure place;
And he shall be for a throne of honour to his father's house.
24. And they shall hang upon him all the glory of his father's house, the offspring and the issue, all vessels of small quantity, from the vessels of cups even to all the vessels of flagons.
25. In that day, saith the LORD of hosts, shall the peg that was fastened in a sure place give way; and it shall be hewn down, and fall, and the burden that was upon it shall be cut off; for the LORD hath spoken it.

Shebna and to declare that Eliakim will be put in his place. Shebna and Eliakim are mentioned in II Kings. (18:18) When Sennacherib besieged Jerusalem, these two officials spoke to the Assyrian general, Rabshakeh. They are mentioned also in II Kings (19:2) when king Hezekiah sent Eliakim to speak to Isaiah.

22 : 24 *All vessels.* Rashi explains it as follows: All the children of his household will be proud of him. So does Ibn Ezra.

22 : 25 *Shall the peg . . . give way.* This does not refer to Eliakim who will be firmly established but goes back to Shebna who will be displaced. Rashi, Kimchi, and Ibn Ezra also explain it this way.

23

THE "BURDEN" of Tyre is the dirge in Chapter 23. This prophecy is directed at the two great Phoenician trading cities. It speaks primarily of Tyre but includes Zidon. The city will be destroyed and after seventy years will slowly begin to recover its status as a mercantile center.

1. The burden of Tyre.
   Howl, ye ships of Tarshish,
   For it is laid waste, so that there is no house, no entering in;
   From the land of Kittim it is revealed to them.

Isaiah 23

23 : 1 *The burden of Tyre.* This dirge against the great seaport of Tyre speaks both of Tyre and Zidon, the other great Phoenician seaport. See Eissfeldt (pp. 322, 3) who gives various opinions as to the dating of this dirge. Some believe that this was a dirge by Isaiah himself, but others say it is as late as the Persian period and refers to the capture of Tyre by Ataxeres the Third (348 B.C.E.), and others say it was still later and refers to the capture of the city by Alexander in the year 322 B.C.E. Ibn Ezra believed that it refers to the capture of the city by Nebuchadnezzar in the sixth century B.C.E. His reason for this dating is the fact that in Verse 13 there is mention of the land of the Chaldeans, i.e., the Babylonians.

Isaiah 23

2. Be still, ye inhabitants of the coastland;
   Thou whom the merchants of Zidon, that pass over
      the sea, have replenished.
3. And on great waters the seed of Shihor,
   The harvest of the Nile, was her revenue;
   And she was the mart of nations.
4. Be thou ashamed, O Zidon; for the sea hath spoken,
   The stronghold of the sea, saying:
   'I have not travailed, nor brought forth,
   Neither have I reared young men, nor brought up
      virgins.'
5. When the report cometh to Egypt,
   They shall be sorely pained at the report of Tyre.
6. Pass ye over to Tarshish;
   Howl, ye inhabitants of the coastland.
7. Is this your joyous city,
   Whose feet in antiquity,
   In ancient days,
   Carried her afar off to sojourn?

Howl, ye ships of Tarshish. The Phoenicians founded trading posts as far west as Spain where they established the town of Tarshish. Their largest vessels were those that went all the way west to Tarshish. Hence frequently in Scripture large ships are referred to as "ships of Tarshish," as in America in earlier days people would speak of "China Clippers."

From the land of Kittim it is revealed to them. Kittim is the island of Cyprus. The great ships of Tarshish on their long return journey from the west put in at Cyprus; and there the tragic news was revealed to them that Tyre, their home port, was destroyed. Hence, "Howl, ye ships of Tarshish." They had no home port left.

23 : 2 *Coastland... whom the merchants of Zidon... replenished.* Here the dirge turns from Tyre to the other great Phoenician port, Zidon. But Rashi makes this reference consistent with the rest of the dirge by translating it as follows: Ye coastal towns, which had been kept prosperous (replenished) by Zidon, weep ye also for Tyre, for with Tyre gone Zidon will soon fall also.

23 : 3 *Seed of Shihor... harvest of the Nile.* Shihor is another

8. Who hath devised this against Tyre, the crowning city,
    Whose merchants are princes,
    Whose traffickers are the honourable of the earth?
9. The LORD of hosts hath devised it,
    To pollute the pride of all glory,
    To bring into contempt all the honourable of the earth.
10. Overflow thy land as the Nile,
    O daughter of Tarshish! there is no girdle any more.
11. He hath stretched out His hand over the sea,
    He hath shaken the kingdoms;
    The LORD hath given commandment concerning Canaan,
    To destroy the strongholds thereof;
12. And He said: 'Thou shalt no more rejoice.'
    O thou oppressed virgin daughter of Zidon,
    Arise, pass over to Kittim;
    Even there shalt thou have no rest.

Isaiah 23

name for the Nile. Tyre and Zidon were the main marts for Egyptian merchandise.

23 : 4 *I have not ... reared young men.* In her desolation the ruined city says: I am completely bereaved; it is as if I never did have any sons or daughters. Kimchi offers a similar explanation.

23 : 6 *Pass ... over to Tarshish.* Flee to the remotest part of your trading world, to the western end of the sea. Ehrlich emends this to read, "Pass by, ye ships of Tarshish," meaning, "Your home harbor and your home city are no longer in existence."

23 : 7 *Is this your joyous city, whose feet in antiquity ... carried her afar off?* Are these ruins all that is left of that city whose adventurous merchant sailors once carried it on far off journeys?

23 : 10 *Overflow thy land as the Nile ... there is no girdle any more.* Just as the Nile floods the land all over, so flee ye now, in all directions. You have no support any more (i.e., girdle); you have no home port to return to.

23 : 11 *Canaan.* The Phoenicians are the Canaanites.

23 : 12 *Pass over to Kittim.* Flee to the island of Cyprus.

Isaiah 23

13. Behold, the land of the Chaldeans—this is the people that was not, when Asshur founded it for shipmen—they set up their towers, they overthrew the palaces thereof; it is made a ruin.
14. Howl, ye ships of Tarshish,
    For your stronghold is laid waste.
15. And it shall come to pass in that day, that Tyre shall be forgotten seventy years, according to the days of one king; after the end of seventy years it shall fare with Tyre as in the song of the harlot:
16. Take a harp,
    Go about the city,

23 : 13 *The Chaldeans.* This verse seems irrelevant. Krauss suggests that the word for "Chaldeans" (Kasdim) should be amended to Kittim, Cyprus, and would then harmonize with the preceding verse. It is this mention of Chaldeans that led Ibn Ezra to date this dirge to the time of the destruction of the city by the Babylonians. Kimchi passes over the apparent irrelevance of the mention of the Chaldeans here and explains the verse as it stands, as follows: The Chaldeans never were a real nation. The Assyrians started it when they established it as a shipping depot.

Isaiah 23

   Thou harlot long forgotten;
   Make sweet melody,
   Sing many songs,
   That thou mayest be remembered.
17. And it shall come to pass after the end of seventy years, that the LORD will remember Tyre, and she shall return to her hire, and shall have commerce with all the kingdoms of the world upon the face of the earth.
18. And her gain and her hire shall be holiness to the LORD; it shall not be treasured nor laid up; for her gain shall be for them that dwell before the LORD, to eat their fill, and for stately clothing.

23 : 15-16 *Tyre shall be forgotten seventy years ... [then] Tyre as in the song of the harlot.* After seventy years of desolation, the mercantile spirit of Tyre will begin to revive and she will begin to search around for new trade "like a forgotten harlot making sweet melody."

23 : 17-18 *She shall return to her hire ... her hire shall be holiness to the Lord.* Tyre will be restored as a great trading mart, but now its wealth will be a blessing unto the righteous.

24

CHAPTERS 24 to 27 constitute a unit. They all are what is called apocalyptic. This is a form of literature of which some examples are found in Scripture as, for example, the Book of Daniel. But most of it is in Greek Jewish writing, preserved outside of the Bible. The word "apocalypse" means "revelation." (The Book of Revelations in the New Testament is a classic example of an apocalypse.) The purpose of apocalypse is to reveal the great catastrophe that will overcome the human race at some distant date, with the salvation of a chosen few. Almost invariably the secret is told to a prophet by an angel. Also involved at the end of time is the resurrection of the dead. This section, Chapters 24 to 27, is clearly apocalyptic in its nature. It speaks of angels in heaven, it refers to the resurrection of the dead (26:19), and another evidence of the late date of this section is the fact that by the time this was written the people of Israel was already spread far and wide over the earth. (27:12-14) Ibn Ezra also is aware of this section as a revelation of a distant premessianic day, because he says that the prophecies here refer to the great wars of Gog and Magog (Ezekiel 38, 39) which will come before the messianic day. Chapter 24 says that even the moon and the sun will be eclipsed.

Of course this ascription to the wars of Gog and Magog gives us no definite date; in fact the modern critical scholars present a wide area of disagreement as to when it was written. Generally they place it late in the postexilic era. (See Eissfeldt, pp. 323ff.)

Isaiah 24

1. Behold, the Lord maketh the earth empty and maketh it waste,
   And turneth it upside down, and scattereth abroad the inhabitants thereof.
2. And it shall be, as with the people, so with the priest;
   As with the servant, so with his master;
   As with the maid, so with her mistress;
   As with the buyer, so with the seller;
   As with the lender, so with the borrower;
   As with the creditor, so with the debtor.
3. The earth shall be utterly emptied, and clean despoiled;
   For the Lord hath spoken this word.
4. The earth fainteth and fadeth away,
   The world faileth and fadeth away,
   The lofty people of the earth do fail.
5. The earth also is defiled under the inhabitants thereof;
   Because they have transgressed the laws, violated the statute,
   Broken the everlasting covenant.
6. Therefore hath a curse devoured the earth,
   And they that dwell therein are found guilty;
   Therefore the inhabitants of the earth waste away,
   And men are left few.

24 : 1-4 *The earth . . . waste . . . utterly emptied.* All the preceding "burdens" were each of them against some individual nation which was to be overthrown. But here the entire population of the earth is under threat of destruction. This worldwide nature of the calamity is characteristic of apocalyptic writing. So the prophet here speaks of the entire earth being destroyed and all classes of humanity (priest and people, servant and master, etc.) will perish.

24 : 5 *Transgressed the laws . . . the everlasting covenant.* Ibn Ezra notes that the word "laws" is in the plural (when usually we say "the law of God") and that the word "olam" (translated here "everlasting covenant") can be translated "the laws of the world." It means that all nations will be destroyed because they have violated God's law as revealed in the world of nature.

Isaiah 24

7. The new wine faileth, the vine fadeth,
   All the merry-hearted do sigh.
8. The mirth of tabrets ceaseth,
   The noise of them that rejoice endeth,
   The joy of the harp ceaseth.
9. They drink not wine with a song;
   Strong drink is bitter to them that drink it.
10. Broken down is the city of wasteness;
    Every house is shut up, that none may come in.
11. There is a crying in the streets amidst the wine;
    All joy is darkened,
    The mirth of the land is gone.
12. In the city is left desolation,
    And the gate is smitten unto ruin.
13. For thus shall it be in the midst of the earth, among the peoples,
    As at the beating of an olive-tree,
    As at the gleanings when the vintage is done.
14. Those yonder lift up their voice, they sing for joy;
    For the majesty of the Lord they shout from the sea:
15. 'Therefore glorify ye the Lord in the regions of light,
    Even the name of the Lord, the God of Israel, in the isles of the sea.'
16. From the uttermost part of the earth have we heard

24 : 7-12 *The wine faileth ... mirth ... ceaseth.* In the terrible days that are coming, all the joys of living will be gone. Nothing will taste good any more.

24 : 14 *Those yonder ... sing for joy.* Who is it that can be singing in the midst of world calamity? Rashi says it means that after the calamity is over the few who are left will praise the Lord. And so does Ibn Ezra.

24 : 15 *In the regions of light.* Hardly any of the traditional commentators translate the word "urim" here as light, except Krauss who says it means in the east, where the dawn light comes, praise the Lord. Rashi says the word means in the crevices, where those who had escaped fled to hide from the oppressors. Kimchi says it means in the valleys. Ibn Ezra says it means in the various countries. Ehrlich emends the word to read "ba-umim," "among the nations." Tur Sinai (Torczyner) simply emends the word

songs: 'Glory to the righteous.'
But I say: I waste away, I waste away, woe is me!
The treacherous deal treacherously;
Yea, the treacherous deal very treacherously.
17. Terror, and the pit, and the trap, are upon thee,
    O inhabitant of the earth.
18. And it shall come to pass, that he who fleeth from
      the noise of the terror shall fall into the pit;
    And he that cometh up out of the midst of the pit
      shall be taken in the trap;
    For the windows on high are opened,
    And the foundations of the earth do shake;
19. The earth is broken, broken down,
    The earth is crumbled in pieces,
    The earth trembleth and tottereth;
20. The earth reeleth to and fro like a drunken man,
    And swayeth to and fro as a lodge;
    And the transgression thereof is heavy upon it,
    And it shall fall, and not rise again.
21. And it shall come to pass in that day,
    That the LORD will punish the host of the high
      heaven on high,
    And the kings of the earth upon the earth.
22. And they shall be gathered together, as prisoners

Isaiah
24

"urim" to "harim," meaning "among the mountains" praise the Lord.

24 : 16 *Glory to the righteous . . . but . . . I waste away.* The word "razi," translated here "waste away," can also mean "secret." Rashi follows the Targum by having the prophet say, "I have been imparted two secret prophecies, one as to the redemption, the other as to the destruction." Hence the apparent contradiction between "glory" and "waste away." But our translation here follows Ibn Ezra who takes the word "razi" to mean "waste away."

24 : 18 *He who fleeth . . . shall fall.* There can be no escape in those days when "the earth is crumbled to pieces." (Verse 19)

24 : 21-23 *The Lord will punish the host of heaven . . . the moon shall be confounded.* It is this reference to the heavenly hosts of angels which is characteristic of the apocalyptic writings. Ibn

133

Isaiah 24

are gathered in the dungeon,
And shall be shut up in the prison,
And after many days shall they be punished.
23. Then the moon shall be confounded, and the sun ashamed;
For the LORD of hosts will reign in mount Zion, and in Jerusalem,
And before His elders shall be Glory.

Ezra connects the idea of the angels with the destruction of the kingdoms of the earth, by referring to the belief that each earthly kingdom has its protective angel in heaven. Thus, with their heavenly protection gone, the earthly kingdoms cannot escape destruction. Then he adds, because of the words "the moon shall be confounded," that this rebuke of the heavenly hosts may mean the eclipse of the moon. (So also Kimchi.)

25

THIS CHAPTER continues the apocalyptic vision of the destruction of the earth and is the beginning of the restoration after the world's cataclysm. In the messianic days death will be abolished. (Verse 8) The chapter ends with rejoicing in Zion and the defeat of Moab, which seems to symbolize all the enemies.

1. O LORD, Thou art my God,
   I will exalt Thee, I will praise Thy name,
   For Thou hast done wonderful things;
   Even counsels of old, in faithfulness and truth.
2. For Thou hast made of a city a heap,
   Of a fortified city a ruin;
   A castle of strangers to be no city,
   It shall never be built.
3. Therefore shall the strong people glorify Thee,
   The city of the terrible nations shall fear Thee.

Isaiah 25

25 : 1-2 *I will exalt Thee ... for Thou hast made of a city a heap.* God is here praised for the destruction of some great hostile city. Most commentators believe it refers to the destruction of Babylon by the Persians. Some place this almost three hundred years later, as referring to the capture of Samaria by John Hyrcanus.

25 : 3 *The strong people glorify Thee.* Ibn Ezra explains this to mean that those who will prove to be strong enough to sur-

Isaiah 25

4. For Thou hast been a stronghold to the poor,
   A stronghold to the needy in his distress,
   A refuge from the storm, a shadow from the heat;
   For the blast of the terrible ones was as a storm against the wall.
5. As the heat in a dry place, Thou didst subdue the noise of strangers;
   As the heat by the shadow of a cloud, the song of the terrible ones was brought low.
6. And in this mountain will the LORD of hosts make unto all peoples
   A feast of fat things, a feast of wines on the lees,
   Of fat things full of marrow, of wines on the lees well refined.
7. And He will destroy in this mountain
   The face of the covering that is cast over all peoples,
   And the veil that is spread over all nations.
8. He will swallow up death for ever;
   And the LORD GOD will wipe away tears from off all faces;

vive will praise God. Kimchi, who ascribes this whole upheaval to the premessianic wars of Gog and Magog, says that those who will survive those final wars will praise God.

25 : 5 *Heat in a dry place ... heat by the shadow.* Kimchi calls attention to the fact that those two contrasting phrases are to be applied thus: "the burning heat" against the oppressors and "the sheltering cloud" for the oppressed people of Israel.

25 : 6 *In the mountain ... a feast of fat things.* Kimchi consistently applies this to the wars of Gog and Magog and finds his justification in the fact that in Ezekiel 39:2 the prophet says that god "will bring thee [Gog] from the north to the mountains of Israel." Ibn Ezra makes substantially the same comment. Then Kimchi explains "the feast of fat things," etc.: the nations who come to invade will be given a meal they cannot digest and wine that will make them reel. They will be stupefied and defeated.

25 : 7 *He will destroy ... the veil ... spread over all nations.* God will remove the covering and the protection which has until now kept these nations from destruction. (Kimchi)

And the reproach of His people will He take away
   from off all the earth;
For the LORD hath spoken it.
9. And it shall be said in that day:
'Lo, this is our God,
For whom we waited, that He might save us;
This is the LORD, for whom we waited,
We will be glad and rejoice in His salvation.'
10. For in this mountain will the hand of the LORD rest,
And Moab shall be trodden down in his place,
Even as straw is trodden down in the dunghill.
11. And when he shall spread forth his hands in the midst thereof,
As he that swimmeth spreadeth forth his hands to swim,
His pride shall be brought down together with the cunning of his hands.
12. And the high fortress of thy walls will He bring down, lay low,
And bring to the ground, even to the dust.

25 : 8 *He will swallow up death for ever.* Kimchi says that this does not mean that people will not die any more. It means that, though there will always be natural death, it is violent death due to war and crime that God will abolish. So specifically here it means that the violence that Israel suffered in exile will now cease. Krauss gives the same explanation. Ehrlich takes this in a sense similar to Kimchi's interpretation but interprets it to refer to the death-dealing invader. But Ibn Ezra changes the meaning of the verse completely. Instead of the word "death" being the object of the verb "to swallow," he takes it to be the subject of the verb and understands the verse to mean, "Death will swallow up the oppressors forever."

25 : 10-12 *As a swimmer spreadeth forth his hands.* These verses are a small "burden" of doom against Moab. Ibn Ezra and Kimchi say it means God will spread forth His hands to destroy them.

26

CHAPTER 26 is mostly devoted to the great days after the world cataclysm and speaks (Verse 19) of the resurrection of the dead. The chapter ends (Verses 20, 21) with a warning to the people to go into hiding during the time of world cataclysm, so as to live through to the better days.

Isaiah 26

1. In that day shall this song be sung in the land of Judah:
   We have a strong city;
   Walls and bulwarks doth He appoint for salvation.
2. Open ye the gates,
   That the righteous nation that keepeth faithfulness may enter in.
3. The mind stayed on Thee Thou keepest in perfect peace;
   Because it trusteth in Thee.
4. Trust ye in the LORD for ever,

26 : 3 *The mind stayed on Thee.* Rashi amplified this as follows: He who stays firm in his reliance upon God and does not abandon his faith when troubles come (will be in perfect peace). Krauss gives substantially the same explanation and points to the parallel idea in Psalm 112:7: "His heart is steadfast, trusting in the Lord."

For the LORD is GOD, an everlasting Rock.
5. For He hath brought down them that dwell on high,
The lofty city,
Laying it low, laying it low even to the ground,
Bringing it even to the dust.
6. The foot shall tread it down,
Even the feet of the poor, and the steps of the needy.
7. The way of the just is straight;
Thou, Most Upright, makest plain the path of the just.
8. Yea, in the way of Thy judgments,
O LORD, have we waited for Thee;
To Thy name and to Thy memorial is the desire of our soul.
9. With my soul have I desired Thee in the night;
Yea, with my spirit within me have I sought Thee earnestly;
For when Thy judgments are in the earth,
The inhabitants of the world learn righteousness.
10. Let favour be shown to the wicked, yet will he not learn righteousness;
In the land of uprightness will he deal wrongfully,
And will not behold the majesty of the LORD.

Isaiah 26

26 : 8 *Yea, in the way of Thy judgments ... have we waited for Thee.* The word "af" translated here as "yea" generally means "also." It is this meaning of the word which guides the traditional commentators. And thus the Targum and Rashi render the verse, "Just as we look for Thy favor, so also we await the destruction of the wicked." Kimchi connects it with the statement in Verse 9, "When Thy judgments are in the earth, the inhabitants learn righteousness," and therefore translates the word "af" as "even when." The verse then means, "Even when Thou didst bring misfortune to us, it was a lesson to us."

26 : 10 *Let favour be shown to the wicked ... he will not learn.* Only those who seek righteousness and hold on to their faith have the power to learn from their misfortunes. Kimchi explains that the wicked never learn because they do not believe that there is any sense to what happens to people on earth. It is all a matter of chance. They say, "There is neither justice nor a judge." If

Isaiah 26

11. LORD, Thy hand was lifted up, yet they see not;
    They shall see with shame Thy zeal for the people;
    Yea, fire shall devour Thine adversaries.
12. LORD, Thou wilt establish peace for us;
    For Thou hast indeed wrought all our works for us.
13. O LORD our God, other lords beside Thee have had dominion over us;
    But by Thee only do we make mention of Thy name.
14. The dead live not, the shades rise not;
    To that end hast Thou punished and destroyed them, and made all their memory to perish.
15. Thou hast gotten Thee honour with the nations, O LORD,
    Yea, exceeding great honour with the nations;

they had believed that there was a divine purpose behind the events of life, then their experience might have brought them some moral guidance.

26:13 *Other lords ... have had dominion ... but Thee only do we mention.* In spite of the persecutions, we have held on to our faith in Thee. (Verse 3) Ibn Ezra says it means, "We have never worshiped any other master but Thee, even when other masters had dominion over us." Ehrlich emends the word "bealunu" "have dominion" to the word "gaalanu" meaning "despise" and translates as follows: "O Lord, we have despised every other master but Thee."

26:14 *The dead live not.* The Targum connects this with the preceding verse of worshiping other masters and says it means, "We worship the living God, but they worship those who are dead and who live not." So, too, Kimchi. Ibn Ezra gives a slightly different tone to the meaning, though his explanation is virtually what the Targum said: "Those mortal masters whom we had refused to worship are all dead and live not." Krauss, who ascribes this whole chapter to the time of Alexander the Great, calls attention to the fact that after Alexander died his followers said that he was a god and was immortal; therefore the writer here refers to the deified Alexander and says, "We did not worship him. He is mortal and really dead."

26:15 *Thou hast gotten Thee honour with the nations, O Lord.* The connection here is difficult. The Jewish commentators refer

Thou art honoured unto the farthest ends of the earth.

Isaiah 26

16. LORD, in trouble have they sought Thee,
Silently they poured out a prayer when Thy chastening was upon them.
17. Like as a woman with child, that draweth near the time of her delivery,
Is in pain and crieth out in her pangs;
So have we been at Thy presence, O LORD.
18. We have been with child, we have been in pain,
We have as it were brought forth wind;
We have not wrought any deliverance in the land;
Neither are the inhabitants of the world come to life.
19. Thy dead shall live, my dead bodies shall arise—

this to Israel, "Thou hast greatly honoured Israel." The Hebrew does not have the plural "nations," as in our translation, but "nation." Hence it is possible to explain this as "God has added honour to Israel." Ibn Ezra amplifies this thought and calls attention to the latter part of the verse, "Thou art honoured unto the farthest ends of the earth." This would then mean (following the traditional explanation): "Even when Thou hast exiled Thy people all over the world, they still continue to honour Thee."

26:16 *When Thy chastening was upon them.* Even in times of trouble, they never grumbled against Thine actions. (Rashi and Kimchi)

26:18 *We have not wrought any deliverance ... neither are the inhabitants ... come to life.* The word "yiplu" translated here "come to life" is generally translated as "fallen." So Kimchi and Ibn Ezra take this sentence to mean, "In the time of our misfortunes, all through our exiles, no deliverance seemed to be coming to us, nor did our adversaries fall."

26:19 *Thy dead shall live ... awake and sing.* Rashi takes this as a prayer, "O may the dead revive!" Kimchi with his preference for placing prophecies at the messianic time says, "It means when the great deliverance will come the dead will revive," and he cites Daniel: "And many of them that sleep in the dust of the earth shall awaken." (12:2) Ibn Ezra does not take this as individual resurrection but as a national revival. He connects it with Verse 14 in which the rulers of the nations are said to

Isaiah 26

Awake and sing, ye that dwell in the dust—
For Thy dew is as the dew of light,
And the earth shall bring to life the shades.
20. Come, my people, enter thou into thy chambers,
And shut thy doors about thee;
Hide thyself for a little moment,
Until the indignation be overpast.
21. For, behold, the LORD cometh forth out of His place
To visit upon the inhabitants of the earth their iniquity;
The earth also shall disclose her blood,
And shall no more cover her slain.

"live not," and he explains the verse (or rather the two parallel Verses 14 and 19) as follows: "The oppressors will not live, but Thy dead, namely we who have been considered as dead, are living today."

Thy dew is as the dew of light and the earth shall bring to life the shades. Again here the word "tapil" "bring to life" is usually translated "to cast down." So the Targum gives its favorite symbolic interpretation, taking the word "light" to refer to the light of the Torah, and therefore takes the verse to mean, "Those who live by the light of the Torah will survive, and those who neglect the light will be cast down." But Kimchi takes the word "tapil" as translated here, "will cast (or bring) forth," and therefore takes it to mean, "The earth will cast away the wicked."

26:20 *Come, my people ... hide thyself.* The clear meaning of the verse is, "Be patient, my people. Concentrate your inner forces and you will outlive the coming evils." Rashi says it means that the prophet advises the people to keep on going to the synagogues and the schools, or else it means, "Look into the inner chamber of your heart," i.e., examine your conscience. Kimchi consistently applies this to the war of Gog and Magog and says that, when those awful days come, rely upon the inner strength of decent living; this will sustain you.

27

CHAPTER 27 concludes the apocalyptic portion, especially Verse 13, with the ingathering of the exiles.

> 1. In that day the LORD with His sore and great and strong sword will punish leviathan the slant serpent, and leviathan the tortuous serpent; and He will slay the dragon that is in the sea.
> 2. In that day sing ye of her:
> 'A vineyard of foaming wine!'

Isaiah 27

27 : 1 *Leviathan ... the serpent ... the dragon.* Most modern scholars date this section as late as the Maccabean era. Therefore they identify these three fabulous beasts which are destined for destruction as the three kingdoms into which the Hellenic world was divided after the death of Alexander the Great. (See Eissfeldt, p. 325, and also Krauss.)

27 : 2 *In that day sing ye of her: 'A vineyard ... '* On that day of redemption people will sing of Israel as the fruitful vine. (Targum and Rashi) Kimchi calls attention to the parallel with Chapter 5, where the prophet had compared Israel to a vineyard but had denounced her for producing evil grapes. But now he prophesies that the redeemed Israel will produce the good wine of a righteous life. Ibn Ezra, too, gives the same explanation.

Isaiah 27

3. I the Lord do guard it,
   I water it every moment;
   Lest Mine anger visit it,
   I guard it night and day.
4. Fury is not in Me;
   Would that I were as the briers and thorns in flame!
   I would with one step burn it altogether.
5. Or else let him take hold of My strength,
   That he may make peace with Me;
   Yea, let him make peace with Me.
6. In days to come shall Jacob take root,
   Israel shall blossom and bud;
   And the face of the world shall be filled with fruitage.
7. Hath He smitten him as He smote those that smote him?
   Or is he slain according to the slaughter of them that were slain by Him?
8. In full measure, when Thou sendest her away, Thou dost contend with her;
   He hath removed her with His rough blast in the day of the east wind.

27 : 3 *I water it every moment; lest Mine anger visit it.* Rashi explains: "During the Exile I punished you, little by little, lest you despair." Kimchi suggests that instead of "Mine anger," it means, "lest the enemy's anger destroy Israel." Ibn Ezra cites this same explanation as coming from Moses Ha-Kohen whom he frequently quotes and he agrees with this interpretation.

27 : 4 *Fury is not in Me . . . I would with one step burn it.*
Kimchi here cites his father's explanation, namely, God says that if I would give full vent to My anger when I find sin in Israel (i.e., "weeds") I would burn the entire vineyard. But I do not do so. There is no such anger in Me. Krauss interprets it similarly.

27 : 5 *Let him take hold of My strength . . . make peace with Me.*
The Targum here makes his favorite paraphrase: Let Israel hold fast to the Torah and I shall give him peace. (So does Kimchi.) Rashi says, "Let Israel seek no other fortress but Me."

27 : 6 *In days to come shall Jacob take root.* From here to the

9. Therefore by this shall the iniquity of Jacob be expiated,
And this is all the fruit of taking away his sin:
When he maketh all the stones of the altar as chalkstones that are beaten in pieces,
So that the Asherim and the sun-images shall rise no more.
10. For the fortified city is solitary,
A habitation abandoned and forsaken, like the wilderness;
There shall the calf feed, and there shall he lie down,
And consume the branches thereof.
11. When the boughs thereof are withered, they shall be broken off;
The women shall come, and set them on fire;
For it is a people of no understanding;
Therefore He that made them will not have compassion upon them,
And He that formed them will not be gracious unto them.
12. And it shall come to pass in that day,
That the LORD will beat off [His fruit]

Isaiah 27

end of the chapter, the prophet seems to speak of the Northern Kingdom, its destruction, and its eventual restoration. In those days, says Kimchi, means in the days when I will ultimately bring salvation to the Northern Kingdom. The language here continues the metaphor of the fruitful vine.

27 : 7 *Hath He smitten him . . . ?* God punished Israel for his sins, but not as completely as He destroyed the nations who oppressed Israel. Israel has been exiled for his sins but can yet purify himself by destroying all idolatry in his midst. ("So that the sun-images shall rise no more.")

27 : 11 *The boughs . . . are withered . . . He . . . will not have compassion.* Kimchi explains this to mean that, although there will ultimately be redemption, Israel as yet has not come to understand the true cleansing purpose of God's punishment; and so for the present he will receive no mercy.

27 : 12 *The Lord will beat off [His fruit].* God will yet bring in the harvest of His scattered children.

145

Isaiah 27

From the flood of the River unto the Brook of Egypt,
And ye shall be gathered one by one, O ye children of Israel.

13. And it shall come to pass in that day,
That a great horn shall be blown;
And they shall come that were lost in the land of Assyria,
And they that were dispersed in the land of Egypt;
And they shall worship the LORD in the holy mountain at Jerusalem.

27 : 13 *Assyria ... Egypt ... worship ... in the holy mountain at Jerusalem.* When the exiled tribes will be brought in from their various lands of exile, the Northern Kingdom will no longer be in existence; so all of Israel will worship together with Judah in the Temple of Jerusalem.

28

ONE OF THE CLASSIC preachments of Isaiah is found in Chapter 28. It begins with a denunciation of the licentious life of upper classes in the Northern Kingdom and applies his messages (beginning with Verse 14) to his own city of Jerusalem. In Verses 9 through 13, there is a scornful description of the moral illiteracy of the people which has to be retaught, "precept by precept, line by line." (Verse 10) The last section (23 to 29) expounds to the scoffers in Jerusalem, God's plans in history. Isaiah uses an extended metaphor describing the agricultural process in the raising of various types of cereal grain.

1. Woe to the crown of pride of the drunkards of Ephraim,
And to the fading flower of his glorious beauty,
Which is on the head of the fat valley of them that are smitten down with wine!

Isaiah 28

28 : 1 *Woe to the crown of ... drunkards of Ephraim.* Perhaps because Isaiah begins this chapter as a dirge with the word "woe," the preceding dirges against the nations beginning in the same way were appropriately inserted before this chapter. This dirge was uttered before Samaria was captured and the Northern Kingdom destroyed in the year 722 B.C.E. Rashi says that the Samaritans indulged in the good wine of Prugita, which was a

Isaiah 28

2. Behold, the Lord hath a mighty and strong one,
As a storm of hail, a tempest of destruction,
As a storm of mighty waters overflowing,
That casteth down to the earth with violence.
3. The crown of pride of the drunkards of Ephraim
Shall be trodden under foot;
4. And the fading flower of his glorious beauty,
Which is on the head of the fat valley,
Shall be as the first-ripe fig before the summer,
Which when one looketh upon it,
While it is yet in his hand he eateth it up.
5. In that day shall the LORD of hosts be
For a crown of glory, and for a diadem of beauty,
Unto the residue of His people;
6. And for a spirit of judgment to him that sitteth in judgment,
And for strength to them that turn back the battle at the gate.

district that produced especially fine wine. Rashi, living in the wine-producing champagne country of France, would naturally comment on varieties of wine; but, actually, he bases this statement on a tradition in the Talmud (Sabbath 147b) that it was the wine of Prugita that was the ruination of the Ten Tribes. Kimchi says that the people of the Ten Tribes grew fat with self-indulgence, and he mentions the passage in Deuteronomy: "And Jeshurun waxed fat and kicked . . . and forsook God." (32:15)

28 : 2 *The Lord hath a mighty and strong one.* Kimchi says it means that God has, waiting, a day of might which will come like a storm. Krauss says it refers to Assyria and means: God hath a mighty instrument, namely, Assyria. (Compare 10:5: "O Assyria, rod of Mine anger.")

28 : 4 *First-ripe fig before the summer.* Kimchi follows Rashi in the explanation that a first-ripe fig in the summer is immediately noticeable. As soon as a passerby observes it, he snatches it up and swallows it.

28 : 5 *Shall the Lord of hosts be . . . a crown of glory.* The Targum with its usual avoidance of anthropomorphisms here translates: God's Messiah will be a crown of glory. Kimchi and Ibn Ezra (and Krauss) say that it means that, after the Ten

7. But these also reel through wine,
And stagger through strong drink;
The priest and the prophet reel through strong drink,
They are confused because of wine,
They stagger because of strong drink;
They reel in vision, they totter in judgment.
8. For all tables are full of filthy vomit,
And no place is clean.
9. Whom shall one teach knowledge?
And whom shall one make to understand the message?
Them that are weaned from the milk,
Them that are drawn from the breasts?
10. For it is precept by precept, precept by precept,
Line by line, line by line;
Here a little, there a little.

Isaiah 28

Tribes will have been destroyed, the people of Judah, grateful for having been spared, will glorify God through their righteous king Hezekiah.

28:7 *Reel in vision ... totter in judgment.* This verse resumes the denunciation of the Northern Kingdom which continues through the rest of the chapter. If we consider Verses 5 and 6 as a pious and consolatory interruption, Verse 4 continues logically with Verse 7 through the rest of the chapter. Kimchi: The verse means, the prophets give them wrong visions and the priests give them perverted justice.

28:9 *Whom shall one teach ... ? Them that are weaned?* Kimchi and Ibn Ezra agree on the following interpretation: Who is there left for the prophet now to teach among all these self-indulgent drunkards? They have no more intelligence than newly-weaned babies. But Krauss says that these words are the words of the drunkards themselves, scornfully addressing the prophet as follows: "Whom are you trying to teach? Are we then little children?"

28:10 *Precept by precept.* Rashi interprets this verse as if it reads: precept against precept. He says that it means, "The prophet gives them God's precepts but they weigh against it (and prefer) the idolatrous precepts." But Ibn Ezra and Kimchi

Isaiah 28

11. For with stammering lips and with a strange tongue
 Shall it be spoken to this people;
12. To whom it was said: 'This is the rest,
 Give ye rest to the weary;
 And this is the refreshing';
 Yet they would not hear.
13. And so the word of the LORD is unto them
 Precept by precept, precept by precept,
 Line by line, line by line;
 Here a little, there a little;
 That they may go, and fall backward, and be broken,
 And snared, and taken.
14. Wherefore hear the word of the LORD, ye scoffers,
 The ballad-mongers of this people which is in Jerusalem:

say: They are like little children, of limited intelligence; teach them by slow degrees, one precept after another. This interpretation is borne out by the closing phrase of the verse: "Here a little, there a little."

28 : 11 *For with stammering lips and with a strange tongue shall it be spoken.* Rashi and Kimchi say that this means that what the prophet speaks is not understood by the people. To them it has as little meaning as if the prophet were stammering. But Ibn Ezra says it describes how one should speak to the people. What is translated here as "strange speech" may literally be translated as "other" or "alternate" speech. Therefore, he says, a teacher must look for simpler words, alternate expressions, to make things clear to the child.

28 : 12 *It was said: 'This is the rest.'* Rashi and Kimchi say the prophet said to them, "Live justly and you will find rest." But they did not listen.

28 : 13 *The word of the Lord . . . line by line . . . that they may be snared.* Rashi and Kimchi: God will punish them line by line, measure for measure, for each sin a punishment. Ibn Ezra reverts to his pedagogic explanation in Verse 10 and says that this means the word of the Lord was to them only a schoolroom exercise.

15. Because ye have said: 'We have made a covenant with death,
    And with the nether-world are we at agreement;
    When the scouring scourge shall pass through,
    It shall not come unto us;
    For we have made lies our refuge,
    And in falsehood have we hid ourselves';
16. Therefore thus saith the Lord GOD:
    Behold, I lay in Zion for a foundation a stone,
    A tried stone, a costly corner-stone of sure foundation;
    He that believeth shall not make haste.
17. And I will make justice the line,
    And righteousness the plummet;
    And the hail shall sweep away the refuge of lies,
    And the waters shall overflow the hiding-place.

Isaiah 28

28 : 15 *We have made a covenant with death.* Ibn Ezra: They said we shall not die, at least not now.

For we have made lies our refuge. Rashi and Kimchi: The people say we have made the idols our refuge. But it is Isaiah who in quoting them calls the idols "lies" and their spokesmen false prophets.

28 : 16 *He that believeth shall not make haste.* The Targum: He who has faith will not be shaken in time of trouble. But Rashi and Kimchi give the verse a slightly different meaning: He who has faith will learn to wait for God's salvation. Ibn Ezra says it means that you had better be patient because this prophecy is for the distant future.

28 : 16-17 *In Zion ... a foundation ... a corner-stone ... justice the line ... righteousness the plummet.* Ibn Ezra connects these two verses. Since God speaks of laying a firm foundation, He therefore speaks also of the tools which the builders use. So Rashi explains: These tools keep the walls straight for the builders; thus righteousness will always march before you and straighten your path (i.e., as the builder's line keeps the wall straight).

The builder uses these tools constantly during the building of the wall. The prophet therefore means that justice and righteousness must be constantly used as the test of a society.

151

Isaiah 28

18. And your covenant with death shall be disannulled,
And your agreement with the nether-world shall not stand;
When the scouring scourge shall pass through,
Then ye shall be trodden down by it.
19. As often as it passeth through, it shall take you;
For morning by morning shall it pass through,
By day and by night;
And it shall be sheer terror to understand the message.
20. For the bed is too short for a man to stretch himself;
And the covering too narrow when he gathereth himself up.
21. For the LORD will rise up as in mount Perazim,
He will be wroth as in the valley of Gibeon;
That He may do His work, strange is His work,
And bring to pass His act, strange is His act.
22. Now therefore be ye not scoffers,
Lest your bands be made strong;
For an extermination wholly determined have I heard from the Lord, the GOD of hosts,
Upon the whole land.
23. Give ye ear, and hear my voice;

28:19 *Sheer terror to understand the message.* Rashi says: "So awesome will be the punishment that it will be terrifying even to hear the prophet announce it." Kimchi gives it a slightly different meaning: "At present they do not understand the message of the prophet but, once they do, they will be shocked and terrified."

28:20 *The bed is too short ... to stretch himself.* Rashi: The oppressor will make such far-reaching demands that you will never be able to meet them. Kimchi: When the Assyrians ravage the countryside and then surround Jerusalem, the world suddenly will appear cramped and small to the people.

28:21 *As in mount Perazim ... Gibeon.* Where God led David to great victories over the Philistines. (I Chronicles 14:16, II Samuel 3:12)

Attend, and hear my speech.
24. Is the plowman never done with plowing to sow,
   With the opening and harrowing of his ground?
25. When he hath made plain the face thereof,
   Doth he not cast abroad the black cummin, and scatter the cummin,
   And put in the wheat in rows and the barley in the appointed place
   And the spelt in the border thereof?
26. For He doth instruct him aright;
   His God doth teach him.
27. For the black cummin is not threshed with a threshing-sledge,
   Neither is a cart-wheel turned about upon the cummin;
   But the black cummin is beaten out with a staff,
   And the cummin with a rod.
28. Is bread corn crushed?
   Nay, he will not ever be threshing it;
   And though the roller of his wagon and its sharp edges move noisily,
   He doth not crush it.
29. This also cometh forth from the LORD of hosts:
   Wonderful is His counsel, and great His wisdom.

Isaiah 28

Strange is His work. Rashi: God's action will seem strange to you; and Kimchi adds, because it will be unprecedented.

28:22 *Your bands.* I.e., your chains.

28:24-28 This describes the farmer, proceeding step by step through the process of raising various types of cereal grain, from the plowing to the threshing. The whole process is so logical a sequence that we feel like saying: "God doth teach him." (Verse 26) But no single step in the process is a permanent one. Each one leads to the next step. So Kimchi explains the metaphor as the description of the steps necessary in preparing the people of Israel to receive and to further God's teachings.

29

A PREACHMENT against the city of Jerusalem, Chapter 29 refers to the coming siege of the city and ends up in Verses 22 to 24 with words of consolation.

Isaiah 29

1. Ah, [a]Ariel, Ariel, the city where David encamped!
Add ye year to year,
Let the feasts come round!

29 : 1 *Ah, Ariel, Ariel, the city where David encamped!* That Ariel is Jerusalem is clear from the next phrase, "city where David encamped." But the exact meaning of the word itself is uncertain. Ibn Ezra calls attention to the fact that the altar in the Temple was called "the hearth" and specifically "harel" (Ezekiel 43:13); hence, Ibn Ezra says, Ariel means "city of the altar hearth." But both Krauss and Tur Sinai connect the name with "aryeh," the "lion," and thus Jerusalem is called here "the lion city," or "the mighty city."

Add ye year to year, let the feasts come round! Kimchi: "You come to the Temple year after year but your festal offerings are an abomination; they are all idolatrous." Krauss and Tur Sinai: "Add one year to this one and, when the calendar comes around, I will carry out My decree." Ehrlich takes it, therefore, to mean, "in two years time."

[a] That is, *The hearth of God.*

2. Then will I distress Ariel,
   And there shall be mourning and moaning;
   And she shall be unto Me as a hearth of God.
3. And I will encamp against thee round about,
   And will lay siege against thee with a mound,
   And I will raise siege works against thee.
4. And brought down thou shalt speak out of the ground,
   And thy speech shall be low out of the dust;
   And thy voice shall be as of a ghost out of the ground,
   And thy speech shall chirp out of the dust.
5. But the multitude of thy foes shall be like small dust,
   And the multitude of the terrible ones as chaff that passeth away;
   Yea, it shall be at an instant suddenly—
6. There shall be a visitation from the LORD of hosts
   With thunder, and with earthquake, and great noise,
   With whirlwind and tempest, and the flame of a devouring fire.
7. And the multitude of all the nations that war against Ariel,
   Even all that war against her, and the bulwarks about her, and they that distress her,
   Shall be as a dream, a vision of the night.
8. And it shall be as when a hungry man dreameth, and, behold, he eateth,
   But he awaketh, and his soul is empty;

Isaiah 29

29 : 2 *She shall be unto Me as a hearth.* Ibn Ezra and Kimchi: The city will be captured. She will be unto Me as an altar of sacrifice, a place of slaughter.

29 : 3-7 A description of the siege of the city.

29 : 4 *Thy speech ... low ... as of a ghost out of the ground.* You will feel humbled and speak in whispers as the whispering voice which the necromancers claim to hear when the dead speak to them from the ground.

29 : 7-8 *Shall be as a dream.* Krauss: The vast hosts of the enemy will simply be unbelievable, as unreal as a dream. But

Isaiah 29

Or as when a thirsty man dreameth, and, behold, he drinketh,
But he awaketh, and, behold, he is faint, and his soul hath appetite—
So shall the multitude of all the nations be,
That fight against mount Zion.

9. Stupefy yourselves, and be stupid!
Blind yourselves, and be blind!
Ye that are drunken, but not with wine,
That stagger, but not with strong drink.

10. For the LORD hath poured out upon you the spirit of deep sleep,
And hath closed your eyes;
The prophets, and your heads, the seers, hath He covered.

11. And the vision of all this is become unto you as the words of a writing that is sealed, which men deliver to one that is learned, saying: 'Read this, I pray thee'; and he saith: 'I cannot, for it is sealed'; 12. and the writing is delivered to him that is not learned, saying: 'Read this, I pray thee'; and he saith: 'I am not learned.'

13. And the Lord said: Forasmuch as this people draw near,

Ibn Ezra says that a dream seems real during the night but vanishes away in the morning. So it was with the Assyrian army besieging Jerusalem. They were terrifying and real in the night, but by the morning they had vanished.

29 : 9 *Stupefy yourselves, and be stupid!* Kimchi says this prophecy was made in the days of the wicked king Ahaz, the father of the good Hezekiah; the prophet says to them, "You are unable to believe or even to understand that the Assyrian army will vanish away because you have stupefied yourselves and are blind."

29 : 11 *The vision ... as the words of a writing.* You are unable to read the words of the prophecy either because the book is sealed for you or because you are illiterate.

29 : 13 *A commandment ... learned by rote.* Their worship of Me is not sincere. It is merely a mechanical ceremonial.

And with their mouth and with their lips do honour Me,

But have removed their heart far from Me,

And their fear of Me is a commandment of men learned by rote;

14. Therefore, behold, I will again do a marvellous work among this people,

Even a marvellous work and a wonder;

And the wisdom of their wise men shall perish,

And the prudence of their prudent men shall be hid.

15. Woe unto them that seek deep to hide their counsel from the LORD,

And their works are in the dark,

And they say: 'Who seeth us? and who knoweth us?'

16. O your perversity!

Shall the potter be esteemed as clay;

That the thing made should say of him that made it: 'He made me not';

Or the thing framed say of him that framed it: 'He hath no understanding?'

17. Is it not yet a very little while,

And Lebanon shall be turned into a fruitful field,

And the fruitful field shall be esteemed as a forest?

Isaiah
29

29 : 15 *Woe unto them . . . who seeth us?* Woe to them who imagine they can hide their hypocrisy from God.

29 : 16 *O your perversity!* Ibn Ezra says that this word means: "It is the reverse of the truth" (that you can conceal your inner thoughts from Me). This interpretation is borne out by what follows: Should the thing that is made say of Him, who had made it, He made me not? God who created us knows our thoughts.

29 : 17 *Lebanon . . . turned into a . . . field . . . and the field . . . as a forest.* Our translation here puts this in the form of a question, but the meaning is still not clear. The Targum and Rashi interpret this to mean: The wooded Lebanon will become a fruitful field and the open field will be so crowded with cities that it will look like a forest. Ibn Ezra says that the whole verse means that food will become scarce and explains the passage as follows: Lebanon, which produces most food, will become Carmel, which produces less; Carmel will become like a forest which produces

Isaiah 29

18. And in that day shall the deaf hear the words of a book,
And the eyes of the blind shall see out of obscurity and out of darkness.
19. The humble also shall increase their joy in the LORD,
And the neediest among men shall exult in the Holy One of Israel.
20. For the terrible one is brought to nought,
And the scorner ceaseth,
And all they that watch for iniquity are cut off;
21. That make a man an offender by words,
And lay a snare for him that reproveth in the gate,
And turn aside the just with a thing of nought.

no food at all. Tur Sinai supports this interpretation and says that the word "yaar," usually translated "forest," is cognate to the Arabic word which means a place full of rocks and with no living plants. However, Ibn Ezra's explanation seems difficult because the verse appears to be an introduction to the consolatory verses which follow and therefore ought to mean fruitfulness rather than sterility.

29 : 18 *In that day.* From this verse to the end of the chapter the prophet speaks of the consolation of better days that are coming.

29 : 20 *The terrible one is brought to nought.* The oppressor.

22. Therefore thus saith the Lord, who redeemed
Abraham, concerning the house of Jacob:
Jacob shall not now be ashamed,
Neither shall his face now wax pale;
23. When he seeth his children, the work of My hands,
in the midst of him,
That they sanctify My name;
Yea, they shall sanctify the Holy One of Jacob,
And shall stand in awe of the God of Israel.
24. They also that err in spirit shall come to understanding,
And they that murmur shall learn instruction.

Isaiah 29

They that watch for iniquity. Rashi explains this to mean those who plan and wait for opportunities to do evil.

29 : 21 *Make a man an offender by words.* Instead of "by words" Ibn Ezra translates "for a word," and it means those evil ones who listen to catch any word that a man may utter in order to accuse him. Rashi says it means the false prophets who by their words lead men to sin.

29 : 24 *They that murmur.* Rashi and Ibn Ezra make reference here to Deuteronomy 1:27: "And ye murmured in your tents (against God)." The prophet refers to those who had always complained against God's justice but who now at last will learn wisdom.

30

THE BACKGROUND of Chapters 30 and 31 is the alliance which Judah and Jerusalem were attempting to make with Egypt for help against Assyria. The prophet declares that Egypt can be of no use to them in their trouble. Chapter 30 (Verses 19 through 26) depicts, as many do, a messianic picture; from Verse 27 to the end is a statement that God himself will destroy Assyria. The whole theme is a basic one in Isaiah's preaching—that the small nation of Judah should not participate in any world alliance but should trust in God for strength to endure.

Isaiah 30

1. Woe to the rebellious children, saith the LORD,
That take counsel, but not of Me;
And that form projects, but not of My spirit,
That they may add sin to sin;

30:1 *That form projects, but not of My spirit.* The word translated here "form projects" comes from the root which means "to cover" or "to anoint." Both the Targum and Rashi take the word to mean "anoint" and say that the verse means, "They anoint kings without consulting My prophets." Rashi, basing his opinion on the general contents of this chapter, says it is Pharaoh whom they meant to make their king. Ibn Ezra takes the word to mean that they take counsel from others but not from God. Krauss takes the word to mean "libation," and calls attention to

Isaiah 30

2. That walk to go down into Egypt,
   And have not asked at My mouth;
   To take refuge in the stronghold of Pharaoh,
   And to take shelter in the shadow of Egypt!
3. Therefore shall the stronghold of Pharaoh turn to your shame,
   And the shelter in the shadow of Egypt to your confusion.
4. For his princes are at Zoan,
   And his ambassadors are come to Hanes.
5. They shall all be ashamed of a people that cannot profit them,
   That are not a help nor profit,
   But a shame, and also a reproach.
6. The burden of the beasts of the South.
   Through the land of trouble and anguish,
   From whence come the lioness and the lion,
   The viper and flying serpent,
   They carry their riches upon the shoulders of young asses,
   And their treasures upon the humps of camels,
   To a people that shall not profit them.
7. For Egypt helpeth in vain, and to no purpose;

the fact that it was a custom (also among the Greeks) at the ceremony ratifying an alliance to pour out a libation. Therefore the verse means, "They make alliances without consulting Me."

30:4 *For his princes are at Zoan.* All the traditional commentators say that the "princes" mean the princes of the king of Israel who journeyed to this Egyptian town to meet the Egyptian officials. This fits well with the next verse, "They shall all be ashamed of a people that cannot profit them"; in other words, such an alliance will not help them at all against the Assyrians.

30:6 *Burden of the beasts of the South.* This seems to be the beginning of a new thought but the Targum and Rashi connect it with the ambassadors going to Egypt and say that this is a description of the pack animals bringing gifts to the Egyptians and describes ("lions and vipers") the hazards of the desert which the emissaries must cross to get to Egypt.

30:7 *Arrogancy that sitteth still.* The Hebrew phrase is dif-

Isaiah 30

     Therefore have I called her
     Arrogancy that sitteth still.
8. Now go, write it before them on a tablet,
     And inscribe it in a book,
     That it may be for the time to come
     For ever and ever.
9. For it is a rebellious people,
     Lying children,
     Children that refuse to hear the teaching of the LORD;
10. That say to the seers: 'See not,'
     And to the prophets: 'Prophesy not unto us right things,
     Speak unto us smooth things, prophesy delusions;
11. Get you out of the way,
     Turn aside out of the path,
     Cause the Holy One of Israel
     To cease from before us.'
12. Wherefore thus saith the Holy One of Israel:
     Because ye despise this word,
     And trust in oppression and perverseness,
     And stay thereon;

---

ficult, but it is clear that it is some sort of jeering epithet for Egypt. But Ibn Ezra, exceptionally, does not refer this phrase to Egypt; he says it is addressed to Israel and that it means Israel's proud strength will manifest itself in just sitting still (i.e., being confidently calm). He bases this interpretation on Verse 15: "In sitting still shall ye be saved."

30:8 *Write ... on a tablet.* This is the same idea as in Chapter 8, Verses 1 and 2, when Isaiah was told during the invasion by the Assyrians and the Northern Kingdom to write his prophecy upon a scroll.

30:10 *Smooth things, prophesy delusions.* The people prefer to delude themselves with optimistic statements. They demand that the prophets confine themselves to roseate prophecies.

30:11 *Cause the Holy One ... to cease from ... us.* Kimchi clarifies this as follows: The people say to the prophets, "Cease talking to us about the Holy One of Israel." Ibn Ezra gives the same interpretation.

Isaiah 30

13. Therefore this iniquity shall be to you
    As a breach ready to fall, swelling out in a high wall,
    Whose breaking cometh suddenly at an instant.
14. And He shall break it as a potter's vessel is broken,
    Breaking it in pieces without sparing;
    So that there shall not be found among the pieces thereof a sherd
    To take fire from the hearth,
    Or to take water out of the cistern.
15. For thus said the Lord God, the Holy One of Israel:
    In sitting still and rest shall ye be saved,
    In quietness and in confidence shall be your strength;
    And ye would not.
16. But ye said: 'No, for we will flee upon horses';
    Therefore shall ye flee;
    And: 'We will ride upon the swift';
    Therefore shall they that pursue you be swift.
17. One thousand shall flee at the rebuke of one,
    At the rebuke of five shall ye flee;
    Till ye be left as a beacon upon the top of a mountain,
    And as an ensign on a hill.
18. And therefore will the Lord wait, that He may be gracious unto you,

---

30 : 15 *In quietness and in confidence shall be your strength.* This is the basic principle of Isaiah's policy. In the struggle between the great powers (Assyria versus Egypt) alliance with either is a disaster. Rely upon your own moral strength for endurance.

30 : 16 *No, for we will flee upon horses.* Ye say we shall not rely upon God; we shall somehow escape the enemy. We will get help from Egypt. Horses came chiefly from Egypt. See Deuteronomy 17:16, where the people are warned against letting the king have many horses lest, in order to procure them, he sends the people back to Egypt.

30 : 17 *One thousand shall flee.* This sort of stampede is described in Leviticus 26:36 and Deuteronomy 28:25.

Till ye be left as . . . an ensign on a hill. Ibn Ezra says that this is a simile of loneliness. Only a handful will remain.

Isaiah 30

And therefore will He be exalted, that He may have compassion upon you;
For the LORD is a God of justice,
Happy are all they that wait for Him.

19. For, O people that dwellest in Zion at Jerusalem,
Thou shalt weep no more;
He will surely be gracious unto thee at the voice of thy cry,
When He shall hear, He will answer thee.
20. And though the LORD give you sparing bread and scant water,
Yet shall not thy Teacher hide Himself any more,
But thine eyes shall see thy Teacher;
21. And thine ears shall hear a word behind thee, saying:
'This is the way, walk ye in it,
When ye turn to the right hand, and when ye turn to the left.'
22. And ye shall defile thy graven images overlaid with silver,
And thy molten images covered with gold;
Thou shalt put them far away as one unclean;
Thou shalt say unto it: 'Get thee hence.'
23. And He will give the rain for thy seed, wherewith thou sowest the ground,
And bread of the increase of the ground, and it shall be fat and plenteous;

30:20 *Thy Teacher [shall not] hide Himself.* The Targum, with its usual avoidance of human description of God, paraphrases: His Shechinah will no longer depart from the sanctuary. You shall be constantly aware of its presence. Rashi says "your Teacher" means "God who teaches you for your own good." Kimchi and Ibn Ezra say it means, "Your guide and your protector will not hide himself. Your help will not come from afar (i.e., from an alliance with Assyria) to help you in the invasion of Syria and the Northern Kingdom, but your king Hezekiah will be your guide and protector."

30:21 *A word behind thee.* Ibn Ezra: You will listen to the prophets and hear your teachers calling after you.

In that day shall thy cattle feed in large pastures.
24. The oxen likewise and the young asses that till the ground
Shall eat savoury provender,
Which hath been winnowed with the shovel and with the fan.
25. And there shall be upon every lofty mountain, and upon every high hill,
Streams and watercourses,
In the day of the great slaughter, when the towers fall.
26. Moreover the light of the moon shall be as the light of the sun,
And the light of the sun shall be sevenfold, as the light of the seven days,
In the day that the LORD bindeth up the bruise of His people,
And healeth the stroke of their wound.
27. Behold, the name of the LORD cometh from far,
With His anger burning, and in thick uplifting of smoke;
His lips are full of indignation,
And His tongue is as a devouring fire;
28. And His breath is as an overflowing stream,
That divideth even unto the neck,
To sift the nations with the sieve of destruction;
And a bridle that causeth to err shall be in the jaws

---

30 : 24 *Winnowed with the shovel and with the fan.* Rashi: Twice winnowed for extra purity.

30 : 25 *Day of the great slaughter, when the towers fall.* Kimchi: This means the destruction of the Assyrian army which will precede the great prosperity. "The towers" mean "their high chieftains" who will fall on that day.

30 : 26 *The light of the moon . . . as the light of the sun.* Ibn Ezra says this refers to the messianic days. Kimchi agrees but adds that it can also mean the happy days of Hezekiah's reign.

30 : 27-33 The prophet turns again to a picture of the destruction of the Assyrian army as is indicated by Verse 31: "Asshur shall be dismayed."

Isaiah 30

of the peoples.
29. Ye shall have a song
As in the night when a feast is hallowed;
And gladness of heart, as when one goeth with the pipe
To come into the mountain of the LORD, to the Rock of Israel.
30. And the LORD will cause His glorious voice to be heard,
And will show the lighting down of His arm,
With furious anger, and the flame of a devouring fire,
With a bursting of clouds, and a storm of rain, and hailstones.

30 : 29 *A song . . . when a feast is hallowed.* Rashi says, on the basis of a midrash, that on Passover night when the people sing of the deliverance from Egypt, on that same night, the deliverance from the Assyrian besiegers will come.

30 : 32 *Staff . . . with tabrets and harps.* The traditional commentators say that this refers to the angels who were sent to destroy the camp of the besieging Assyrians. They came to their

Isaiah 30

31. For through the voice of the LORD shall Asshur be dismayed,
    The rod with which He smote.
32. And in every place where the appointed staff shall pass,
    Which the LORD shall lay upon him,
    It shall be with tabrets and harps;
    And in battles of wielding will He fight with them.
33. For a hearth is ordered of old;
    Yea, for the king it is prepared,
    Deep and large;
    The pile thereof is fire and much wood;
    The breath of the LORD, like a stream of brimstone, doth kindle it.

task with the sound of music. Krauss: The verse simply means that this great victory should be celebrated by timbrel and harp.

30 : 33 *For a hearth is ordered of old.* The Hebrew word here for "hearth" is "tofta," or "tofet," so Rashi and Kimchi translate the "hearth" as "hell." Ibn Ezra, however, says that "tofet" was the city dump outside of Jerusalem, where refuse was constantly being burned.

31

CHAPTER 31, Verse 1, "Woe to them that go down to Egypt for help," continues the prophet's denunciation of those leaders in Jerusalem who seek an alliance with Egypt. Participating in the struggle between the world giants would only lead to national destruction.

Isaiah 31

1. Woe to them that go down to Egypt for help,
And rely on horses,
And trust in chariots, because they are many,
And in horsemen, because they are exceeding mighty;
But they look not unto the Holy One of Israel,
Neither seek the LORD!
2. Yet He also is wise,
And bringeth evil,
And doth not call back His words;
But will arise against the house of the evil-doers,

31:1 *To Egypt for help, and rely on horses.* Egypt is famous for its horses and chariots. In Deuteronomy 17:16, the people are warned not to permit their king to have too many horses. They seek this alliance instead of counting on God's help ("but they look not unto the Holy One of Israel").

31:2 *He . . . bringeth evil.* Evil here means misfortune or punishment.

And against the help of them that work iniquity.
3. Now the Egyptians are men, and not God,
And their horses flesh, and not spirit;
So when the LORD shall stretch out His hand,
Both he that helpeth shall stumble, and he that is helped shall fall,
And they all shall perish together.
4. For thus saith the LORD unto me:
Like as the lion, or the young lion, growling over his prey,
Though a multitude of shepherds be called forth against him,
Will not be dismayed at their voice,
Nor abase himself for the noise of them;
So will the LORD of hosts come down
To fight upon mount Zion, and upon the hill thereof.
5. As birds hovering,
So will the LORD of hosts protect Jerusalem;
He will deliver it as He protecteth it,
He will rescue it as He passeth over.
6. Turn ye unto Him
Against whom ye have deeply rebelled, O children of Israel.
7. For in that day they shall cast away
Every man his idols of silver, and his idols of gold,
Which your own hands have made unto you for a sin.
8. Then shall Asshur fall with the sword, not of man,
And the sword, not of men, shall devour him;
And he shall flee from the sword,
And his young men shall become tributary.
9. And his rock shall pass away by reason of terror,

Isaiah 31

31 : 4 *The Lord ... to fight upon mount Zion.* That is, to fight in behalf of Mount Zion, or to fight upon Mount Zion against the besieging enemies. Thus in Verse 5: "He will deliver it as He protecteth it."

31 : 9 *His rock shall pass away by ... terror.* Rock is the frequently used symbol for strength and refers, of course, to Assyria whose strength shall fade. Ibn Ezra takes the word "rock" to

Isaiah 31

> And his princes shall be dismayed at the ensign,
> Saith the LORD, whose fire is in Zion,
> And His furnace in Jerusalem.

mean "a fortress," which was usually built upon a rock. He says that "his rock shall pass away" means: "When the Assyrians begin to flee, they will not even stop at their own fortresses but will run on further." In other words, Ibn Ezra translates this as if it reads: "The Assyrian shall run past his fortresses" (in too great a panic to enter them for refuge).

32

THE PROPHET states that only the justice which they perform gives kings and princes the right to exercise their rulership. In Verses 9ff., he returns to the theme of Chapter 3 in which he denounces the luxury-loving women of the upper classes in Jerusalem. The chapter ends with the future reign of justice and it asserts that only justice is the source of national security. Verse 17: "The work of righteousness shall be peace."

1. Behold, a king shall reign in righteousness,
   And as for princes, they shall rule in justice.
2. And a man shall be as in a hiding-place from the wind,
   And a covert from the tempest;
   As by the watercourses in a dry place,
   As in the shadow of a great rock in a weary land.

Isaiah 32

32 : 1 *A king shall reign in righteousness.* Rashi says (and so does Krauss) that the prophet here refers to Hezekiah, recalling by way of contrast king Ahaz, his wicked father.

32 : 2 *And a man shall be . . . a hiding-place.* Rashi and Ibn Ezra and Kimchi all understand the words "a man" as meaning "the man." The verse therefore means: Hezekiah will be the protection for his people.

Isaiah 32

3. And the eyes of them that see shall not be closed,
And the ears of them that hear shall attend.
4. The heart also of the rash shall understand knowledge,
And the tongue of the stammerers shall be ready to speak plainly.
5. The vile person shall be no more called liberal,
Nor the churl said to be noble.
6. For the vile person will speak villany,
And his heart will work iniquity,
To practise ungodliness, and to utter wickedness against the LORD,
To make empty the soul of the hungry,
And to cause the drink of the thirsty to fail.
7. The instruments also of the churl are evil;
He deviseth wicked devices
To destroy the poor with lying words,
And the needy when he speaketh right.
8. But the liberal deviseth liberal things;
And by liberal things shall he stand.
9. Rise up, ye women that are at ease, and hear my voice;
Ye confident daughters, give ear unto my speech.
10. After a year and days shall ye be troubled, ye confident women;

32 : 3-4 *The eyes . . . that see.* The reason for the future tense is that the verse means to say, "Now the people are still blind and deaf to the words of God's prophets, but, under the righteous king, they will see, hear, and attend."

32 : 5 *The vile person shall be no more called liberal.* The standards of social decency will again be established and men will once more be judged by their character.

From Verse 6 to Verse 14 the prophet again speaks of the punishment that will come to the nation; and from Verse 15 to the end of the chapter, he speaks his words of consolation.

32 : 9 *Rise up, ye women that are at ease.* He addresses the women in Jerusalem who live lives of luxury and here tells these pampered women of the punishment and miseries that are to

For the vintage shall fail, the ingathering shall not come.
11. Tremble, ye women that are at ease;
Be troubled, ye confident ones;
Strip you, and make you bare,
And gird sackcloth upon your loins,
12. Smiting upon the breasts
For the pleasant fields, for the fruitful vine;
13. For the land of my people
Whereon thorns and briers come up;
Yea, for all the houses of joy
And the joyous city.
14. For the palace shall be forsaken;
The city with its stir shall be deserted;
The mound and the tower shall be for dens for ever,
A joy of wild asses, a pasture of flocks;
15. Until the spirit be poured upon us from on high,
And the wilderness become a fruitful field,
And the fruitful field be counted for a forest.
16. Then justice shall dwell in the wilderness,
And righteousness shall abide in the fruitful field.
17. And the work of righteousness shall be peace;
And the effect of righteousness quietness and confidence for ever.

Isaiah
32

come, while in Chapter 3, Verses 16 through 26 he catalogued all their jewelry and other ornaments.

32 : 11 *Gird sackcloth.* Usually the sign of mourning. It is also paralleled to Chapter 3, Verse 24, "a girding of sackcloth."

32 : 15 *Until the spirit be poured upon us from on high.* Here the prophet begins to speak of the restoration which will follow the punishment.

Wilderness . . . field . . . forest. This is the same series of changes in the landscape as he mentions in Chapter 29, Verse 17.

32 : 17 *The work of righteousness shall be peace.* This is the classic conviction of prophetic and rabbinic Judaism, namely, that only a just society can ever have stability and help establish world peace. See, too, "Ethics of the Fathers," V, 11: "The sword comes into the world when justice is perverted."

Isaiah 32

18. And my people shall abide in a peaceable habitation,
    And in secure dwellings, and in quiet resting-places.
19. And it shall hail, in the downfall of the forest;
    But the city shall descend into the valley.
20. Happy are ye that sow beside all waters,
    That send forth freely the feet of the ox and the ass.

32 : 19 *It shall hail, in the ... forest ... the city shall descend into the valley.* This verse is not quite clear. Kimchi attempts to connect both parts as being a description of the blessing that will come. The verse means, specifically, that in those blessed days, when it will hail, it will hail only in the forest where it will do no harm. The cities will prosper and grow and expand into the valleys. Tur Sinai says that this verse must be read together with Verse 20, and he translates it as follows: Whether it be on the slopes of the forest, or in the lowlands, happy are ye that sow, etc.

33

THIS CHAPTER deals primarily with God's punishment of the Assyrians and the reign of righteousness which will follow the deliverance of the city of Jerusalem. In this picture there is a section (Verses 7 to 12) which speaks of the wickedness that devastates the land, but the main theme of almost the entire chapter is that the coming of righteousness will bring social stability. Verses 5 and 6: "He hath filled Zion with justice and righteousness and the stability of Thy times..."

1. Woe to thee that spoilest, and thou wast not spoiled;
   And dealest treacherously, and they dealt not treacherously with thee!
   When thou hast ceased to spoil, thou shalt be spoiled;
   And when thou art weary with dealing treacherously, they shall deal treacherously with thee.
2. O LORD, be gracious unto us;

Isaiah 33

33 : 1 *Woe ... that spoilest, and ... wast not spoiled.* Kimchi agrees with Ibn Ezra that this applies to Assyria, but he has an alternate explanation that it refers to the days of the Messiah. The parallel of "treacherously and treacherously," "spoiler and spoiler," are found also in Chapter 21, Verse 2.

33 : 2 *Be Thou their arm every morning.* This is a brief prayer uttered in the midst of the danger.

Isaiah
33

We have waited for Thee;
Be Thou their arm every morning,
Our salvation also in the time of trouble.

3. At the noise of the tumult the peoples are fled;
   At the lifting up of Thyself the nations are scattered.
4. And your spoil is gathered as the caterpillar gathereth;
   As locusts leap do they leap upon it.
5. The LORD is exalted, for He dwelleth on high;
   He hath filled Zion with justice and righteousness.
6. And the stability of thy times shall be
   A hoard of salvation—wisdom and knowledge,
   And the fear of the LORD which is His treasure.
7. Behold, their valiant ones cry without;
   The ambassadors of peace weep bitterly.
8. The highways lie waste,
   The wayfaring man ceaseth;
   He hath broken the covenant,
   He hath despised the cities,
   He regardeth not man.
9. The land mourneth and languisheth;

33 : 3 *Lifting up of Thyself . . . nations are scattered.* When God shows His power, the Assyrians will be scattered. The nations here mean the various national components of the Assyrian army.

33 : 4 *Your spoil is gathered.* Rashi says that this sentence is addressed to the Assyrians. "The spoil which you had taken from the land is now being taken from you by your former victims."

33 : 6 *The stability of thy times.* Kimchi and Ibn Ezra agree that this sentence is addressed to the people of Israel.

33 : 7 *Their valiant ones cry . . . ambassadors . . . weep.* There is considerable discussion as to what the word translated here as "valiant" actually means. Kimchi says both words, "valiant" and "ambassadors," mean "messengers" and refer to the various officials that in times of peace were sent around from Jerusalem to the various Judean cities. Now that the Assyrians have invaded the land, the emissaries from Jerusalem weep. Ibn Ezra gives a similar definition, but he says it means the messengers of all the nations who, at that time, vainly sought peace. Krauss says that

Isaiah
33

Lebanon is ashamed, it withereth;
Sharon is like a wilderness;
And Bashan and Carmel are clean bare.
10. Now will I arise, saith the LORD;
Now will I be exalted;
Now will I lift Myself up.
11. Ye conceive chaff, ye shall bring forth stubble;
Your breath is a fire that shall devour you.
12. And the peoples shall be as the burnings of lime;
As thorns cut down, that are burned in the fire.
13. Hear, ye that are far off, what I have done;
And, ye that are near, acknowledge My might.
14. The sinners in Zion are afraid;
Trembling hath seized the ungodly:
'Who among us shall dwell with the devouring fire?
Who among us shall dwell with everlasting burnings?'
15. He that walketh righteously, and speaketh uprightly;
He that despiseth the gain of oppressions,
That shaketh his hands from holding of bribes,
That stoppeth his ears from hearing of blood,

Hezekiah sent emissaries to Sennacherib hoping to bring back a peace treaty, but the Assyrian king sent them back empty-handed (and in tears).

33 : 8-9 Describe the devastation of the land by the Assyrians.

33 : 11 *Conceive chaff ... your breath is a fire.* Rashi, Kimchi, and Ibn Ezra say that this verse is addressed to the Assyrians. Rashi says it means, "Your destruction will come from your own breath" (from within you).

33 : 12 *The peoples shall be as ... lime.* Again here "the peoples" means the various nations that form part of the Assyrian army.

33 : 14 *The sinners in Zion are afraid ... 'Who ... shall dwell with the ... fire? ...'* Rashi and Kimchi both take the verse to mean that the sinners in Zion, when they see the sudden destruction of the Assyrians, will tremble and say, "Who can protect us against such destructive fires as God has sent down?" Ibn Ezra: "The sinner says, 'Who among us can dwell in the presence of God's devouring flames?'"

177

Isaiah 33

And shutteth his eyes from looking upon evil;
16. He shall dwell on high;
His place of defence shall be the munitions of rocks;
His bread shall be given, his waters shall be sure.
17. Thine eyes shall see the king in his beauty;
They shall behold a land stretching afar.
18. Thy heart shall muse on the terror:
'Where is he that counted, where is he that weighed?
Where is he that counted the towers?'
19. Thou shalt not see the fierce people;
A people of a deep speech that thou canst not perceive,
Of a stammering tongue that thou canst not understand.
20. Look upon Zion, the city of our solemn gatherings;
Thine eyes shall see Jerusalem a peaceful habitation,
A tent that shall not be removed,

33 : 15-16 *He that walketh righteously.* The righteous will feel secure. This picture of the confident security of the righteous is developed from here to the end of the chapter.

33 : 17 *The king in his beauty.* Our translation spells "king" without a capital. It follows Kimchi who says it means Hezekiah. But the Targum says it means God, and it paraphrases the thought in the usual way by saying, "You (the righteous) will behold the Shechinah of the Divine Presence."

33 : 18 *Thy heart shall muse on the terror.* Kimchi explains: You will think back and muse on the days of terror before the defeat of the Assyrians.

'Where is he that counted?' Kimchi says that this is part of the musing of the days during the siege. In those days before the victory, during the siege, the king had imposed a heavy tax on

        The stakes whereof shall never be plucked up,
        Neither shall any of the cords thereof be broken.
21. But there the LORD will be with us in majesty,
    In a place of broad rivers and streams;
    Wherein shall go no galley with oars,
    Neither shall gallant ship pass thereby.
22. For the LORD is our Judge,
    The LORD is our Lawgiver,
    The LORD is our King;
    He will save us.
23. Thy tacklings are loosed;
    They do not hold the stand of their mast,
    They do not spread the sail;
    Then is the prey of a great spoil divided;
    The lame take the prey.
24. And the inhabitant shall not say: 'I am sick';
    The people that dwell therein shall be forgiven their iniquity.

Isaiah 33

all the inhabitants of Jerusalem. Special assessors went through the city, counting every house and tower. Where are they now?

33 : 21 *Wherein shall go no galley with oars.* There will no longer be the ships of the invaders which had come to carry away the spoil.

33 : 23 *Thy tacklings are loosed.* This connects directly with Verse 21 which speaks of the galleys. Verse 22 interrupts the metaphor. The meaning is: The ships of the spoilers are all crippled and the weakest of the Israelites ("the lame") are able to take away from them the spoil which the Assyrians had collected.

33 : 21-24 This group of verses would read better if Verse 22 were moved to the end of the chapter.

34

MODERN SCHOLARS are generally agreed that both Chapters 34 and 35 are late and belong to the apocalyptic section because of their mood and the fact that they are a dirge. Unlike Chapters 13 through 23 (which are addressed to a single nation), they predict the destruction of the entire inhabited world (as do Chapters 24 through 27). Besides, they also speak, as in the apocalyptic, of the angels, the hosts of heaven. Thus Ibn Ezra says that these chapters belong to the messianic time. Chapter 34 (Verse 5) departs from the worldwide apocalyptic denunciation of all nations and becomes a specific "burden" against Edom, the symbol of Israel's prime adversary. It describes, in the frequently used picture, the land of Edom becoming a waste, with only desert animals to inhabit it.

Isaiah 34

1. Come near, ye nations, to hear,
   And attend, ye peoples;
   Let the earth hear, and the fulness thereof,
   The world, and all things that come forth of it.
2. For the LORD hath indignation against all the nations,
   And fury against all their host;
   He hath utterly destroyed them,

34 : 1 *Come near, ye nations, to hear.* The writer addresses himself to all the nations of the world.

He hath delivered them to the slaughter.
3. Their slain also shall be cast out,
And the stench of their carcasses shall come up,
And the mountains shall be melted with their blood.
4. And all the host of heaven shall moulder away,
And the heavens shall be rolled together as a scroll;
And all their host shall fall down,
As the leaf falleth off from the vine,
And as a falling fig from the fig-tree.
5. For My sword hath drunk its fill in heaven;
Behold, it shall come down upon Edom,
And upon the people of My ban, to judgment.
6. The sword of the LORD is filled with blood,
It is made fat with fatness,
With the blood of lambs and goats,
With the fat of the kidneys of rams;
For the LORD hath a sacrifice in Bozrah,
And a great slaughter in the land of Edom.
7. And the wild-oxen shall come down with them,
And the bullocks with the bulls;
And their land shall be drunken with blood,
And their dust made fat with fatness.
8. For the LORD hath a day of vengeance,
A year of recompense for the controversy of Zion.

Isaiah 34

34 : 4 *Host of heaven shall moulder.* Kimchi says that this is imaginative. It expresses a state of mind. When a person is in very great trouble, it seems to him that even the heavens have turned against him.

34 : 5 *My sword hath drunk its fill in heaven.* Both Rashi and Ibn Ezra refer here to the old belief that each nation on earth has its guardian angel in heaven. The verse then means: In order to punish the sinful nations on earth, He will begin by destroying their guardian angels in heaven.

34 : 6 *A sacrifice in Bozrah . . . Edom.* Ibn Ezra: Bozrah is a part of Edom. Krauss explains why in this dirge addressed to all the nations Edom is also separately mentioned. It is because Edom is the bitterest enemy of Israel; and so it is singled out as a type of them all.

Isaiah 34

9. And the streams thereof shall be turned into pitch,
And the dust thereof into brimstone,
And the land thereof shall become burning pitch.
10. It shall not be quenched night nor day,
The smoke thereof shall go up for ever;
From generation to generation it shall lie waste:
None shall pass through it for ever and ever.
11. But the pelican and the bittern shall possess it,
And the owl and the raven shall dwell therein;
And He shall stretch over it
The line of confusion, and the plummet of emptiness.
12. As for her nobles, none shall be there to be called to the kingdom;
And all her princes shall be nothing.
13. And thorns shall come up in her palaces,
Nettles and thistles in the fortresses thereof;
And it shall be a habitation of wild-dogs,
An enclosure for ostriches.

34 : 9-17   These verses describe the land when it will become a permanent wilderness. Only the desert animals (wild cats, jackals, etc.) will inhabit it.

34 : 16   *The book of the Lord, and read . . . none shall want her mate.*   Rashi says "the book of the Lord" here means the book

Isaiah 34

14. And the wild-cats shall meet with the jackals,
    And the satyr shall cry to his fellow;
    Yea, the night-monster shall repose there,
    And shall find her a place of rest.
15. There shall the arrowsnake make her nest, and lay,
    And hatch, and brood under her shadow;
    Yea, there shall the kites be gathered,
    Every one with her mate.
16. Seek ye out of the book of the LORD, and read;
    No one of these shall be missing,
    None shall want her mate;
    For My mouth it hath commanded,
    And the breath thereof it hath gathered them.
17. And He hath cast the lot for them,
    And His hand hath divided it unto them by line;
    They shall possess it for ever,
    From generation to generation shall they dwell therein.

of Genesis. Read how, when God brought the flood to destroy the evil world, the animals who were saved came each one with his mate to the ark.

34 : 17 *He hath cast the lot for them . . . they shall possess it.* God has assigned the land, now a wilderness, to the desert animals.

35

THIS CHAPTER describes the restoration which will follow the world cataclysm (and specifically also the judgment against Edom). The thought and the diction of this chapter is close to that of Chapter 40. David Yellin, in *Chikre Hamikra* (Isaiah) p. 37, has a list of ideas and phrases common to both chapters.

Isaiah 35

1. The wilderness and the parched land shall be glad;
   And the desert shall rejoice, and blossom as the rose.
2. It shall blossom abundantly, and rejoice,
   Even with joy and singing;
   The glory of Lebanon shall be given unto it,
   The excellency of Carmel and Sharon;
   They shall see the glory of the LORD,
   The excellency of our God.
3. Strengthen ye the weak hands,
   And make firm the tottering knees.
4. Say to them that are of a fearful heart: 'Be strong, fear not';
   Behold, your God will come with vengeance,
   With the recompense of God He will come and save you.

Isaiah 35

5. Then the eyes of the blind shall be opened,
   And the ears of the deaf shall be unstopped.
6. Then shall the lame man leap as a hart,
   And the tongue of the dumb shall sing;
   For in the wilderness shall waters break out,
   And streams in the desert.
7. And the parched land shall become a pool,
   And the thirsty ground springs of water;
   In the habitation of jackals herds shall lie down.
   It shall be an enclosure for reeds and rushes.
8. And a highway shall be there, and a way,
   And it shall be called The way of holiness;
   The unclean shall not pass over it; but it shall be
      for those;
   The wayfaring men, yea fools, shall not err therein.
9. No lion shall be there,
   Nor shall any ravenous beast go up thereon,
   They shall not be found there;
   But the redeemed shall walk there;
10. And the ransomed of the LORD shall return,
    And come with singing unto Zion,
    And everlasting joy shall be upon their heads;
    They shall obtain gladness and joy,
    And sorrow and sighing shall flee away.

35 : 1-2 *The wilderness ... shall rejoice ... and blossom.* In the cataclysm, the inhabited world will be turned into a desert; in the restoration, the desert will become a garden again.

35 : 4 *God will come with vengeance ... recompense.* With vengeance against evil and recompense for righteousness.

35 : 8 *A highway shall be there.* This is a symbol of the return of the exiles. The same thought is found in Isaiah 40:4: "Make level in the desert a highway for our God." So, in Verse 10: "The ransomed of the Lord shall return ... unto Him."

36 to 39

THESE FOUR CHAPTERS are an historical narrative taken from the Book of Kings (II Kings 18:13-20:19). It was placed here because, in the events described, Isaiah took a prominent part. The section contains two poetic addresses, one ascribed to Isaiah (37:22-29) and the other to king Hezekiah (38:10-20) when he recovered from his sickness.

Except for a few verses, this historical narrative is clear and straightforward and requires almost no commentary to explain the text.

Isaiah 36

1. Now it came to pass in the fourteenth year of king Hezekiah, that Sennacherib king of Assyria came up against all the fortified cities of Judah, and took them. 2. And the king of Assyria sent Rab-shakeh from Lachish to Jerusalem unto king Hezekiah with a great army. And he stood by the conduit of the upper pool in the highway of the fullers' field. 3. Then came forth unto him Eliakim the son of Hilkiah, that was over the household, and Shebna the scribe, and Joah the son of Asaph the recorder. 4. And Rab-shakeh said unto them: 'Say ye now to Hezekiah: Thus saith the great king, the king of Assyria: What confidence is this wherein thou trustest? 5. I said: It is but vain words; for counsel and strength are for the war. Now on whom dost thou trust, that thou

Isaiah 36

hast rebelled against me? 6. Behold, thou trustest upon the staff of this bruised reed, even upon Egypt; whereon if a man lean, it will go into his hand, and pierce it; so is Pharaoh king of Egypt to all that trust on him. 7. But if thou say unto me: We trust in the LORD our God; is not that He, whose high places and whose altars Hezekiah hath taken away, and hath said to Judah and to Jerusalem: Ye shall worship before this altar? 8. Now therefore, I pray thee, make a wager with my master, the king of Assyria, and I will give thee two thousand horses, if thou be able on thy part to set riders upon them. 9. How then canst thou turn away the face of one captain, even of the least of my master's servants? yet thou puttest thy trust on Egypt for chariots and for horsemen! 10. And am I now come up without the LORD against this land to destroy it? The LORD said unto me: Go up against this land, and destroy it.'

11. Then said Eliakim and Shebna and Joah unto Rab-shakeh: 'Speak, I pray thee, unto thy servants in the Aramean language, for we understand it; and speak not to us in the Jews' language, in the ears of the people that are on the wall.' 12. But Rab-shakeh said: 'Hath my master sent me to thy master, and to thee, to speak these words? hath he not sent me to the men that sit upon the wall, to eat their own dung, and to drink their own water with you?' 13. Then Rab-shakeh stood, and cried with a loud voice in the Jews' language, and said: 'Hear ye the words of the great king, the king of Assyria. 14. Thus saith the king: Let not Hezekiah beguile you, for he will not be able to deliver you; 15. neither let Hezekiah make you trust in the LORD, saying: The LORD will surely deliver us; this city shall not be given into the hand of the king of Assyria. 16. Hearken not to Hezekiah; for thus saith the king of Assyria: Make

---

36 : 12 *Eat their own dung* . . . The people of Jerusalem who must suffer the ultimate stages of starvation during the siege. (Rashi)

Isaiah 36

your peace with me, and come out to me; and eat ye every one of his vine, and every one of his fig-tree, and drink ye every one the waters of his own cistern; 17. until I come and take you away to a land like your own land, a land of corn and wine, a land of bread and vineyards. 18. Beware lest Hezekiah persuade you, saying: The LORD will deliver us. Hath any of the gods of the nations delivered his land out of the hand of the king of Assyria? 19. Where are the gods of Hamath and Arpad? where are the gods of Sepharvaim? and have they delivered Samaria out of my hand? 20. Who are they among all the gods of these countries, that have delivered their country out of my hand, that the LORD should deliver Jerusalem out of my hand?'

21. But they held their peace, and answered him not a word; for the king's commandment was, saying: 'Answer him not.' 22. Then came Eliakim the son of Hilkiah, that was over the household, and Shebna the scribe, and Joah the son of Asaph the recorder, to Hezekiah with their clothes rent, and told him the words of Rab-shakeh.

Isaiah 37

1. And it came to pass, when king Hezekiah heard it, that he rent his clothes, and covered himself with sackcloth, and went into the house of the LORD. 2. And he sent Eliakim, who was over the household, and Shebna the scribe, and the elders of the priests, covered with sackcloth, unto Isaiah the prophet the son of Amoz. 3. And they said unto him: 'Thus saith Hezekiah: This day is a day of trouble, and of rebuke, and of contumely; for the children are come to the birth, and there is not strength to bring forth. 4. It may be the LORD thy God will hear the words of Rab-shakeh, whom the king of Assyria his master hath sent to taunt the living God, and will rebuke the words which the LORD thy God hath

---

36 : 22 *With their clothes rent.* The emissaries, returning frustrated to king Hezekiah, tore their clothes in the usual sign of mourning.

heard; wherefore make prayer for the remnant that is left.' 5. So the servants of king Hezekiah came to Isaiah. 6. And Isaiah said unto them: 'Thus shall ye say to your master: Thus saith the LORD: Be not afraid of the words that thou hast heard, wherewith the servants of the king of Assyria have blasphemed Me. 7. Behold, I will put a spirit in him, and he shall hear a rumour, and shall return unto his own land; and I will cause him to fall by the sword in his own land.'

8. So Rab-shakeh returned, and found the king of Assyria warring against Libnah; for he had heard that he was departed from Lachish. 9. And he heard say concerning Tirhakah king of Ethiopia: 'He is come out to fight against thee.' And when he heard it, he sent messengers to Hezekiah, saying: 10. 'Thus shall ye speak to Hezekiah king of Judah, saying: Let not thy God in whom thou trustest beguile thee, saying: Jerusalem shall not be given into the hand of the king of Assyria. 11. Behold, thou hast heard what the kings of Assyria have done to all lands, by destroying them utterly; and shalt thou be delivered? 12. Have the gods of the nations delivered them, which my fathers have destroyed, Gozan, and Haran, and Rezeph, and the children of Eden that were in Telassar? 13. Where is the king of Hamath, and the king of Arpad, and the king of the city of Sepharvaim, of Hena, and Ivvah?'

14. And Hezekiah received the letter from the hand of the messengers, and read it; and Hezekiah went up unto the house of the LORD, and spread it before the LORD. 15. And Hezekiah prayed unto the LORD, saying: 16. 'O LORD of hosts, the God of Israel, that sittest upon the cherubim, Thou art the God, even Thou alone, of all the kingdoms of the earth; Thou hast made heaven and earth. 17. Incline Thine ear, O LORD, and hear; open Thine eyes, O

37 : 3 *Birth, and there is not strength to bring forth.* This is a frequent biblical metaphor. It means to be in great agony without any hope of relief.

Isaiah 37

Lord, and see; and hear all the words of Sennacherib, who hath sent to taunt the living God. 18. Of a truth, Lord, the kings of Assyria have laid waste all the countries, and their land, 19. and have cast their gods into the fire; for they were no gods, but the work of men's hands, wood and stone; therefore they have destroyed them. 20. Now therefore, O Lord our God, save us from his hand, that all the kingdoms of the earth may know that Thou art the Lord, even Thou only.'

21. Then Isaiah the son of Amoz sent unto Hezekiah, saying: 'Thus saith the Lord, the God of Israel: Whereas thou hast prayed to Me against Sennacherib king of Assyria, 22. this is the word which the Lord hath spoken concerning him:
The virgin daughter of Zion
Hath despised thee and laughed thee to scorn;
The daughter of Jerusalem
Hath shaken her head at thee.
23. Whom hast thou taunted and blasphemed?
And against whom hast thou exalted thy voice?
Yea, thou hast lifted up thine eyes on high,
Even against the Holy One of Israel!
24. By the servants hast thou taunted the Lord,
And hast said: With the multitude of my chariots
Am I come up to the height of the mountains,
To the innermost parts of Lebanon;
And I have cut down the tall cedars thereof,
And the choice cypress-trees thereof;
And I have entered into his farthest height,
The forest of his fruitful field.
25. I have digged and drunk water,
And with the sole of my feet have I dried up
All the rivers of Egypt.
26. Hast thou not heard?
Long ago I made it,
In ancient times I fashioned it;

---

37 : 22-29 These verses are a prophecy of Isaiah, addressed to the king of Assyria.

> Now have I brought it to pass,
> Yea, it is done; that fortified cities
> Should be laid waste into ruinous heaps.
27. Therefore their inhabitants were of small power,
> They were dismayed and confounded;
> They were as the grass of the field,
> And as the green herb,
> As the grass on the housetops,
> And as a field of corn before it is grown up.
28. But I know thy sitting down, and thy going out, and thy coming in,
> And thy raging against Me.
29. Because of thy raging against Me,
> And for that thine uproar is come up into Mine ears,
> Therefore will I put My hook in thy nose,
> And My bridle in thy lips,
> And I will turn thee back by the way
> By which thou camest.
30. And this shall be the sign unto thee: ye shall eat this year that which groweth of itself, and in the second year that which springeth of the same; and in the third year sow ye, and reap, and plant vineyards, and eat the fruit thereof. 31. And the remnant that is escaped of the house of Judah shall again take root downward, and bear fruit upward. 32. For out of Jerusalem shall go forth a remnant, and out of mount Zion they that shall escape; the zeal of the LORD of hosts shall perform this. 33. Therefore thus saith the LORD concerning the king of Assyria: He shall not come unto this city, nor shoot an arrow there, neither shall he come before it with shield, nor cast a mound against it. 34. By the way that he came, by the same shall he return, and he shall not come unto this city, saith the LORD. 35. For I will defend this city to save it, for Mine own sake, and for My servant David's sake.'
36. And the angel of the LORD went forth, and

Isaiah 37

---

37 : 28 *I know thy sitting down.* This is the same thought as in Psalm 139:2.

Isaiah 37

smote in the camp of the Assyrians a hundred and fourscore and five thousand; and when men arose early in the morning, behold, they were all dead corpses. 37. So Sennacherib king of Assyria departed, and went, and returned, and dwelt at Nineveh. 38. And it came to pass, as he was worshipping in the house of Nisroch his god, that Adrammelech and Sarezer his sons smote him with the sword; and they escaped into the land of Ararat. And Esarhaddon his son reigned in his stead.

Isaiah 38

1. In those days was Hezekiah sick unto death. And Isaiah the prophet the son of Amoz came to him, and said unto him: 'Thus saith the LORD: Set thy house in order; for thou shalt die, and not live.' 2. Then Hezekiah turned his face to the wall, and prayed unto the LORD, 3. and said: 'Remember now, O LORD, I beseech Thee, how I have walked before Thee in truth and with a whole heart, and have done that which is good in Thy sight.' And Hezekiah wept sore. 4. Then came the word of the LORD to Isaiah, saying: 5. 'Go, and say to Hezekiah: Thus saith the LORD, the God of David thy father: I have heard thy prayer, I have seen thy tears; behold, I will add unto thy days fifteen years. 6. And I will deliver thee and this city out of the hand of the king of Assyria; and I will defend this city. 7. And this shall be the sign unto thee from the LORD, that the LORD will do this thing that He hath spoken: 8.

38 : 8 *The sun-dial of Ahaz.* Rashi refers to the statement in the Talmud (Sanhedrin 96a) and parallel sources. The talmudic sources say that when the evil king Ahaz died the day was shortened by ten degrees. Then, when Hezekiah was to be restored to health, the day was restored to its normal length.

38 : 12 *He will cut me off from the thrum.* That is, the thread that remains on the loom after the completed piece is cut away. So, says Hezekiah, God will cut me off from the continuity of my life.

38 : 13 *The more ... like ... a lion.* Rashi explains it as follows:

Isaiah 38

behold, I will cause the shadow of the dial, which is gone down on the sun-dial of Ahaz, to return backward ten degrees.' So the sun returned ten degrees, by which degrees it was gone down.

9. The writing of Hezekiah king of Judah, when he had been sick, and was recovered of his sickness.
10. I said: In the noontide of my days I shall go,
    Even to the gates of the nether-world;
    I am deprived of the residue of my years.
11. I said: I shall not see the LORD,
    Even the LORD in the land of the living;
    I shall behold man no more with the inhabitants of the world.
12. My habitation is plucked up and carried away from me
    As a shepherd's tent;
    I have rolled up like a weaver my life;
    He will cut me off from the thrum;
    From day even to night wilt Thou make an end of me.
13. The more I make myself like unto a lion until morning,
    The more it breaketh all my bones;
    From day even to night wilt Thou make an end of me.
14. Like a swallow or a crane, so do I chatter,
    I do moan as a dove;
    Mine eyes fail with looking upward.
    O LORD, I am oppressed, be Thou my surety.

The more I resolve to be as strong as a lion and endure my pain, the more I suffer.

From day even to night wilt Thou make an end of me. The word translated here "make an end of me" can be translated "make peace with me." So Ibn Ezra translates the verse, "From the day to the night, Thou makest peace with me"; that is to say, "The attacks of pain take place during the night, but, during the daylight hours, I find relief and peace."

38 : 14 *Mine eyes . . . looking upward.* Kimchi: I raise mine eyes in prayer.

Isaiah 38

15. What shall I say? He hath both spoken unto me,
    And Himself hath done it;
    I shall go softly all my years for the bitterness of my soul.
16. O Lord, by these things men live,
    And altogether therein is the life of my spirit;
    Wherefore recover Thou me, and make me to live.
17. Behold, for my peace I had great bitterness;
    But Thou hast in love to my soul delivered it
    From the pit of corruption;
    For Thou hast cast all my sins behind Thy back.
18. For the nether-world cannot praise Thee,
    Death cannot celebrate Thee;
    They that go down into the pit cannot hope for Thy truth.
19. The living, the living, he shall praise Thee,
    As I do this day;
    The father to the children shall make known Thy truth.
20. The Lord is ready to save me;
    Therefore we will sing songs to the stringed instruments
    All the days of our life in the house of the Lord.
21. And Isaiah said: 'Let them take a cake of figs, and lay it for a plaster upon the boil, and he shall recover.' 22. And Hezekiah said: 'What is the sign that I shall go up to the house of the Lord?'

38 : 18 *The nether-world cannot praise Thee.* The same thought is expressed in Psalm 115:17: "The dead cannot praise God."

38 : 22 *And Hezekiah said: 'What is the sign?'* This sentence seems to hang in the air. He asks a question and receives no answer. For some reason, the verse is misplaced and has no mean-

Isaiah 39

1. At that time Merodach-baladan the son of Baladan, king of Babylon, sent a letter and a present to Hezekiah; for he heard that he had been sick, and was recovered. 2. And Hezekiah was glad of them, and showed them his treasure-house, the silver, and the gold, and the spices, and the precious oil, and all the house of his armour, and all that was found in his treasures; there was nothing in his house, nor in all his dominion, that Hezekiah showed them not. 3. Then came Isaiah the prophet unto king Hezekiah, and said unto him: 'What said these men? and from whence came they unto thee?' And Hezekiah said: 'They are come from a far country unto me, even from Babylon.' 4. Then said he: 'What have they seen in thy house?' And Hezekiah answered: 'All that is in my house have they seen; there is nothing among my treasures that I have not shown them.' 5. Then said Isaiah to Hezekiah: 'Hear the word of the LORD of hosts: 6. Behold, the days come, that all that is in thy house, and that which thy fathers have laid up in store until this day, shall be carried to Babylon; nothing shall be left, saith the LORD. 7. And of thy sons that shall issue from thee, whom thou shalt beget, shall they take away; and they shall be officers in the palace of the king of Babylon.' 8. Then said Hezekiah unto Isaiah: 'Good is the word of the LORD which thou hast spoken.' He said moreover: 'If but there shall be peace and truth in my days.'

ing at the end of Chapter 38. In the original source of this narrative, this sentence is in II Kings 20:8 and it is followed by Isaiah's answer: "This shall be a sign unto thee, the shadow on the sun-dial . . . " Therefore, it should be in Chapter 38 after Verse 7, where he should ask, "What is the sign?" and Isaiah answer, "The sign is on the sun-dial."

The Second and Third Isaiahs

FOR OVER a century scholars had come to the conclusion that the half of the Book of Isaiah beginning with Chapter 40 was not written by the Prophet Isaiah who lived in the time of the kings Uzziah and Hezekiah and who preached most of the sermons in Chapters 1 through 39. These scholars are also generally agreed that this second part of the book is not a unit in itself, that Chapters 40 to 55 are usually taken to be by one author and 56 to the end of the book by another author or series of authors. In fact, some scholars do not even consider Chapters 40 to 55 as a unit, written by only one "Deutero-Isaiah." The various views as to the different types of subdivisions are recorded in Eissfeldt, p. 332, but he adds: "The general practice has been to ascribe the main body of 40-55 to a single poet-prophet."

The reasons for breaking the continuity of the book at Chapter 40 are many. First of all, while in the earlier part of the book, Chapters 1 through 39, the name of the Prophet Isaiah is often mentioned, here in the latter half of the book no prophet's name is given. Therefore it becomes impossible to identify the author or authors. So for convenience sake, scholars refer to the author of most of Chapters 40 to 55 as "the Second Isaiah" or "Deutero-Isaiah" (although there is no ground for assuming that Isaiah was his name). The author of the rest of the book and of certain chapters within 40 to 55 is referred to as "Third Isaiah" or "Trito-Isaiah." Since the section from Chapter 40 on is by a different author or authors and since even in Chapters 1 through 39 there are parts not written by Isaiah of Jerusalem, scholars look upon the entire book as a miscellaneous assembly of various prophecies by various authors. Thus Isaiah as a book would be analogous to a book of the minor prophets which brings together the works of twelve (or more) separate authors.

That the book was not all written by Isaiah but is a collection is hinted at somewhat vaguely in the statement of the Talmud: "Hezekiah and his group wrote Isaiah (also Proverbs, Song of Songs, and Ecclesiastes)." (Baba Batra 15a) Another reason for the conclusion that the book from Chapter 40 on could not have been written by Isaiah, the son of Amoz, is the nature of the message and of the audience addressed. Isaiah of Jerusalem speaks to a nation still settled in its homeland and ruled by its kings. He therefore discusses national policy, foreign alliances, and so forth. The second half of the book deals with the people in exile and is therefore not concerned with political matters. Also, the second part of the book addresses by name Cyrus, the Persian king, who overthrew the Babylonian Empire which had destroyed Jerusalem in 586, at least one hundred years after the time of Isaiah. Cyrus overthrew Babylon in 538 B.C.E., about two hundred years after the reigns of Uzziah and Hezekiah who ruled when Isaiah preached. Finally, the general mood of the Prophet Isaiah of Jerusalem was denunciatory, whereas the general mood of these latter chapters is purely consolatory and reassuring.

Just when these various authors were put together into our present book is difficult to determine. However it seems fairly certain that by the time the apocryphal book of Ben Sirach (Ecclesiasticus) was written (second century, B.C.E.) the Book of Isaiah was already a unit as we have it today. Ben Sirach says of Isaiah: "Hezekiah did that which was good . . . which Isaiah the Prophet commanded him; he added life unto the king by the spirit of might, he saw the future and comforted the mourners of Zion." (48:22-25) Clearly the Book of Isaiah, which Ben Sirach referred to, included the early part of the book in which Isaiah dealt with King Hezekiah, and the latter part in which he comforted the exiles in Babylon.

In spite of these strong arguments, there are still some writers who argue for the unity of the book, insisting that Isaiah of Jerusalem wrote these latter chapters also. The more traditional authors can be typified by Rachel Margolith in *The Indivisible Isaiah*, New York, 1964 (the book had been previously published in Hebrew).

The Second and Third Isaiahs

She criticizes the entire modern school on the ground that it is too materialistic and assumes that a prophet is no more than a child of his environment concluding that those prophecies which do not harmonize with the environment and the historical situation of a certain era could not possibly be written by a prophet who lived in that era. And on this basis they reject many chapters in the first part of the Book of Isaiah and declare that the chapters from 40 on could not be by Isaiah of Jerusalem. But, she says, these materialistic scholars ignore the fact that a prophet is more than a child of his environment; a prophet is a God-inspired man, and under inspiration he can foresee the future. Did not the Prophet Ezekiel foretell the wars of Gog and Magog which were to occur millennia after his time?

A more sophisticated type of traditional defense of the unity of the book was made by A. Kaminka. (*Mechkarim*, Vol. I, pp. 8ff.) He does not say that the prophet foretold the future. He says that the change of mood from denunciation to consolation was quite possible in the life of one man who lived as long as Isaiah did. It is only the non-Jewish scholars who believe that none of the preexilic prophets ever had a consolatory word for the people of Israel, and therefore, on the basis of this general attitude, they declare all consolatory statements wherever they are found in the Prophets as being necessarily postexilic. As for the mention of Cyrus in two places in Isaiah, these two uses of the name of a Persian king were inserted by a later hand.

These arguments defending the traditional unity of the book are not likely to convince a modern reader. It must however be admitted that the general point of view of the composite nature of the book, while acceptable, is not free of difficulties which have not been solved as yet. Particularly there is the difficulty mentioned by Kaminka, namely, if the author of the latter part were another prophet, who was contemporary and lived among the people whom he consoled, how can it possibly be believed that his name would be entirely forgotten? Isaiah ben Amoz who lived centuries before the Exile was well remembered and details of his life recorded. Furthermore it is indeed strange that Isaiah ben Amoz who denounced the people and whose message was certainly not welcome at the time should be remembered and his writings preserved but the name of this supposed Second Isaiah who preached a message of consolation whose message must have been quite welcome should be forgotten and, indeed, so completely forgotten that we do not even know his name. This objection is a strong one and is strengthened by the fact that we do not even know where he lived. Sheldon Blank and other scholars believe he was born and worked in Babylon. Moses Buttenweiser believes that he was born and worked in Palestine.

One might suggest a possible explanation of how it happened that the biography and even Deutero-Isaiah's name are completely unknown. Because of their structure the preachments in Deutero-Isaiah do not give the impression of having been organized public addresses. They seem to be a sequence of small sections. Some scholars in fact identify as many as sixty separate segments. It is possible (as Buttenweiser suggests) that Deutero-Isaiah lived in Palestine. If that is the case, it may well be that he sent his messages to the exiles in Babylon in the form of unsigned letters. But this is only an hypothesis and the fact remains that his name was unknown or forgotten.

Yet, in spite of this and other difficulties, the later authorship of Chapter 40 to the end must be accepted if only because the traditional theory involves still greater difficulties and because of the basic fact that a prophet is not a prognosticator but a child of his age.

And, in spite of those disagreements about the latter part of Isaiah, especially the last chapters, scholars, by and large, regard Chapters 40 to 55 as a unit and so we can try to describe the leading thoughts contained in them.

Perhaps the most lucid summary of the thoughts in Deutero-Isaiah were made by Sheldon Blank in his "Studies in Deutero-Isaiah," *HUC Annual,* 1940, and later embodied with elaboration in his book, *Prophetic Faith in Isaiah,* New York, 1958. The first and leading thought is absolute monotheism. The God of Israel is not merely Yahweh, a local god distinguished by his name from other local gods, Marduk and Rimon, etc., but He is God, the Creator and Ruler of the world. The proof Deutero-Isaiah gives that God is the God of the world is that He is Master of history; and, because He alone is Master of history, only He predicts and has indeed predicted historical events which were to come. What God had announced through His prophets was fulfilled in history. The proof

The Second and Third Isaiahs

that the idols have no reality is the fact that they cannot predict history. Since God is Lord of the world and His rulership was thus proved in the message of the prophets, specifically in the experience of the people of Israel, both the prophet and the people of Israel are in duty bound to bring the message of God to the world. Both of them are God's servants. The memory of the comparatively recent career of the Prophet Jeremiah and the tragedies of his life make him, as it were, the prototype and, therefore, the indication that God's prophets and His prophetic people Israel were servants suffering for God's plan for the world. (See Eissfeldt, p. 341.) This, then, in general is the thought of Deutero-Isaiah: Monotheism is proved by prophecy of historic events. The prophet and the people of Israel are God's witnesses and God's servants who will suffer if need be to bring the knowledge of the One true God to the world. It is because of this task of witness-servant that God consoles Israel and assures it that its captivity is over and it now begins its true historic career. A clear and somewhat different emphasis in detail of the meaning of the book is given on the basis of much careful research by Julian Morgenstern in his *Message of Deutero-Isaiah*, Cincinnati, 1961.

The composite nature of the Book of Isaiah gives rise to still another problem. If the chapters from 40 on belong to another author or authors, whose name we do not even know, why were they attached to the Book of Isaiah ben Amoz? Some scholars say that the answer to the question is primarily a mechanical one. The scroll of the early Isaiah was much shorter than the scroll of Jeremiah and Ezekiel. The Book of Isaiah, including the historical appendage, contained only thirty-nine chapters. Jeremiah had fifty-two and Ezekiel, forty-eight. It was therefore just a convenience to append these new materials to the shorter scroll, and so these additional chapters became a "Second Isaiah" and a "Third Isaiah."

But the problem was not quite so simple. It is not only these chapters from 40 on which scholars agree do not belong to Isaiah ben Amoz, there are a number of chapters within the first thirty-nine which modern scholars generally agree are not by the older Isaiah; and these chapters, except for the historical Chapters 31 to 39, were not *appended* to the earlier book but were inserted into it. Why were they inserted at all, and why were they inserted just where they were inserted? In other words, if the book is a composite, as modern scholars generally agree, what system if any was followed in assembling the mosaic? (Cf. also Eissfeldt, pp. 345, 6.)

This problem was approached in a rather new fashion by L. J. Liebreich, in the *New Jewish Quarterly Review*, Vols. 46, 47. He shows that the arrangement was essentially stylistic; certain key words and phrases served as a sort of cement to hold the various parts together.

As for the text of the "Second Isaiah," it is generally in good condition. Very few words and sentences have grown confused in the passage of time, and, therefore, there are very few suggested text corrections. It is because the text is in such good condition that some scholars doubt that the works of the "Second Isaiah" were ever delivered as orations to an audience. The orations of the other prophets must have been recorded by auditors or written down later and perhaps imperfectly recalled, or different versions by different auditors came into circulation. Thus the text could easily get confused. But if as is assumed the works of the "Second Isaiah" were not originally orations but epistles or letters written to his brethren, then there was an original text in existence directly from the hands of the author. This would explain the good condition of the text as we have it.

Yet, although the wording is in good condition, the general structure is puzzling. Scholars say that the thought of "Second Isaiah" is broken up into small sections, often of two or three sentences each. Some count as many as sixty such small sections. A special study of these separate sections was made by Menahem Haran in Jerusalem (*Beyn Rishonot L'Hadashot*) who organized the various separate sections into larger unities. Thus, while it may be that where our modern chapters end is not the end of a logical larger unity, it is convenient in the commentary to deal with this section as in the previous sections of the book, chapter by chapter. Where, of course, the thought overleaps the division between certain chapters, that fact will be pointed out.

40

THIS CHAPTER begins the second part of Isaiah, "Deutero-Isaiah." It opens with a call on the prophet to comfort the people in exile. Most commentators, ancient and modern, consider that this exile is the Babylonian Exile, but Ibn Ezra and Kimchi say that it refers to the present diaspora. God calls for a highway back from Babylon across the desert to the Holy Land. God's word is eternal. Human plans made by earthly rulers wither like grass of the fields, but God's plan is eternal and His promise of restoration can therefore be relied upon. He addresses the nations (Verses 12 to 26) assuring them their idols are as nothing, that God is the Creator of the world; and, if they would just lift up their eyes and see the heavens, they would realize that. If the nations may be convinced of the absurdity of their idols and the omnipotence of God, then surely the people of Israel who had been taught by God's prophets can fully rely on His promise of consolation and redemption. (Verse 31)

1. Comfort ye, comfort ye My people,
   Saith your God.

Isaiah 40

40 : 1 *Comfort ye ... My people.* In Ibn Ezra's commentary to this verse there is a hint that from here on the prophecies are by a different prophet. Ibn Ezra's statement is not quite clear. He says that in later years people will find encouragement from the

Isaiah 40

2. Bid Jerusalem take heart,
   And proclaim unto her,
   That her time of service is accomplished,
   That her guilt is paid off;
   That she hath received of the LORD's hand
   Double for all her sins.
3. Hark! one calleth:
   'Clear ye in the wilderness the way of the LORD,
   Make plain in the desert
   A highway for our God.

consolations uttered by the prophet even after he is dead. This makes it likely that this comment (the text of which seems to be confused) did indicate that this passage was written much later than it purports to be. Ibn Ezra ends his comment with the cryptic expression, "And he who is knowledgeable will understand." He uses a similarly cryptic expression, when he points out an anachronism in other texts, to indicate that the verse was written much later than it purports to have been written. Thus, in Genesis 12:6, describing the coming of Abram to Canaan, the text says, "And the Canaanite was *then* in the land," indicating that when this verse was written the Canaanites had already vanished from the land, which of course took place many centuries after the time of Abram. To this verse, Ibn Ezra says, "There is a secret involved here and he who understands it will be silent." Thus, by his cryptic remark here in Isaiah, he is intimating that this was written long after the time of Isaiah ben Amoz.

As to the meaning of the words, "Comfort ye My people," nearly all the classic commentators give it a slightly different sense from the way we usually understand it. We take this verse to be addressed to the people. God tells the people to be comforted. But the classic commentators note that the next words begin, "Bid Jerusalem take heart and proclaim unto her." Now who is told here to proclaim the message to Jerusalem? Clearly it is the prophets who must make the proclamation of consolation. Hence the first verse, likewise, is addressed not to Israel but to the prophets, and it means, according to the classic commentators, "O ye prophets, give ye comfort to My people." In other words, "My people" is not being addressed here but is the

4. Every valley shall be lifted up,
And every mountain and hill shall be made low;
And the rugged shall be made level,
And the rough places a plain;
5. And the glory of the LORD shall be revealed,
And all flesh shall see it together;
For the mouth of the LORD hath spoken it.'
6. Hark! one saith: 'Proclaim!'
And he saith: 'What shall I proclaim?'
'All flesh is grass,

Isaiah **40**

object of the verb "comfort." This explanation goes back to the Targum and is followed by all the classic commentators.

40 : 2 *She hath received ... double for all her sins.* The Targum inserts an idea here that is not found in the text. It says, "She will receive from God the double cup of consolation, corresponding to the double punishment she has received." Rashi explains why the Targum inserts "the cup of consolation"; he says it is because the Targum needs to explain how a just God could give Israel twice as much punishment as she has deserved, and therefore he balances it with saying that God will also give them corresponding consolation.

40 : 3 *A highway for our God.* The phrase troubles the commentators. God needs no highway to be built for Him. So the Targum says, "Prepare a road for the people of God." Rashi says, "Prepare the road to Jerusalem," i.e., to the *city* of God. So Ibn Ezra says, "Prepare the way to the Temple," the *house* of God. But Kimchi understands that the phrase is metaphoric and refers to the fact that God himself, as it were, would be their Leader on their return home.

40 : 5 *The mouth of the Lord hath spoken.* The Targum, in its usual, careful avoidance of any human characteristics being ascribed to God, translates "mouth," as "The *word* of the Lord has been spoken."

40 : 6 *All flesh is grass.* These three sentences (Verses 6-8), which speak of the brevity of human life and the transiency of all human effort, are referred by the classic commentators to the hostile nations or to the wicked or, specifically, to the Babylonian power. The verses mean, therefore, that all attempts by earthly

205

Isaiah 40

And all the goodliness thereof is as the flower of the field;
7. The grass withereth, the flower fadeth;
Because the breath of the Lord bloweth upon it—
Surely the people is grass.
8. The grass withereth, the flower fadeth;
But the word of our God shall stand for ever.'
9. O thou that tellest good tidings to Zion,
Get thee up into the high mountain;
O thou that tellest good tidings to Jerusalem,
Lift up thy voice with strength;
Lift it up, be not afraid;
Say unto the cities of Judah:
'Behold your God!'
10. Behold, the Lord God will come as a Mighty One,
And His arm will rule for Him;

powers to prevent the fulfillment of God's plan of restoration of Israel are bound to be unavailing against God's eternal strength and purpose. Only God's plan would be fulfilled. Ibn Ezra calls attention to a similar reference to the fleeting nature of human effort when contrasted with God's eternity. Psalm 90 speaks of God who existed "before the mountains were brought forth" and contrasts this with man's transiency: "In the morning they are like grass which groweth up. In the evening it is cut down and withereth." (Verses 5, 6) So the passage here means that only God's purpose is eternal. Any attempt to resist it on the part of the nations of the earth will be transient and futile. "But the word of our God shall stand forever." (Verse 8)

40 : 9 *O thou that tellest good tidings . . . say . . . 'Behold your God!'* The word for "who tellest good tidings" is feminine and therefore requires explanation. Kimchi says it is Zion who proclaims good tidings. Ibn Ezra says the feminine word for "congregation" is implied. The Malbim explains the feminine word thus: O Zion, proclaim . . . "Behold your God." The Targum, as usual, avoids the idea that God is physically visible and translates, "Behold God's dominion."

40 : 10 *His reward is with Him.* Kimchi explains this to mean, "God who comes to redeem brings with Him a reward for those of His people who kept their faith in Him during the Exile." But

Behold, His reward is with Him,
And His recompense before Him.
11. Even as a shepherd that feedeth his flock,
That gathereth the lambs in his arm,
And carrieth them in his bosom,
And gently leadeth those that give suck.
12. Who hath measured the waters in the hollow of his hand,
And meted out heaven with the span,
And comprehended the dust of the earth in a measure,
And weighed the mountains in scales,
And the hills in a balance?
13. Who hath meted out the spirit of the LORD?
Or who was His counsellor that he might instruct Him?

Isaiah 40

Ibn Ezra takes this phrase in an entirely different way. He says it means, "God has His own reward; He does not need our rewards for the blessings that He brings us." So Ibn Ezra connects his explanation with the next verse: "God is like a gentle shepherd who, out of sheer loving care, protects the weak of the flock."

Verses 12 to 26 contain the thought frequently found in Deutero-Isaiah—the greatness of God contrasted with the nothingness of human-made idols and God's eternity contrasted with the transiency of man. To whom is this declaration addressed? Most of the commentators understand that this large passage is addressed to the nations of the earth. Since in Deutero-Isaiah's thought God is not only the God of Israel (as other gods are the gods of their respective peoples) but is truly the God of the entire universe and of all humanity, it becomes necessary for the prophet to address the nations, to convince them of the futility of their man-made idols, and tell them to look at nature and see itself and learn from it that there is only One God. More specifically, since God the Eternal now intends to redeem His people from exile, all the earthly power of all the nations and their gods are helpless to oppose His intention.

As Verses 12 to 26 are addressed to the nations, Verses 27 to the end are addressed to the people of Israel. They should not

Isaiah 40

14. With whom took He counsel, and who instructed Him,
And taught Him in the path of right,
And taught Him knowledge,
And made Him to know the way of discernment?
15. Behold, the nations are as a drop of a bucket,
And are counted as the small dust of the balance;
Behold, the isles are as a mote in weight.
16. And Lebanon is not sufficient fuel,
Nor the beasts thereof sufficient for burnt-offerings.
17. All the nations are as nothing before Him;
They are accounted by Him as things of nought, and vanity.
18. To whom then will ye liken God?
Or what likeness will ye compare unto Him?
19. The image perchance, which the craftsman hath melted,
And the goldsmith spread over with gold,
The silversmith casting silver chains?
20. A holm-oak is set apart,
He chooseth a tree that will not rot;
He seeketh unto him a cunning craftsman
To set up an image, that shall not be moved.
21. Know ye not? hear ye not?

need to be convinced of the power of the One true God. They had been taught of Him in the past: "Hast thou not known, hast thou not heard?" (Verse 28) Therefore, whether the nations are convinced or not of the futility of their idols, the exiled people of Israel certainly must be confident of God's help.

40 : 14 *With whom took He counsel . . . and taught Him knowledge.* The Targum takes this verse in a strange and unusual way. It translates it to mean: "Who placed the holy spirit in the mouth of the prophets? The righteous who fulfill His word will make it known." But the other commentators take it virtually the way it is translated here.

40 : 15 *As a drop of a bucket.* The thought in Verse 15 continues directly to Verse 17, "Nations are as nothing"; thus Verse 16 seems to interrupt the thought. But Rashi makes a connection

Isaiah 40

Hath it not been told you from the beginning?
Have ye not understood the foundations of the earth?

22. It is He that sitteth above the circle of the earth,
And the inhabitants thereof are as grasshoppers;
That stretcheth out the heavens as a curtain,
And spreadeth them out as a tent to dwell in;

23. That bringeth princes to nothing;
He maketh the judges of the earth as a thing of nought.

24. Scarce are they planted,
Scarce are they sown,
Scarce hath their stock taken root in the earth;
When He bloweth upon them, they wither,
And the whirlwind taketh them away as stubble.

25. To whom then will ye liken Me, that I should be equal?
Saith the Holy One.

26. Lift up your eyes on high,
And see: who hath created these?
He that bringeth out their host by number,
He calleth them all by name;
By the greatness of His might, and for that He is strong in power,
Not one faileth.

---

as follows: "There is not enough wood and not enough sacrificial animals to atone for the sin of the Babylonians." Kimchi: "Those nations who think they can hinder God's purposes will commit so great a sin thereby that the Lebanon and its beasts will not be sufficient for sacrifices of atonement in their behalf."

40:18 *To whom . . . will ye liken God?* Kimchi properly connects this question with the description of the man-made idols in the next two verses. God says to the nations: "Do you imagine that I am as powerless as your idols?"

40:21 *Know ye not?* Still addressing the nations, God says: Does not history teach you that God is Master of the world? "He bringeth princes to nought." (Verse 23) Does not nature teach the same lesson? "Lift up your eyes on high." (Verse 26)

Isaiah 40

27. Why sayest thou, O Jacob,
    And speakest, O Israel:
    'My way is hid from the LORD,
    And my right is passed over from my God'?
28. Hast thou not known? hast thou not heard
    That the everlasting God, the LORD,
    The Creator of the ends of the earth,
    Fainteth not, neither is weary?
    His discernment is past searching out.
29. He giveth power to the faint;
    And to him that hath no might He increaseth strength.
30. Even the youths shall faint and be weary,
    And the young men shall utterly fall;
31. But they that wait for the LORD shall renew their strength;
    They shall mount up with wings as eagles;
    They shall run, and not be weary;
    They shall walk, and not faint.

40 : 27 *Why sayest thou, O Jacob?* Rashi: "Why, O Israel, in your exile do you doubt God's power? You were taught of His intentions, and you must surely know that He will bring you strength in your present weakness."

40 : 31 *Mount up with wings as eagles.* Tur Sinai (Torczyner) here recalls the widespread legend of the phoenix, the bird which is believed to renew its youth magically, and he indicates that the phoenix legend is referred to here as a symbol of Israel's rejuvenation; only, instead of a phoenix, the Hebrew legend speaks of the eagle: "Thy youth is renewed like the eagle." (Psalm 103, Verse 5) So here exiled Israel will "renew their strength" (Verse 3) "and mount up with wings as eagles."

41

THE CHAPTER begins with the thought, dominant in Deutero-Isaiah, that the proof of God's uniqueness is that He is Master of history. Let the worshipers of idols try to prove that their idols had predicted, as God has done, the events of current history, the march of victorious Cyrus. Yet, in spite of this clear proof from history of the nothingness of the idols, the nations continue to make idols. So this passage repeats the description of the technique of idol-making found in Chapter 40, Verses 19 and 20. "The carpenter encouraged the goldsmith." (Verses 6, 7) Their persistent idolatry is in contrast with Israel, "My servant whom God has chosen of old." (Verse 8) He need not fear any longer. God will redeem him and destroy the oppressors, as harvesters thresh wheat. (Verses 14-16) As Israel journeys back home through the desert, God will bring forth in the "dry lands springs of water." (Verse 18) The prophet then reverts to the challenge to the idol worshipers to prove that their gods could "announce things to come." (Verse 22) Now God will send a harbinger of good tidings unto Zion (Verse 27) and then the idol worshipers will know "their molten images are wind and confusion." (Verse 29)

1. Keep silence before Me, O islands,
   And let the peoples renew their strength;
   Let them draw near, then let them speak;

Isaiah 41

41 : 1 *Keep silence.* The Hebrew implies more than silence; it means, as the commentators point out, "Keep silent, ye nations,

211

Isaiah 41

Let us come near together to judgment.
2. Who hath raised up one from the east,
At whose steps victory attendeth?
He giveth nations before him,
And maketh him rule over kings;
His sword maketh them as the dust,
His bow as the driven stubble.
3. He pursueth them, and passeth on safely;
The way with his feet he treadeth not.
4. Who hath wrought and done it?
He that called the generations from the beginning.
I, the Lord, who am the first,
And with the last am the same.
5. The isles saw, and feared;
The ends of the earth trembled;
They drew near, and came.
6. They helped every one his neighbour;

in order to listen to what I shall say." Therefore a better translation might be, "Hearken unto Me."

41 : 2 *Who hath raised up . . . from the east.* Clearly this refers to the victorious march of Cyrus, as Ibn Ezra indicates. (See, also, Krauss.) However, the Targum says that the victorious conqueror refers to father Abraham whom God called "from the east." Rashi agrees with the Targum that it is Abraham who is referred to here. But then Rashi must explain the meaning of Verse 2 which says that he conquered many nations. Rashi therefore says that it refers to the four kings whom Abraham conquered. (See Genesis 14.) But the verses obviously refer to Cyrus and therefore Ibn Ezra explains how the Targum and subsequently Krauss come to this explanation. He says: "The ancients were led to this explanation because Verse 8 says, 'but thou, Israel, seed of Abraham, my friend.'" When Ibn Ezra says "the ancients," he must be referring to the tradition recorded in the Midrash (Genesis Rabah 43:3) although there too the verse is used to refer to the kings who came from the east and fought with Abraham. However, if we follow Ibn Ezra and all the modern commentators, the whole chapter works out consistently as referring to the march of Cyrus.

41 : 5 *The isles saw . . . they drew near, and came.* The distant

And every one said to his brother:
'Be of good courage.'

7. So the carpenter encouraged the goldsmith,
And he that smootheth with the hammer him that smiteth the anvil,
Saying of the soldering: 'It is good';
And he fastened it with nails, that it should not be moved.

8. But thou, Israel, My servant,
Jacob whom I have chosen,
The seed of Abraham My friend;

9. Thou whom I have taken hold of from the ends of the earth,
And called thee from the uttermost parts thereof,
And said unto thee: 'Thou art My servant,
I have chosen thee and not cast thee away';

10. Fear thou not, for I am with thee,
Be not dismayed, for I am thy God;

Isaiah
41

land. The victorious march of Cyrus made a world impact and the prophet says: "All the distant nations came to a realization of God as the Master of history." But Kimchi, who follows the midrashic interpretation, says this refers to Abraham, that the verse means that kings (i.e., the king of Sodom) came to appeal for help to Abraham; Rashi, likewise, says that they came to Abraham who brought them near to God.

41 : 6-7 *The carpenter encouraged the goldsmith.* This repeats the technique of idol-building given in Chapter 40, Verses 19, 20: "goldsmith," "silversmith," "set up an image," etc. The sequence of thought means that the nations in their first terror at the onward march of Cyrus turn once more in panic to their idols.

41 : 8 *But thou, Israel, My servant.* They turned to their idols, terrified by the tremendous events of present history; but you, O Israel, know that you are My servant. This is the first statement in Deutero-Isaiah of one of his leading thoughts, that Israel is selected as God's servant and God's witness to the nations of the world. This thought runs through the entire book. (See 42:1, 44:26, 49:3, 5 etc.)

41 : 10 *I strengthen thee.* The verb in the Hebrew text is from the root "chazak," "strong," meaning, "I hold thee firmly." It

213

Isaiah 41

I strengthen thee, yea, I help thee;
Yea, I uphold thee with My victorious right hand.
11. Behold, all they that were incensed against thee
Shall be ashamed and confounded;
They that strove with thee
Shall be as nothing, and shall perish.
12. Thou shalt seek them, and shalt not find them,
Even them that contended with thee;
They that warred against thee
Shall be as nothing, and as a thing of nought.
13. For I the LORD thy God
Hold thy right hand,
Who say unto thee: 'Fear not, I help thee.'
14. Fear not, thou worm Jacob,
And ye men of Israel;
I help thee, saith the LORD,
And thy Redeemer, the Holy One of Israel.
15. Behold, I make thee a new threshing-sledge
Having sharp teeth;
Thou shalt thresh the mountains, and beat them small,

means more specifically "I have taken thee for Mine own." In the Hebrew text the verb is in the past tense, but Kimchi, who interprets the entire prophecy of this part of Isaiah as referring to the redemption from the present exile, says the verb is to be translated as if it were a future, "I will take thee." But Ibn Ezra says that it should be translated as it stands because it does refer to the past, the redemption that took place when the people were in Babylon. The fact that Ibn Ezra says "They *were* in Babylon" may be taken as another obscure hint on his part that these chapters were written much later than the earlier chapters.

41 : 11-12 *They ... shall be as nothing ... thou ... shalt not find them.* The Babylonians who now oppress you will be defeated and will disappear entirely from history.

41 : 14 *Thou worm Jacob.* The Targum simply sidesteps explaining this curious metaphor and says, "Ye tribes of Jacob." But Rashi says it means that at the time the prophets spoke to them they were as weak as a worm. Ibn Ezra says that the Babylonians considered them merely as worms. But Krauss calls atten-

And shalt make the hills as chaff.
16. Thou shalt fan them, and the wind shall carry them away,
And the whirlwind shall scatter them;
And thou shalt rejoice in the Lord,
Thou shalt glory in the Holy One of Israel.
17. The poor and needy seek water and there is none,
And their tongue faileth for thirst;
I the Lord will answer them,
I the God of Israel will not forsake them.
18. I will open rivers on the high hills,
And fountains in the midst of the valleys;
I will make the wilderness a pool of water,
And the dry land springs of water.
19. I will plant in the wilderness the cedar, the acacia-tree,
And the myrtle, and the oil-tree;
I will set in the desert the cypress, the plane-tree, and the larch together;
20. That they may see, and know,
And consider, and understand together,

Isaiah 41

tion to the fact that the use of the noun "worm" occurs elsewhere in Scripture as depicting helplessness or worthlessness. So Psalm 22:7: "I am as a worm, despised of the people" and Job 25:6: "How much less man, that is a worm." The phrase simply means, "Thou poor, helpless, and despised people."

41 : 15-16 *Threshing-sledge ... fan.* Kimchi explains the metaphor fully and says that it means that just as the various harvest tools break up the grains and blow away the chaff so will the evil oppressors be scattered when Israel is redeemed.

41 : 17-20 *The needy seek water ... I will make the wilderness a pool of water.* The Targum and Rashi describe all this as a metaphor referring to those who thirst for the word of God. God will hear their earnest prayer and refresh their souls. Rashi calls attention, then, to the use of the word "thirst" to indicate the spiritual longing for the word of God. He refers to Amos 8:11, "Not a thirst for water, but hearing the words of the Lord." But Kimchi and Ibn Ezra take this more literally as referring to those exiles returning from Babylon across the desert, which is

Isaiah 41

        That the hand of the Lord hath done this,
        And the Holy One of Israel hath created it.
21. Produce your cause, saith the Lord;
        Bring forth your reasons, saith the King of Jacob.
22. Let them bring them forth, and declare unto us
        The things that shall happen;
        The former things, what are they?
        Declare ye, that we may consider,
        And know the end of them;
        Or announce to us things to come.
23. Declare the things that are to come hereafter,
        That we may know that ye are gods;
        Yea, do good, or do evil,
        That we may be dismayed, and behold it together.
24. Behold, ye are nothing,
        And your work a thing of nought;
        An abomination is he that chooseth you.
25. I have roused up one from the north, and he is come,

of course consistent with the beginning of Chapter 40 in which God calls for a highway across the desert for the return of the exiles.

41 : 21-26 *Produce your cause.* This section again challenges the nations who still believe in idols to prove that their idols could have predicted these historic events. The fact that it was only God who could "declare the things that are to come hereafter" (Verse 25) proves that God alone is the Master of history; only He can, through His prophets, predict future events.

41 : 27 *A harbinger unto Zion.* The chapter would read easier

From the rising of the sun one that calleth upon My name;
And he shall come upon rulers as upon mortar,
And as the potter treadeth clay.
26. Who hath declared from the beginning, that we may know?
And beforetime, that we may say that he is right?
Yea, there is none that declareth,
Yea, there is none that announceth,
Yea, there is none that heareth your utterances.
27. A harbinger unto Zion will I give: 'Behold, behold them,'
And to Jerusalem a messenger of good tidings.
28. And I look, but there is no man;
Even among them, but there is no counsellor,
That, when I ask of them, can give an answer.
29. Behold, all of them,
Their works are vanity and nought;
Their molten images are wind and confusion.

Isaiah 41

if this verse were moved to the end of the chapter. Thus the description of the nothingness of the idols would constitute an unbroken sequence and the chapter would end as Chapter 40 ended with the resurrection of the people of Israel. The "harbinger unto Zion" is literally "the first for Zion." (Rishon le Zion) Kimchi and Ibn Ezra both explain it as follows: The first of the exiles to return to Zion will announce and say, "Behold, here come the returning exiles."

42

THIS CHAPTER is devoted entirely to the thought hinted at in Chapter 41, Verse 6, "Israel, My servant." Israel is God's servant and is given His task to the nations. Although God has given the task for Israel to be "a covenant of the people, a light to the nations," (Verse 6) Israel is still blind to its task, "Who is blind, but My servant?" (Verse 19) and has not learned the lesson to be derived from its own suffering, namely, that God himself "gave Jacob for a spoil and Israel to the robbers" (Verse 24) in order to purify Israel from sin.

Verses 1 through 4 are counted by the scholars as the first of four Servant Songs, or Songs of the Servant of God. The other three are Verses 1-6 in Chapter 49, Verses 4-9 in Chapter 50, and Chapter 52, Verse 13 through Chapter 53, Verse 12. The songs are a subject of wide disagreement among scholars, ancient as well as modern. Who is the "servant of God"? Some of the ancient commentators say it means the Messiah; others say it is the Prophet Isaiah himself. Saadia believed it was the Prophet Jeremiah. But most of them agree (with the reading in Septuagint) that it has a collective meaning—the people of Israel as servant of God. (See commentary note to Verse 1.) Non-Jewish scholars also present a wide variety of identifications of the "servant." The older Christian theologians said it was a prophecy of Jesus. Modern scholars have identified the "servant" with at least a half dozen personalities, royal, prophetic, etc.

In recent years a number of scholars have tended to deprecate the importance of these four Servant Songs. Harry Orlinsky, in his *Studies of the Second Part of the Book of Isaiah* (Leyden, 1967), has an original and radical approach to the whole question. He considers the entire widespread discussion an overemphasis due to the influence of Christian theology. He denies that there can be in prophetic thought any such idea as vicarious atonement. He identified the "servant" with the prophet himself. This denial of the possibility in prophetic thought of vicarious atonement was made by Kimchi. (See commentary note to 53:4.) It is evident that the debate over the meaning of the Servant Songs will continue for a long time. (For a summary of a debate, see Krauss in his commentary to Chapter 52 and Eissfeldt, pp. 333-6.) The dominant point of view, both among Jewish and Christian scholars, is that the "servant of God" is to be identified with the people of Israel.

Isaiah 42

1. Behold My servant, whom I uphold;
   Mine elect, in whom My soul delighteth;
   I have put My spirit upon him,
   He shall make the right to go forth to the nations.
2. He shall not cry, nor lift up,
   Nor cause his voice to be heard in the street.
3. A bruised reed shall he not break,
   And the dimly burning wick shall he not quench;

42 : 1 *Behold My servant.* Not all of the classic commentators accept the interpretation that God's servant here means the whole people of Israel. For example, both the Targum and Kimchi say the servant means the Messiah. Ibn Ezra also says that the servant means the prophet himself. But the oldest of the translations, the Septuagint, takes it for granted that the servant means Israel, because it simply paraphrases this verse and reads it as follows: "Behold Jacob, My servant, and Israel, My messenger." Rashi, too, says that the servant refers to Israel and he supports this opinion with a citation from Psalm 135:4: "For the Lord hath chosen Jacob." (See, also, Krauss.)

42 : 2 *He shall not cry, nor lift . . . his voice.* Rashi says it means: He will not need to shout to call the nations to him; they will come of their own accord.

42 : 3 *A bruised reed.* Kimchi explains this metaphor: Even the

Isaiah 42

He shall make the right to go forth according to the truth.

4. He shall not fail nor be crushed,
Till he have set the right in the earth;
And the isles shall wait for his teaching.
5. Thus saith God the LORD,
He that created the heavens, and stretched them forth,
He that spread forth the earth and that which cometh out of it,
He that giveth breath unto the people upon it,
And spirit to them that walk therein:
6. I the LORD have called thee in righteousness,
And have taken hold of thy hand,
And kept thee, and set thee for a covenant of the people,
For a light of the nations;
7. To open the blind eyes,
To bring out the prisoners from the dungeon,
And them that sit in darkness out of the prison-house.
8. I am the LORD, that is My name;
And My glory will I not give to another,
Neither My praise to graven images.
9. Behold, the former things are come to pass,

weakest and the most helpless will receive tender consideration and full justice.

42 : 6 *For a light of the nations.* Although Rashi holds with most commentators that the servant means the people of Israel, nevertheless in this verse ("I the Lord have called thee") he believes the reference is to the Prophet Isaiah, and therefore he is compelled to translate a "covenant of the *nations*" as meaning the various tribes of Israel, since each tribe could be called a nation. But it is clear that the thought here is the same as in Chapter 49, Verse 8, "a covenant of the peoples," and means as Kimchi explains it: "Just as My covenant is with you, so will you through your moral influence establish a covenant of all the nations with Me." As an example of this moral influence of Israel upon the nations, Kimchi refers to "the seven command-

And new things do I declare;
Before they spring forth I tell you of them.
10. Sing unto the Lord a new song,
And His praise from the end of the earth;
Ye that go down to the sea, and all that is therein,
The isles, and the inhabitants thereof.
11. Let the wilderness and the cities thereof lift up their voice,
The villages that Kedar doth inhabit;
Let the inhabitants of Sela exult,
Let them shout from the top of the mountains.
12. Let them give glory unto the Lord,
And declare His praise in the islands.
13. The Lord will go forth as a mighty man,
He will stir up jealousy like a man of war;
He will cry, yea, He will shout aloud,
He will prove Himself mighty against His enemies.
14. I have long time held My peace,
I have been still, and refrained Myself;
Now will I cry like a travailing woman,
Gasping and panting at once.
15. I will make waste mountains and hills,
And dry up all their herbs;
And I will make the rivers islands,
And will dry up the pools.

Isaiah 42

ments of the Sons of Noah," the basic moral law which all nations will learn to observe.

42 : 8 *My glory will I not give ... to graven images.* God will not allow the world to remain sunk in the mire of idolatry. Therefore the time will come when the inhabitants of the isles will "sing a new song to the Lord." (Verse 10)

42 : 14 *I have ... held My peace.* Rashi and Kimchi: "I have been quiet all these years while My people were in exile." But the whole chapter speaks of the world being redeemed from idolatry and the verse seems to mean that God's patience with the blindness of the world has come to an end and He will now lead the world to knowledge of Him. So Verse 16: "These things will I do," until the idolators shall be greatly ashamed, "that say unto molten images: 'Ye are our gods.'"

221

Isaiah 42

16. And I will bring the blind by a way that they knew not,
    In paths that they knew not will I lead them;
    I will make darkness light before them,
    And rugged places plain.
    These things will I do,
    And I will not leave them undone.
17. They shall be turned back, greatly ashamed,
    That trust in graven images,
    That say unto molten images:
    'Ye are our gods.'
18. Hear, ye deaf,
    And look, ye blind, that ye may see.
19. Who is blind, but My servant?
    Or deaf, as My messenger that I send?
    Who is blind as he that is wholehearted,
    And blind as the LORD's servant?
20. Seeing many things, thou observest not;
    Opening the ears, he heareth not.

42 : 19 *Who is blind, but My servant?* Malbim gives an acceptable explanation of what is meant by calling Israel blind. He says that there is none so blind as those who have the faculty of sight and yet willfully close their eyes and refuse to see. Israel who has been taught by all the prophets and refuses to see the meaning of God's law is truly blind. In fact, Rashi in Verse 20 says: "I (says the Lord) try to open your eyes through My messengers, the prophets, but not one of you listens to My words."

21. The Lord was pleased, for His righteousness' sake,
    To make the teaching great and glorious.
22. But this is a people robbed and spoiled,
    They are all of them snared in holes,
    And they are hid in prison-houses;
    They are for a prey, and none delivereth,
    For a spoil, and none saith: 'Restore.'
23. Who among you will give ear to this?
    Who will hearken and hear for the time to come?
24. Who gave Jacob for a spoil, and Israel to the robbers?
    Did not the Lord?
    He against whom we have sinned,
    And in whose ways they would not walk,
    Neither were they obedient unto His law.
25. Therefore He poured upon him the fury of His anger,
    And the strength of battle;
    And it set him on fire round about, yet he knew not,
    And it burned him, yet he laid it not to heart.

Isaiah 42

42 : 24 *Who gave Jacob for a spoil?* The Targum: "Is it not God himself who made Israel suffer because of their sins, and yet they did not turn back to God's law." And in this explanation the Targum is followed by all the classic commentators. The people of Israel are punished for their sins and should so learn God's purpose to purify them, until they learn this, "Who is blind like My servant and deaf like My messenger?" (Verse 19)

43

GOD will redeem Israel so that Israel may become His witness. But Israel forgets the lesson of the unhappy past: Because Israel has sinned, God sent punishment for its purification.

Isaiah 43

1. But now thus saith the LORD that created thee, O Jacob,
And He that formed thee, O Israel:
Fear not, for I have redeemed thee,
I have called thee by thy name, thou art Mine.
2. When thou passest through the waters, I will be with thee,
And through the rivers, they shall not overflow thee;
When thou walkest through the fire, thou shalt not be burned,
Neither shall the flame kindle upon thee.

43 : 1 *But now . . . I have redeemed thee.* Kimchi follows his father's opinion that this refers to God's redemption of Jerusalem from the armies of Sennacherib. But he notes that other commentators say that it refers to the coming redemption from Babylon through Cyrus the Persian king. Ibn Ezra holds (and so does Krauss) to the latter explanation because in Verse 3 it speaks of "Egypt and Ethiopia," which would be conquered by the Persians.

3. For I am the L{\sc ord} thy God,
   The Holy One of Israel, thy Saviour;
   I have given Egypt as thy ransom,
   Ethiopia and Seba for thee.
4. Since thou art precious in My sight, and honourable,
   And I have loved thee;
   Therefore will I give men for thee,
   And peoples for thy life.
5. Fear not, for I am with thee;
   I will bring thy seed from the east,
   And gather thee from the west;
6. I will say to the north: 'Give up,'
   And to the south: 'Keep not back,
   Bring My sons from far,
   And my daughters from the end of the earth;
7. Every one that is called by My name,
   And whom I have created for My glory,
   I have formed him, yea, I have made him.'
8. The blind people that have eyes shall be brought forth,
   And the deaf that have ears.

Isaiah 43

43 : 3-4 *Egypt as thy ransom ... peoples for thy life.* Ibn Ezra and Krauss explain the idea of ransom: that the Persians will take the Egyptians, etc., into captivity as a ransom, in a sense, for Israel whom Cyrus will set free.

43 : 5-6 *From the east ... the west ... the north ... the south.* Kimchi, who explains the redemption as being that of Jerusalem from Sennacherib, must now explain why the prophet speaks of Israel being restored from all the distant lands. He says that the defeat of Sennacherib was proof to convince Israel that God would now redeem its far-scattered exiles. Krauss says that it means the redemption from Babylon; and the points of the compass are mentioned because Babylon was a worldwide empire.

43 : 8 *The blind ... that have eyes.* Both Rashi and Kimchi say that this refers to the fact that the people of Israel has become weak and blind in its exile. But clearly the idea of Israel's blindness is a restatement of the thought in Chapter 42, Verses 18, 19, "Look, ye blind, that ye may see. Who is blind, but My servant?" In other words, Israel in the exile is blind to the real meaning

Isaiah 43

9. All the nations are gathered together,
And the peoples are assembled;
Who among them can declare this,
And announce to us former things?
Let them bring their witnesses, that they may be justified;
And let them hear, and say: 'It is truth.'
10. Ye are My witnesses, saith the LORD,
And My servant whom I have chosen;
That ye may know and believe Me, and understand
That I am He;
Before Me there was no God formed,
Neither shall any be after Me.
11. I, even I, am the LORD;
And beside Me there is no saviour.
12. I have declared, and I have saved,
And I have announced,
And there was no strange god among you;
Therefore ye are My witnesses, saith the LORD, and I am God.
13. Yea, since the day was I am He,

---

of God's purpose. Nevertheless, though still ignorant, blind, and deaf, Israel will be redeemed.

43 : 9 *Nations are gathered together.* The thought is a restatement of that expressed in previous chapters. Let the nations come together, as if at some great legal trial, and try to prove the power of their idols.

43 : 10 *Ye are My witnesses.* The nations may try to prove the reality of their idols but ye, O Israel, are My witnesses because you have seen My works in your own history. You were taught and you know that I am God. No one knows as you do that "I have declared, and I have saved." (Verse 12)

43 : 14 *For your sake I have sent to Babylon.* Whom did God send to Babylon? Ibn Ezra says it really means: As it were, I Myself have come to Babylon to save you. But then he adds that "a learned man in Spain" said that God sent His divine glory, His Shechinah, to join Israel in Babylon.

It is on the basis of this understanding of the verse (that God sent His Shechinah to Babylon) that the Talmud (b. Megillah

And there is none that can deliver out of My hand;
I will work, and who can reverse it?
14. Thus saith the LORD, your Redeemer,
The Holy One of Israel:
For your sake I have sent to Babylon,
And I will bring down all of them as fugitives,
Even the Chaldeans, in the ships of their shouting.
15. I am the LORD, your Holy One,
The Creator of Israel, your King.
16. Thus saith the LORD, who maketh a way in the sea,
And a path in the mighty waters;
17. Who bringeth forth the chariot and horse,
The army and the power—
They lie down together, they shall not rise,
They are extinct, they are quenched as a wick:
18. Remember ye not the former things,
Neither consider the things of old.

Isaiah 43

29a) develops the general idea that to whatever land Israel is exiled the Shechinah joins it in the exile.

The Targum paraphrases the verse: Because of your sins I exiled you to Babylon and the Chaldeans carried you away in their ships. (See end of verse.) Rashi repeats the opinion of the Targum. But this explanation fits poorly with the first part of the verse, "Thus saith your Redeemer." Kimchi comes to the correct explanation. He connects the words "Thus saith your Redeemer" with the words "For your sake I have sent to Babylon," and interprets: In your behalf I sent Cyrus to Babylon to conquer it, for I am the Lord your Redeemer.

43 : 16 *A path in the mighty waters.* Rashi: This refers to the path which God made for Israel through the mighty waters of the Red Sea. Kimchi elaborates and says: Just as God thus redeemed them from the Egyptians, so He will now redeem them from the Babylonians. But Ibn Ezra says "the path in the waters" is the path which will be followed by the Persian ships who will come and conquer Babylon.

43 : 18 *Remember . . . not the former things.* Forget all the miseries of the past. Now I will bring you deliverance. (Verse 19: "I will do a new thing.")

Isaiah 43

19. Behold, I will do a new thing;
    Now shall it spring forth; shall ye not know it?
    I will even make a way in the wilderness,
    And rivers in the desert.
20. The beasts of the field shall honour Me,
    The jackals and the ostriches;
    Because I give waters in the wilderness,
    And rivers in the desert,
    To give drink to My people, Mine elect;
21. The people which I formed for Myself,
    That they might tell of My praise.
22. Yet thou hast not called upon Me, O Jacob,
    Neither hast thou wearied thyself about Me, O Israel.
23. Thou hast not brought Me the small cattle of thy burnt-offerings;
    Neither hast thou honoured Me with thy sacrifices.
    I have not burdened thee with a meal-offering,
    Nor wearied thee with frankincense.

43 : 19-20 *Rivers in the desert.* The same idea as expressed in Chapter 41, Verse 17, God will provide water for Israel as it returns across the desert back to its home.

43 : 23 *Thou hast not brought Me ... cattle.* Rashi emphasizes the word "Me" as follows: It is not to Me that you brought your sacrifices but to the idols. And Kimchi adds, but on the contrary you burdened Me with your sins. Ibn Ezra explains it rather prosaically: In Babylon you could bring Me no offerings (but only your sins).

24. Thou hast bought Me no sweet cane with money,
Neither hast thou satisfied Me with the fat of thy sacrifices;
But thou hast burdened Me with thy sins,
Thou hast wearied Me with thine iniquities.
25. I, even I, am He that blotteth out thy transgressions for Mine own sake;
And thy sins I will not remember.
26. Put Me in remembrance, let us plead together;
Declare thou, that thou mayest be justified.
27. Thy first father sinned,
And thine intercessors have transgressed against Me.
28. Therefore I have profaned the princes of the sanctuary,
And I have given Jacob to condemnation,
And Israel to reviling.

Isaiah 43

43 : 25-26 *Thy sins I will not remember. Put Me in remembrance.* I will indeed forget and forgive but you should never forget your past iniquities.

43 : 27 *Thy first father sinned.* Kimchi says this refers to the sin of Adam, but Rashi says this refers actually to Abraham who doubted God's promise. Genesis 15:8: Abraham asked, How shall I know that I shall inherit the land? Krauss and Tur Sinai (Torczyner) agree with Rashi's explanation.

43 : 28 *The princes of the sanctuary.* Krauss explains that that means the priests. He refers to I Chronicles 24:5: "Thus they (the priests) were divided by lot; for they were princes of the sanctuary."

44

IN FUTURE generations Israel, God's chosen servant, will be fully devoted to the Lord. (Verse 5: "I am the Lord's.") The chapter continues with the previously mentioned theme of God's exclusive knowledge of future events. Then follows the technical description of the process of idol-making; here this description has an added element, a strong concluding note of sarcasm. Then God returns to address Israel, promising to forgive its sins, have Jerusalem rebuilt, and at the end of the chapter mentions, for the first time by name, Cyrus the Persian king who will be "God's shepherd" and will cause Jerusalem to be rebuilt.

Isaiah 44

1. Yet now hear, O Jacob My servant,
   And Israel, whom I have chosen;
2. Thus saith the Lord that made thee,

44 : 1-2 *Jacob My servant ... formed thee from the womb.* Ibn Ezra says that this verse refers to the fact that God gave Jacob strength in his mother's womb to hold on to Esau. Kimchi here quotes Ibn Ezra by name, as he does elsewhere in his commentary to this book ("the sage Abraham Ibn Ezra") and he says the verse means: As God had helped your father Jacob in the womb, so will He help you now.

But these limited explanations of the verse do not fit with the close of the verse: "My servant Israel, whom I have chosen."

And formed thee from the womb, who will help thee:
Fear not, O Jacob My servant,
And thou, Jeshurun, whom I have chosen.
3. For I will pour water upon the thirsty land,
And streams upon the dry ground;
I will pour My spirit upon thy seed,
And My blessing upon thine offspring;
4. And they shall spring up among the grass,
As willows by the watercourses.
5. One shall say: 'I am the LORD's';
And another shall call himself by the name of Jacob;
And another shall subscribe with his hand unto the LORD,
And surname himself by the name of Israel.
6. Thus saith the LORD, the King of Israel,
And his Redeemer the LORD of hosts:
I am the first, and I am the last,
And beside Me there is no God.

Isaiah 44

The verse must have a wider meaning. The expression "formed thee from the womb" was applied to the Prophet Jeremiah: "Before thou camest forth out of the womb, I have appointed thee a prophet unto the nations." (Jeremiah 1:5) Now, here, the same idea is applied to the entire people of Israel and means that from its very beginning Israel was chosen to be God's servant. (See also Verse 24.) Evidently what Deutero-Isaiah had in mind was that the entire nation would now take up the role of prophecy.

Jeshurun. Another name for Israel. It occurs also in Deuteronomy, Chapter 32, Verse 15; Chapter 23, Verses 5 and 26.

44 : 3 *My spirit upon thy seed.* Hitherto the description of God bringing water to the desert meant that He would make the desert safe for the returning exiles. But here He adds that the descendants of Israel will become spiritually fruitful: "I will pour My spirit upon thy seed." (Verse 3)

44 : 4-5 *Willows by the watercourses . . . surname himself . . . Israel.* Rashi says this luxurious growth refers to the many proselytes who will come to join the house of Israel. Ibn Ezra has the same explanation and cites Zachariah: "Men of the nations will say, 'We will go with you for we have heard that God is with you.'" (8:23)

Isaiah

44

7. And who, as I, can proclaim—
   Let him declare it, and set it in order for Me—
   Since I appointed the ancient people?
   And the things that are coming, and that shall come to pass, let them declare.
8. Fear ye not, neither be afraid;
   Have I not announced unto thee of old, and declared it?
   And ye are My witnesses.
   Is there a God beside Me?
   Yea, there is no Rock; I know not any.
9. They that fashion a graven image are all of them vanity,
   And their delectable things shall not profit;
   And their own witnesses see not, nor know;
   That they may be ashamed.
10. Who hath fashioned a god, or molten an image
    That is profitable for nothing?
11. Behold, all the fellows thereof shall be ashamed;
    And the craftsmen skilled above men;
    Let them all be gathered together, let them stand up;
    They shall fear, they shall be ashamed together.
12. The smith maketh an axe,
    And worketh in the coals, and fashioneth it with hammers,
    And worketh it with his strong arm;
    Yea, he is hungry, and his strength faileth;
    He drinketh no water, and is faint.
13. The carpenter stretcheth out a line;
    He marketh it out with a pencil;
    He fitteth it with planes,
    And he marketh it out with the compasses,
    And maketh it after the figure of a man,

44 : 7 *I appointed the ancient people.* Rashi and Kimchi say that this means: Since I created mankind of old. But in modern Hebrew writing, this phrase, "am olam," is taken to mean "the eternal people" and refers to Israel.

44 : 9-17 A more detailed description of the fabrication of an idol. It ends with the sarcastic thought that a man takes a block of wood, half of which he uses to make a fire to warm himself:

According to the beauty of a man, to dwell in the house.
14. He heweth him down cedars,
And taketh the ilex and the oak,
And strengtheneth for himself one among the trees of the forest;
He planteth a bay-tree, and the rain doth nourish it.
15. Then a man useth it for fuel;
And he taketh thereof, and warmeth himself;
Yea, he kindleth it, and baketh bread;
Yea, he maketh a god, and worshippeth it;
He maketh it a graven image, and falleth down thereto.
16. He burneth the half thereof in the fire;
With the half thereof he eateth flesh;
He roasteth roast, and is satisfied;
Yea, he warmeth himself, and saith: 'Aha,
I am warm, I have seen the fire';
17. And the residue thereof he maketh a god, even his graven image;
He falleth down unto it and worshippeth, and prayeth unto it,
And saith: 'Deliver me, for thou art my god.'
18. They know not, neither do they understand;
For their eyes are bedaubed, that they cannot see,
And their hearts, that they cannot understand.
19. And none considereth in his heart,
Neither is there knowledge nor understanding to say:
'I have burned the half of it in the fire;
Yea, also I have baked bread upon the coals thereof;
I have roasted flesh and eaten it;
And shall I make the residue thereof an abomination?
Shall I fall down to the stock of a tree?'

Isaiah 44

"Aha, I am warm" (Verse 16) and the other half he carves into a god to whom he says: "Deliver me, thou art my god." (Verse 17)

44 : 19 *Shall I make the residue ... an abomination?* I.e., a god. Either this is a euphemism for a god or it means: Should not the idol-maker realize that it is merely an abomination?

Isaiah 44

20. He striveth after ashes,
    A deceived heart hath turned him aside,
    That he cannot deliver his soul, nor say:
    'Is there not a lie in my right hand?'
21. Remember these things, O Jacob,
    And Israel, for thou art My servant;
    I have formed thee, thou art Mine own servant;
    O Israel, thou shouldest not forget Me.
22. I have blotted out, as a thick cloud, thy transgressions,
    And, as a cloud, thy sins;
    Return unto Me, for I have redeemed thee.
23. Sing, O ye heavens, for the LORD hath done it;
    Shout, ye lowest parts of the earth;
    Break forth into singing, ye mountains,
    O forest, and every tree therein;
    For the LORD hath redeemed Jacob,
    And doth glorify Himself in Israel.
24. Thus saith the LORD, thy Redeemer,

---

44 : 20 *Striveth after ashes.* Rashi explains: If half of the block of wood which he makes into a fire to warm himself ends up as ashes, should he not realize that the god is equally worthless?

44 : 25 *Tokens of the imposters . . . diviners mad.* Rashi: The Babylonians constantly relied upon their astrology but God who made the heavens frustrates their predictions. (See also Kimchi.)

44 : 26 *That confirmeth . . . the counsel of His messengers.* Rashi and Kimchi say this means the prophets, Isaiah and others, who predicted the rebuilding of Jerusalem.

44 : 28 *Cyrus . . . My shepherd.* Kimchi: As My shepherd he will lead My flock back home. Krauss raises the question: How could the prophet, who spoke before the conquest of Babylon

And He that formed thee from the womb:
I am the Lord, that maketh all things;
That stretched forth the heavens alone;
That spread abroad the earth by Myself;
25. That frustrateth the tokens of the impostors,
And maketh diviners mad;
That turneth wise men backward,
And maketh their knowledge foolish;
26. That confirmeth the word of His servant,
And performeth the counsel of His messengers;
That saith of Jerusalem: 'She shall be inhabited';
And of the cities of Judah: 'They shall be built,
And I will raise up the waste places thereof';
27. That saith to the deep: 'Be dry,
And I will dry up thy rivers';
28. That saith of Cyrus: 'He is My shepherd,
And shall perform all My pleasure';
Even saying of Jerusalem: 'She shall be built';
And to the temple: 'Thy foundation shall be laid.'

Isaiah 44

by Cyrus, predict that Cyrus, after conquering Babylon, would order Jerusalem to be rebuilt? He answers his question as follows: The prophet and his contemporaries already knew of the onward march of the Persians, which was ever-victorious; and so Deutero-Isaiah voices an enthusiastic conviction as to what would be the blessed outcome for the exiled people of Israel.

The thought that God would use a heathen king for His purposes is not unusual. In Isaiah 10:5, when God determines to punish Israel, He makes use of the Assyrian king: "O Assyria, rod of Mine anger." As the Assyrian was God's instrument for the punishing of Israel, so now the Persian will be His instrument for Israel's redemption.

45

THIS CHAPTER develops the theme mentioned for the first time in the last sentence of the preceding chapter. Cyrus, the king of Persia, will be God's instrument for the deliverance of Israel. He will conquer many nations who will then turn to Israel and make obeisance to God. (Verse 22: "Look unto Me and be ye saved, all the ends of the earth.")

Isaiah 45

1. Thus saith the LORD to His anointed,
   To Cyrus, whose right hand I have holden,
   To subdue nations before him,
   And to loose the loins of kings;
   To open the doors before him,
   And that the gates may not be shut:
2. I will go before thee,
   And make the crooked places straight;
   I will break in pieces the doors of brass,
   And cut in sunder the bars of iron;
3. And I will give thee the treasures of darkness,
   And hidden riches of secret places,

45 : 2   *The doors of brass, and . . . bars of iron.*   According to Herodotus, the gates of Babylon were thus constructed. (See Krauss.)

45 : 3   *Who call thee by thy name.*   Both Rashi and Kimchi,

That thou mayest know that I am the LORD,
Who call thee by thy name, even the God of Israel.
4. For the sake of Jacob My servant,
And Israel Mine elect,
I have called thee by thy name,
I have surnamed thee, though thou hast not known Me.
5. I am the LORD, and there is none else,
Beside Me there is no God;
I have girded thee, though thou hast not known Me;
6. That they may know from the rising of the sun, and from the west,
That there is none beside Me;
I am the LORD, and there is none else;
7. I form the light, and create darkness;
I make peace, and create evil;
I am the LORD, that doeth all these things.
8. Drop down, ye heavens, from above,
And let the skies pour down righteousness;
Let the earth open, that they may bring forth salvation,

Isaiah 45

holding of course to the idea that the whole Book of Isaiah was written by Isaiah ben Amoz, say that the prophet here refers to Cyrus by name, even though Cyrus was not yet born. (In fact, Cyrus lived two hundred years after the First Isaiah.)

45 : 4 *For the sake of Jacob ... I have called thee by ... name ... though thou hast not known Me.* It is for the sake of the redemption of the people of Israel that God gives this power to Cyrus even though, of course, Cyrus himself does not know that his strength comes from God. The axe is not aware of him who wields it.

45 : 7 *I form ... light, and ... darkness.* Both Rashi and Ibn Ezra explain these two nouns as distributive. So Rashi says: Light is for Israel, darkness for Babylon; and Ibn Ezra: Light is for Cyrus and darkness for Babylon. But Krauss calls attention to the opinion of Saadia, who said that this statement is a refutation of Persian religion which is a dualism, teaching that one power creates light and the other power creates darkness. God here says: I create both light and darkness.

237

Isaiah 45

And let her cause righteousness to spring up together;
I the LORD have created it.

9. Woe unto him that striveth with his Maker,
As a potsherd with the potsherds of the earth!
Shall the clay say to him that fashioneth it: 'What makest thou?'
Or: 'Thy work, it hath no hands'?

10. Woe unto him that saith unto his father: 'Wherefore begettest thou?'
Or to a woman: 'Wherefore travailest thou?'

11. Thus saith the LORD,
The Holy One of Israel, and his Maker:
Ask Me of the things that are to come;
Concerning My sons, and concerning the work of My hands, command ye Me.

12. I, even I, have made the earth,
And created man upon it;
I, even My hands, have stretched out the heavens,
And all their host have I commanded.

13. I have roused him up in victory,
And I make level all his ways;
He shall build My city,
And he shall let Mine exiles go free,
Not for price nor reward,
Saith the LORD of hosts.

14. Thus saith the LORD:
The labour of Egypt, and the merchandise of Ethiopia,

45 : 9 *Shall the clay say ... 'What makest thou?'* It is not clear just who is quoted as making this skeptical statement. Krauss says that it is Israel which is complaining to God that He uses a heathen king for its deliverance when He should have reestablished a Judean king. But Malbim says it refers back to Verse 7, where God says: "I form the light, and create darkness." The complainers are those people who grumble at the fact that God has not made the world all light with no darkness and all good with no evil.

45 : 11 *Ask Me of the things that are to come.* Since I alone am

And of the Sabeans, men of stature,
Shall come over unto thee, and they shall be thine;
They shall go after thee, in chains they shall come over;
And they shall fall down unto thee,
They shall make supplication unto thee:
Surely God is in thee, and there is none else,
There is no other God.
15. Verily Thou art a God that hidest Thyself,
O God of Israel, the Saviour.
16. They shall be ashamed, yea, confounded, all of them;
They shall go in confusion together that are makers of idols.
17. O Israel, that art saved by the LORD with an everlasting salvation;
Ye shall not be ashamed nor confounded world without end.
18. For thus saith the LORD that created the heavens,
He is God;
That formed the earth and made it,
He established it,
He created it not a waste, He formed it to be inhabited:
I am the LORD, and there is none else.
19. I have not spoken in secret,
In a place of the land of darkness;
I said not unto the seed of Jacob:
'Seek ye Me in vain';

the Creator and the Ruler of the universe, only I know the future.

45 : 13 *I have roused him up in victory.*   I determine the future of history by calling upon Cyrus and giving him victory.

45 : 14 *Egypt ... Ethiopia ... Sabeans.*   All these will be conquered by Cyrus. In this statement the prophet was somewhat overoptimistic. Egypt was conquered by the Persian king Cambyses, successor of Cyrus.

These conquered nations will turn to Israel saying: "Surely God is in thee." (Verse 14)

Isaiah 45

I the Lord speak righteousness,
I declare things that are right.

20. Assemble yourselves and come, draw near together,
Ye that are escaped of the nations;
They have no knowledge that carry the wood of their graven image,
And pray unto a god that cannot save.

21. Declare ye, and bring them near,
Yea, let them take counsel together:
Who hath announced this from ancient time,
And declared it of old?
Have not I the Lord?
And there is no God else beside Me;
A just God and a Saviour;
There is none beside Me.

22. Look unto Me, and be ye saved,
All the ends of the earth;
For I am God, and there is none else.

23. By Myself have I sworn,
The word is gone forth from My mouth in righteousness,
And shall not come back,
That unto Me every knee shall bow,
Every tongue shall swear.

24. Only in the Lord, shall one say of Me, is victory and strength;
Even to Him shall men come in confusion,
All they that were incensed against Him.

25. In the Lord shall all the seed of Israel
Be justified, and shall glory.

---

45 : 24 *In the Lord, shall one say of Me.* Rashi says that this verse is in some disorder. Kimchi here again cites Abraham Ibn Ezra who reads the verse as follows: Surely in God alone (who spoke to me) is there righteousness and strength. In other words, the word "me" should not be capitalized; it refers to the prophet, who is the speaker.

45 : 25 *In the Lord shall ... Israel be justified.* Ibn Ezra: Only through its belief in God will Israel be justified.

46

THIS BRIEF chapter makes use of all the themes of the earlier chapters of Deutero-Isaiah, the nothingness of the idols, especially the idols of Babylon: I the Lord alone predict history; I have called to Cyrus to achieve the redemption of Israel, and this redemption is at hand.

1. Bel boweth down, Nebo stoopeth;
   Their idols are upon the beasts, and upon the cattle;
   The things that ye carried about are made a load,
   A burden to the weary beast.
2. They stoop, they bow down together,
   They could not deliver the burden;
   And themselves are gone into captivity.

Isaiah 46

46:1 *Bel boweth ... Nebo stoopeth.* The gods of Babylon are now prostrate and their statues will be carried away by burdened beasts and weary carriers.

46:2 *Themselves are gone into captivity.* Bel and Nebo, the gods themselves, are gone into captivity. Since the ancients believed that when a people was defeated its gods were also defeated, then just as the people was taken away by the victor into exile so are its gods carried away. Kimchi says: Since the gods themselves are now captives, how can they possibly help their worshipers?

Isaiah 46

3. Hearken unto Me, O house of Jacob,
   And all the remnant of the house of Israel,
   That are borne [by Me] from the birth,
   That are carried from the womb:
4. Even to old age I am the same,
   And even to hoar hairs will I carry you;
   I have made, and I will bear;
   Yea, I will carry, and will deliver.
5. To whom will ye liken Me, and make Me equal,
   And compare Me, that we may be like?
6. Ye that lavish gold out of the bag,
   And weigh silver in the balance;
   Ye that hire a goldsmith, that he make it a god,
   To fall down thereto, yea, to worship.
7. He is borne upon the shoulder, he is carried,
   And set in his place, and he standeth,
   From his place he doth not remove;
   Yea, though one cry unto him, he cannot answer,
   Nor save him out of his trouble.

46 : 3 *House of Jacob ... borne ... from the birth.* By contrast to the description of the idols being carried away and borne by carriers, I the Lord have carried you, O Israel, from the very beginning of your history (i.e., from birth). Rashi says: From the time that the various tribes of Israel were born in the house of Laban, the father-in-law of Jacob.

46 : 4 *Even to old age.* Ibn Ezra: This is just figurative and it means: I the Lord will maintain Israel as My people forever.

46 : 5-7 These verses repeat the description of the helplessness of the man-made idol.

8. Remember this, and stand fast;
   Bring it to mind, O ye transgressors.
9. Remember the former things of old:
   That I am God, and there is none else;
   I am God, and there is none like Me;
10. Declaring the end from the beginning,
    And from ancient times things that are not yet done;
    Saying: 'My counsel shall stand,
    And all My pleasure will I do';
11. Calling a bird of prey from the east,
    The man of My counsel from a far country;
    Yea, I have spoken, I will also bring it to pass,
    I have purposed, I will also do it.
12. Hearken unto Me, ye stout-hearted,
    That are far from righteousness:
13. I bring near My righteousness, it shall not be far off,
    And My salvation shall not tarry;
    And I will place salvation in Zion
    For Israel My glory.

Isaiah 46

46 : 10 *Declaring the end from the beginning.* God tells the future events, being the sole Master of history.

46 : 11 *Calling a bird of prey from the east.* Rashi does not take this to mean a rapacious bird. He refers it to Abraham whom God called to Canaan out of the east. But Kimchi and Ibn Ezra both take this to mean Cyrus, and the "rapacious bird" is an epithet for his conquering power. So Jeremiah speaks of conquest in "Behold he shall come up and swoop down as a vulture" (49:22) and Ezekiel speaks of a conqueror as "a great eagle." (17:3)

47

CHAPTER 47 is a dirge for Babylon. The prophet describes her as a "pampered queen" who now will become a slave woman grinding corn. All her astrologers and counselors will be unable to help her. They will all desert her. The description of Babylon, the queen, who will become a slave is the reverse of the change described at the beginning of Chapter 52, where Zion, now a slave (Verse 2: "O captive daughter of Zion"), will soon put on her royal garments again. (Cf. Chapters 13, 14.)

Isaiah 47

1. Come down, and sit in the dust,
   O virgin daughter of Babylon,
   Sit on the ground without a throne,
   O daughter of the Chaldeans;
   For thou shalt no more be called
   Tender and delicate.
2. Take the millstones, and grind meal;

47 : 1 *Tender and delicate.* At the end of Chapter 3, Isaiah denounces the daughter of Zion as luxury-loving and pampered. The same basic metaphor is here now used for Babylon facing her doom. A similar phrase is found also in Deuteronomy: "The tender and delicate woman who would not even set the sole of her foot upon the ground." (28:56)

47 : 2 *Grind meal.* Rashi says: You will now be a slave to the

Isaiah 47

Remove thy veil,
Strip off the train, uncover the leg,
Pass through the rivers.
3. Thy nakedness shall be uncovered,
Yea, thy shame shall be seen;
I will take vengeance,
And will let no man intercede.
4. Our Redeemer, the LORD of hosts is His name,
The Holy One of Israel.
5. Sit thou silent, and get thee into darkness,
O daughter of the Chaldeans;
For thou shalt no more be called
The mistress of kingdoms.
6. I was wroth with My people,
I profaned Mine inheritance,
And gave them into thy hand;
Thou didst show them no mercy;
Upon the aged hast thou very heavily
Laid thy yoke.
7. And thou saidst:
'For ever shall I be mistress';
So that thou didst not lay these things to thy heart,
Neither didst remember the end thereof.
8. Now therefore hear this, thou that art given to pleasures,
That sittest securely,
That sayest in thy heart:
'I am, and there is none else beside me;
I shall not sit as a widow,

---

kings of Persia, and Kimchi adds: You will be given hard labor as all captives are given.

47 : 4 *Our Redeemer.* This verse is a sort of pious exclamation interrupting the flow of thought which continues the address to Babylon in Verse 5.

47 : 6 *I was wroth with My people ... Thou didst show them no mercy.* If it was God who had punished Israel for its sins by sending it into exile, why then should Babylon be punished for being its captor? Because "thou didst show no mercy." Babylon could have treated its Jewish captives with less cruelty.

Isaiah 47

Neither shall I know the loss of children';
9. But these two things shall come to thee in a moment
In one day,
The loss of children, and widowhood;
In their full measure shall they come upon thee,
For the multitude of thy sorceries,
And the great abundance of thine enchantments.
10. And thou hast been secure in thy wickedness,
Thou hast said: 'None seeth me';
Thy wisdom and thy knowledge,
It hath perverted thee;
And thou hast said in thy heart:
'I am, and there is none else beside me.'
11. Yet shall evil come upon thee;
Thou shalt not know how to charm it away;
And calamity shall fall upon thee;
Thou shalt not be able to put it away;
And ruin shall come upon thee suddenly,
Before thou knowest.
12. Stand now with thine enchantments,

47 : 9 *For the multitude of thy sorceries.* "For" does not mean "because" of thy sorceries, but as Kimchi explains it: In spite of all thy sorceries, thy misfortunes will come upon thee. The same thought is expressed in Verse 11: "Evil shall come . . . thou shalt not know how to charm it away."

47 : 14 *Stubble . . . not a coal to warm at.* Rashi says it means that the fire will be like a fire of stubble which blazes up for an

Isaiah 47

      And with the multitude of thy sorceries,
      Wherein thou hast laboured from thy youth;
      If so be thou shalt be able to profit,
      If so be thou mayest prevail.
13. Thou art wearied in the multitude of thy counsels;
      Let now the astrologers, the stargazers,
      The monthly prognosticators,
      Stand up, and save thee
      From the things that shall come upon thee.
14. Behold, they shall be as stubble;
      The fire shall burn them;
      They shall not deliver themselves
      From the power of the flame;
      It shall not be a coal to warm at,
      Nor a fire to sit before.
15. Thus shall they be unto thee
      With whom thou hast laboured;
      They that have trafficked with thee from thy youth
      Shall wander every one to his quarter;
      There shall be none to save thee.

instant but gives no warmth. Kimchi says: All the help that your astrologers will give you will be as worthless as the flash flame of stubble. Ibn Ezra explains it somewhat differently: It will not be a fire to warm you but a fire of destruction, a devouring flame.

47 : 15 *They that have trafficked with thee.* Babylon was a great mercantile center. Merchants flocked to it from many lands. Now they will desert her.

247

48

HAVING ADDRESSED Babylon and foretold its doom, God now addresses the people of Israel in exile. He speaks of its pride of ancestry but says it is a false pride, since Israel has always sinned and therefore is unworthy of its past. Nevertheless God has refined it "in the furnace of affliction" (Verse 10) and assured redemption for His own sake. (Verse 9) God has already foretold this development of events, so now the prophet visualizes the redemption and says to the people, "Go forth from Babylon." (Verse 20)

Isaiah 48

1. Hear ye this, O house of Jacob,
   Who are called by the name of Israel,
   And are come forth out of the fountain of Judah;
   Who swear by the name of the LORD,
   And make mention of the God of Israel,
   But not in truth, nor in righteousness.
2. For they call themselves of the holy city,

48:1 *From the fountain of Judah.* The same metaphor for ancestry is found in Psalm 68:7: "Ye that are from the fountain of Israel."

But not in truth. Not sincerely. Rashi cites as parallel the verse in Jeremiah: "They say as the Lord liveth, surely they swear falsely." (5:2) Kimchi explains: They are like a man who swears by the name of his king and yet rebels against him.

And stay themselves upon the God of Israel,
The LORD of hosts is His name.
3. I have declared the former things from of old;
Yea, they went forth out of My mouth, and I announced them;
Suddenly I did them, and they came to pass.
4. Because I knew that thou art obstinate,
And thy neck is an iron sinew,
And thy brow brass;
5. Therefore I have declared it to thee from of old;
Before it came to pass I announced it to thee;
Lest thou shouldest say: 'Mine idol hath done them,
And my graven image, and my molten image, hath commanded them.'
6. Thou hast heard, see, all this;
And ye, will ye not declare it?
I have announced unto thee new things from this time,
Even hidden things, which thou hast not known.
7. They are created now, and not from of old,
And before this day thou heardest them not;
Lest thou shouldest say: 'Behold, I knew them.'
8. Yea, thou heardest not;
Yea, thou knewest not;
Yea, from of old thine ear was not opened;

Isaiah
48

48 : 3-7 *I have declared former things . . . I knew thou art obstinate . . . Mine idol hath done them.* Rashi: I have declared the previous deliverances before they occurred, the deliverance from Egypt and the deliverance from Sennacherib when he besieged Jerusalem. If I had not predicted the events beforehand, you, stubborn as you are in your idolatry, would say, "My idol had delivered me."

48 : 4 *Thy brow brass.* A brow of brass is a metaphor for shameless impudence. Thus Jeremiah 3:3: "Thou hast a harlot's forehead. Thou refusest to be ashamed."

48 : 8 *A transgressor from the womb.* Rashi: From the very beginning of your history, even in Egypt, did you rebel and transgress against Me; as Ezekiel explains: "I said to them, 'Defile not yourself with the idols of Egypt; but they rebelled against Me.

Isaiah 48

> For I knew that thou wouldest deal very treacherously,
> And wast called a transgressor from the womb.
> 9. For My name's sake will I defer Mine anger,
> And for My praise will I refrain for thee,
> That I cut thee not off.
> 10. Behold, I have refined thee, but not as silver;
> I have tried thee in the furnace of affliction.
> 11. For Mine own sake, for Mine own sake, will I do it;
> For how should it be profaned?
> And My glory will I not give to another.
> 12. Hearken unto Me, O Jacob,
> And Israel My called:
> I am He; I am the first,
> I also am the last.
> 13. Yea, My hand hath laid the foundation of the earth,
> And My right hand hath spread out the heavens;
> When I call unto them,
> They stand up together.
> 14. Assemble yourselves, all ye, and hear;
> Which among them hath declared these things?
> He whom the LORD loveth shall perform His pleasure on Babylon,
> And show His arm on the Chaldeans.
> 15. I, even I, have spoken, yea, I have called him;
> I have brought him, and he shall make his way prosperous.

They did not forsake the idol of Egypt.'" (20:7, 8) Kimchi gives an analogous explanation: From the beginning of their history they rebelled against God. Many times did they rebel in the desert.

48 : 10 *I have refined thee, but not as silver . . . in the furnace of affliction.* Their sufferings were to be a purifying fire, burning away the evil. The phrase "not as silver" is somewhat difficult. Kimchi explains it as follows: When silver is refined, all the dross is removed and only pure silver remains. But in the exile while the afflictions purified there still, of course, was some sinfulness.

Isaiah 48

16. Come ye near unto Me, hear ye this:
    From the beginning I have not spoken in secret;
    From the time that it was, there am I;
    And now the Lord GOD hath sent me, and His spirit.
17. Thus saith the LORD, thy Redeemer,
    The Holy One of Israel:
    I am the LORD thy God,
    Who teacheth thee for thy profit,
    Who leadeth thee by the way that thou shouldest go.
18. Oh that thou wouldest hearken to My commandments!
    Then would thy peace be as a river,
    And thy righteousness as the waves of the sea;
19. Thy seed also would be as the sand,
    And the offspring of thy body like the grains thereof;
    His name would not be cut off
    Nor destroyed from before Me.
20. Go ye forth from Babylon,
    Flee ye from the Chaldeans;
    With a voice of singing
    Declare ye, tell this,
    Utter it even to the end of the earth;
    Say ye: 'The LORD hath redeemed
    His servant Jacob.
21. And they thirsted not
    When He led them through the deserts;
    He caused the waters to flow

---

48 : 12-14 *He whom God loveth.* Cyrus is here called "he whom the Lord loveth." (Rashi)

48 : 16 *From the beginning I have not spoken in secret.* Rashi quoting the Midrash says that this refers to the grand revelation on Mount Sinai. According to Kimchi the verse means that all the prophecies of redemption in the past were never made in secret but were always publicly proclaimed by the prophet.

God hath sent me, and His spirit. Kimchi fills out the sentence as follows: God has sent me and set His spirit within me.

251

Isaiah
48

Out of the rock for them;
He cleaved the rock also,
And the waters gushed out.'
22. There is no peace,
Saith the LORD concerning the wicked.

48 : 22 *No peace ... for the wicked.* This seems to be a jarring ending to the chapter following the joyous description of the redemption. Ibn Ezra says it means there will be no peace for the wicked of Israel. Kimchi and Rashi say there will be no peace for the wicked oppressors, Babylon and the king Nebuchadnezzar and his followers.

49

NOW ISRAEL addresses the nations, "Hearken, ye people," and speaks of the task which God has imposed upon Israel to enlighten the nations. Then God assures Israel that though now it is despised it will be honored by the rulers of the earth, who will send back the exiles from all the distant lands and will make respectful obeisance.

1. Listen, O isles, unto me,
   And hearken, ye peoples, from far:
   The LORD hath called me from the womb,
   From the bowels of my mother hath He made mention of my name;
2. And He hath made my mouth like a sharp sword,
   In the shadow of His hand hath He hid me;
   And He hath made me a polished shaft,
   In His quiver hath He concealed me;

Isaiah 49

49 : 1 *Hath called me from the womb.* Echoes the thought of Chapter 44, Verse 1: "Jacob My servant ... formed thee from the womb." (See commentary note there.)

49 : 2 *My mouth a sharp sword ... a polished shaft.* Rashi says it means a sword to rebuke the wicked; but Kimchi refers it to the emotion of the prophet. The prophet says: I cannot refrain from prophesying; God has made my speech sharp and incisive.

In the shadow of His hand hath He hid me. Ibn Ezra ex-

253

Isaiah 49

3. And He said unto me: 'Thou art My servant,
   Israel, in whom I will be glorified.'
4. But I said: 'I have laboured in vain,
   I have spent my strength for nought and vanity;
   Yet surely my right is with the LORD,
   And my recompense with my God.'
5. And now saith the LORD
   That formed me from the womb to be His servant,
   To bring Jacob back to Him,
   And that Israel be gathered unto Him—
   For I am honourable in the eyes of the LORD,
   And my God is become my strength—
6. Yea, He saith: 'It is too light a thing that thou
      shouldest be My servant
   To raise up the tribes of Jacob,
   And to restore the offspring of Israel;
   I will also give thee for a light of the nations,
   That My salvation may be unto the end of the earth.'
7. Thus saith the LORD,
   The Redeemer of Israel, his Holy One,
   To him who is despised of men,
   To him who is abhorred of nations,
   To a servant of rulers:
   Kings shall see and arise,
   Princes, and they shall prostrate themselves;
   Because of the LORD that is faithful,
   Even the Holy One of Israel, who hath chosen thee.
8. Thus saith the LORD:
   In an acceptable time have I answered thee,
   And in a day of salvation have I helped thee;
   And I will preserve thee, and give thee

plains: In spite of the sharpness of my rebukes, no one shall harm me (the prophet) for God protects me.

49 : 6 *Too light a thing . . . to restore . . . Israel . . . a light of the nations.* Kimchi: God will do more than restore Israel; He will turn the nations to righteousness.

49 : 7 *Despised of men . . . princes . . . shall prostrate themselves.* Kimchi explains: Kings will hear thy words and will turn to God. He cites Zechariah: "Men of all nations (will say) 'We will

Isaiah 49

For a covenant of the people,
To raise up the land,
To cause to inherit the desolate heritages;
9. Saying to the prisoners: 'Go forth';
To them that are in darkness: 'Show yourselves';
They shall feed in the ways,
And in all high hills shall be their pasture;
10. They shall not hunger nor thirst,
Neither shall the heat nor sun smite them;
For He that hath compassion on them will lead them,
Even by the springs of water will He guide them.
11. And I will make all My mountains a way,
And My highways shall be raised on high.
12. Behold, these shall come from far;
And, lo, these from the north and from the west,
And these from the land of Sinim.
13. Sing, O heavens, and be joyful, O earth,
And break forth into singing, O mountains;
For the Lord hath comforted His people,
And hath compassion upon His afflicted.
14. But Zion said: 'The Lord hath forsaken me,
And the Lord hath forgotten me.'
15. Can a woman forget her sucking child,
That she should not have compassion on the son of her womb?
Yea, these may forget,
Yet will not I forget thee.
16. Behold, I have graven thee upon the palms of My hands;
Thy walls are continually before Me.

---

go with you, for we have heard that God is with you.' " (8:23)

49 : 8 *To inherit the desolate heritages.* To reconvert the old neglected fields into heritable, productive lands.

49 : 11 *I will make My mountains a way . . . highways.* This echoes the thought of Chapter 40, Verse 4: "Every valley shall be lifted up" (to make a highway for the redeemed).

49 : 16 *I have graven thee upon the palms of My hands.* The metaphor is a troublesome one. How can an engraving be made

255

Isaiah 49

17. Thy children make haste;
    Thy destroyers and they that made thee waste shall go forth from thee.
18. Lift up thine eyes round about, and behold:
    All these gather themselves together, and come to thee.
    As I live, saith the LORD,
    Thou shalt surely clothe thee with them all as with an ornament,
    And gird thyself with them, like a bride.
19. For thy waste and thy desolate places
    And thy land that hath been destroyed—
    Surely now shalt thou be too strait for the inhabitants,
    And they that swallowed thee up shall be far away.
20. The children of thy bereavement
    Shall yet say in thine ears:
    'The place is too strait for me;
    Give place to me that I may dwell.'
21. Then shalt thou say in thy heart:
    'Who hath begotten me these,
    Seeing I have been bereaved of my children, and am solitary,
    An exile, and wandering to and fro?
    And who hath brought up these?
    Behold, I was left alone;
    These, where were they?'
22. Thus saith the Lord GOD:

---

upon a hand? Besides, there is the difficulty of speaking of God's hand in this way. Ibn Ezra cites Saadia to the effect that the word used here does not mean "hand" at all but means the clouds; namely, that God has written Israel's name upon the clouds and so the name is constantly before Him. But Ibn Ezra says simply that it is an anthropomorphism, using human terms and applying them to God. Perhaps the metaphor means: I have engraved thee on a signet ring which is on My hand. Tur Sinai has this explanation in mind, but, in the second half of the verse, he emends the word "walls" and translates it: Thy "seal" is ever before me.

Behold, I will lift up My hand to the nations,
And set up Mine ensign to the peoples,
And they shall bring thy sons in their bosom,
And thy daughters shall be carried upon their shoulders.

Isaiah 49

23. And kings shall be thy foster-fathers,
And their queens thy nursing mothers;
They shall bow down to thee with their face to the earth,
And lick the dust of thy feet;
And thou shalt know that I am the LORD,
For they shall not be ashamed that wait for Me.
24. Shall the prey be taken from the mighty,
Or the captives of the victorious be delivered?
25. But thus saith the LORD:
Even the captives of the mighty shall be taken away,
And the prey of the terrible shall be delivered;
And I will contend with him that contendeth with thee,
And I will save thy children.
26. And I will feed them that oppress thee with their own flesh;
And they shall be drunken with their own blood, as with sweet wine;
And all flesh shall know that I the LORD am thy Saviour,
And thy Redeemer, the Mighty One of Jacob.

---

49 : 17 *Thy destroyers . . . shall go forth.* Kimchi: The evil ones among you who are the cause of your suffering will now leave you.

49 : 18-23 A description of the returning exiles, expressed in the metaphor of lost children being returned to their mother: Kings and queens will bring Thy children back and will take good care of them and make respectful obeisance to Thee. This future reverence for Israel is a contrast to the former state expressed in Verse 7: "To him who is abhorred of nations, a servant of rulers."

49 : 24-27 *Shall the prey be taken away from the mighty?* Kimchi says it is the oppressing nations who say this in scorn.

Can anyone be strong enough to take our captives from us? But Ibn Ezra says that the children of Israel in their hopelessness say these words and the answer comes, "Yes," and the oppressors in turn will suffer: "I will feed them their own flesh." (Verse 26) Rashi finds this metaphor somewhat strong and he explains it to mean: I will feed their flesh to the beasts of the field.

50

GOD now calls upon Israel to admit that the exile was due to Israel's sins. Then the prophet says that God had taught him to speak and he has followed his God-given task in spite of persecution. He ends with the thought that God will justify him and the violent oppressors will be punished.

1. Thus saith the LORD:
   Where is the bill of your mother's divorcement,
   Wherewith I have put her away?
   Or which of My creditors is it
   To whom I have sold you?
   Behold, for your iniquities were ye sold,
   And for your transgressions was your mother put away.

Isaiah 50

50: 1 *Where is the bill of your mother's divorcement?* The exiling of Israel is described as a formal divorce. This is consistent with the metaphor frequently found in the Prophets, describing the relation between God and Israel as that of husband and wife. The metaphor is found first in Hosea and in Jeremiah 3, and it is used throughout in Deutero-Isaiah.

Which of My creditors ... have I sold you? This now does not refer to Israel as wife but to the individuals as children of the marriage. Men were often sold to pay for debt. Daughters were

Isaiah 50

2. Wherefore, when I came, was there no man?
   When I called, was there none to answer?
   Is My hand shortened at all, that it cannot redeem?
   Or have I no power to deliver?
   Behold, at My rebuke I dry up the sea,
   I make the rivers a wilderness;
   Their fish become foul, because there is no water,
   And die for thirst.
3. I clothe the heavens with blackness,
   And I make sackcloth their covering.
4. The Lord God hath given me
   The tongue of them that are taught,
   That I should know how to sustain with words him
     that is weary;
   He wakeneth morning by morning,
   He wakeneth mine ear
   To hear as they that are taught.
5. The Lord God hath opened mine ear,
   And I was not rebellious,
   Neither turned away backward.
6. I gave my back to the smiters,
   And my cheeks to them that plucked off the hair;
   I hid not my face from shame and spitting.

thus sold by their fathers: "If a man sell his daughter to be a maid-servant." (Exodus 21:7) This did not mean actual slavery. The "eved Ivri," the Hebrew slave (more correctly, Hebrew servant), was merely indentured to work out the debt for a fixed number of years, as indentured servants were sent from England to Virginia in colonial times.

For your transgressions was your mother put away. That is to say: I did not divorce your mother or sell you to be bond-servants because I hated her or you but because of your sins.

50:2 *Wherefore, when I came.* The Targum again avoids the anthropomorphism of God personally coming by translating: Why when I sent My prophets did ye not respond? Also the Targum translates the anthropomorphism, "Is My hand shortened" as, Is My power not strong enough to deliver?

50:4 *The tongue of them that are taught.* The prophet speaks of God as if He were a teacher Who taught him daily, and he de-

260

7. For the Lord God will help me;
   Therefore have I not been confounded;
   Therefore have I set my face like a flint,
   And I know that I shall not be ashamed.
8. He is near that justifieth me;
   Who will contend with me? let us stand up together;
   Who is mine adversary? let him come near to me.
9. Behold, the Lord God will help me;
   Who is he that shall condemn me?
   Behold, they all shall wax old as a garment,
   The moth shall eat them up.
10. Who is among you that feareth the Lord,
    That obeyeth the voice of His servant?
    Though he walketh in darkness,
    And hath no light,
    Let him trust in the name of the Lord,
    And stay upon his God.
11. Behold, all ye that kindle a fire,
    That gird yourselves with fire-brands,
    Begone in the flame of your fire,
    And among the brands that ye have kindled.
    This shall ye have of My hand;
    Ye shall lie down in sorrow.

Isaiah 50

scribes himself as an obedient pupil. (Verse 5: "I was not rebellious.")

50 : 6 *I gave my back to the smiters.* Kimchi calls attention to the fact that there is no evidence anywhere in Scripture that Isaiah was ever persecuted for the unpopularity of his message; therefore he concludes that the verse means: Even if I had been persecuted, I would never have failed to utter the message that God had taught me to give.

50 : 7 *I set my face like a flint.* I shall not be frightened nor even flinch.

50: 10 *Though he walketh in darkness.* Hitherto you did not listen to my words but "ye walked in darkness." (Kimchi)

50 : 11 *All ye that kindle a fire.* Rashi: All you who refuse to listen to the prophet's word. Kimchi indicates that the word "all" must not be taken literally; it means "those of you" who do not listen.

261

51

THE PROPHET assures the exiles that God, who made Abraham their father into a great nation and who controls all nature, has ample power to redeem them. Therefore let them not forget their Creator nor fear the oppressor who is only mortal.

Isaiah 51

1. Hearken to Me, ye that follow after righteousness,
   Ye that seek the LORD;
   Look unto the rock whence ye were hewn,
   And to the hole of the pit whence ye were digged.
2. Look unto Abraham your father,
   And unto Sarah that bore you;
   For when he was but one I called him,
   And I blessed him, and made him many.

51 : 1 *Ye that follow after righteousness.* "Tzedek." The same phrase is in Deuteronomy: "Justice, justice ("tzedek") shall you follow." (16:2)

51 : 2 *Abraham . . . Sarah . . . and made him many.* Rashi and Kimchi: Though Abraham was all alone and a stranger, God multiplied his descendants and made Abraham great. So you who are now alone and strangers in exile will be redeemed for a great future.

As God promised Abraham that his descendants would be as numerous as the sands of the sea, so God now blesses Zion as in

3. For the L ORD hath comforted Zion;
   He hath comforted all her waste places,
   And hath made her wilderness like Eden,
   And her desert like the garden of the L ORD;
   Joy and gladness shall be found therein,
   Thanksgiving, and the voice of melody.
4. Attend unto Me, O My people,
   And give ear unto Me, O My nation;
   For instruction shall go forth from Me,
   And My right on a sudden for a light of the peoples.
5. My favour is near,
   My salvation is gone forth,
   And Mine arms shall judge the peoples;
   The isles shall wait for Me,
   And on Mine arm shall they trust.
6. Lift up your eyes to the heavens,
   And look upon the earth beneath;
   For the heavens shall vanish away like smoke,
   And the earth shall wax old like a garment,
   And they that dwell therein shall die in like manner;
   But My salvation shall be for ever,
   And My favour shall not be abolished.

Isaiah 51

Chapter 49, Verses 20, 21, that the land will become far too small for the populous people of Israel.

51 : 4 *My right on a sudden.* The word "argiya" used here and translated "sudden" is translated by Rashi and Ibn Ezra as "my right I will bring about or establish." Our translation here as "sudden" follows an alternative translation cited by Ibn Ezra.

51 : 5 *The isles . . . on Mine arm shall they trust.* A favorite idea of Deutero-Isaiah: The day will come when all the nations will abandon their idolatry and begin to trust in God.

51 : 6 *Heavens shall vanish . . . earth . . . wax old . . . and they that dwell therein shall die . . . but My salvation shall be for ever.* Ibn Ezra says that from this passage a philosopher has derived a proof of the immortality of the soul. (See Friedlander's note in his translation of Ibn Ezra on this passage.) The proof was as follows: If all the people on earth will die, then what meaning will there be to God's salvation which is said to endure forever? Clearly it must mean that only their bodies will die but the souls

Isaiah 51

7. Hearken unto Me, ye that know righteousness,
   The people in whose heart is My law;
   Fear ye not the taunt of men,
   Neither be ye dismayed at their revilings.
8. For the moth shall eat them up like a garment,
   And the worm shall eat them like wool;
   But My favour shall be for ever,
   And My salvation unto all generations.
9. Awake, awake, put on strength,
   O arm of the LORD;
   Awake, as in the days of old,
   The generations of ancient times.
   Art thou not it that hewed Rahab in pieces,
   That pierced the dragon?
10. Art thou not it that dried up the sea,
    The waters of the great deep;
    That made the depths of the sea a way
    For the redeemed to pass over?
11. And the ransomed of the LORD shall return,
    And come with singing unto Zion,
    And everlasting joy shall be upon their heads;
    They shall obtain gladness and joy,
    And sorrow and sighing shall flee away.

will live to enjoy God's salvation. To which Ibn Ezra says that the doctrine of immortality is right, but it is not to be proved from this verse. The verse is simply a poetic statement of the general idea that, whatever else may vanish, God's word will endure.

51 : 9 *Art thou not ... that hewed Rahab ... pierced the dragon?* The Targum: Art thou not the one who overcame Pharaoh and his followers who were strong as dragons? This translation is based on the fact that, in Isaiah 30:7, Pharaoh is indeed called "Rahab," "the proud." Rashi and Kimchi accept this identification. But Krauss calls attention to the fact that this is a reference to an ancient Semitic legend. According to the Assyrian legend, the god Marduk defeated the great sea monsters, Rahab, and the dragon. The prophet, using this ancient legend, wishes to say merely that it is not Marduk or any other idol that is all-powerful and all-conquering but God himself.

12. I, even I, am He that comforteth you;
    Who art thou, that thou art afraid of man that shall die,
    And of the son of man that shall be made as grass;
13. And hast forgotten the LORD thy Maker,
    That stretched forth the heavens,
    And laid the foundations of the earth;
    And fearest continually all the day
    Because of the fury of the oppressor,
    As he maketh ready to destroy?
    And where is the fury of the oppressor?
14. He that is bent down shall speedily be loosed;
    And he shall not go down dying into the pit,
    Neither shall his bread fail.
15. For I am the LORD thy God,
    Who stirreth up the sea, that the waves thereof roar;
    The LORD of hosts is His name.
16. And I have put My words in thy mouth,
    And have covered thee in the shadow of My hand,
    That I may plant the heavens,
    And lay the foundations of the earth,
    And say unto Zion: 'Thou art My people.'

51:10 *Dried up the sea.* This refers to the division of the Red Sea in the deliverance from Egypt.

51:11 *The ransomed of the Lord shall return.* As once in Egypt, so now God will rescue the exiles in Babylon.

51:13 *Where is the fury of the oppressor?* Rashi says it means that when tomorrow comes the oppressor will be no more. He will be completely forgotten after the redemption. Kimchi refers this to Sennacherib who besieged Jerusalem: Where is that tyrant now?

51:16 *The foundations of the earth . . . 'Thou art My people.'* The Targum unites both halves of the verse as follows: God, who promised that Israel will be as numerous as the stars of the heavens and the sands of the earth, will certainly rescue His people from exile. But Kimchi explains the verses somewhat differently. He says that when God will redeem Israel the world will seem to them to be a new heaven and a new earth.

Isaiah 51

17. Awake, awake,
    Stand up, O Jerusalem,
    That hast drunk at the hand of the LORD
    The cup of His fury;
    Thou hast drunken the beaker, even the cup of staggering,
    And drained it.
18. There is none to guide her
    Among all the sons whom she hath brought forth;
    Neither is there any that taketh her by the hand
    Of all the sons that she hath brought up.
19. These two things are befallen thee;
    Who shall bemoan thee?
    Desolation and destruction, and the famine and the sword;
    How shall I comfort thee?
20. Thy sons have fainted, they lie at the head of all the streets,

51 : 17-23 *Awake, awake . . . the cup of His fury.* Ibn Ezra explains: Israel in exile is like a drunken man, staggering about and bewildered. Therefore God calls upon him to awake from the stupor of exile. The idea of nations being given a cup to drink is rather frequently used in the biblical literature. Jeremiah says: "Take this cup of fury, and cause the nations to drink."

Isaiah 51

   As an antelope in a net;
   They are full of the fury of the Lord,
   The rebuke of thy God.
21. Therefore hear now this, thou afflicted,
    And drunken, but not with wine;
22. Thus saith thy Lord the Lord,
    And thy God that pleadeth the cause of His people:
    Behold, I have taken out of thy hand
    The cup of staggering;
    The beaker, even the cup of My fury,
    Thou shalt no more drink it again;
23. And I will put it into the hand of them that afflict thee;
    That have said to thy soul:
    'Bow down, that we may go over';
    And thou hast laid thy back as the ground,
    And as the street, to them that go over.

(25:15) So Lamentations: "O Edom, the cup shall pass over unto thee; thou shalt be drunk." (4:21) Therefore the symbol means: The people of Israel in exile is drunk with misfortunes. (Verse 21: "Thou afflicted, drunken but not with wine.") God will now take away this cup of confusion: "I will put it into the hands of them that afflict thee." (Verse 23)

52

THE PROPHET calls upon Jerusalem to rise from its ruins and put on its royal garments again. The people will return and Zion will be restored.

Isaiah 52

1. Awake, awake,
   Put on thy strength, O Zion;
   Put on thy beautiful garments,
   O Jerusalem, the holy city;
   For henceforth there shall no more come into thee
   The uncircumcised and the unclean.
2. Shake thyself from the dust;

52 : 1 *The uncircumcised and the unclean.* Krauss says that this does not mean that Gentiles would not be permitted in Jerusalem, which was never the case, but that no hostile army will ever again invade it.

Because the prophet here depicts a state of perfect peace, Ibn Ezra believes that it cannot mean the redemption from Babylon but it must refer to the ideal messianic redemption. He interprets as messianic nearly all references of redemption in Deutero-Isaiah, but he admits that Verse 11, "Depart ye, depart ye, go ye out from thence," does seem to refer to the departure from the Babylonian Exile.

52 : 2 *The bands of thy neck.* The captive girl sits in the dust with a rope around her neck.

Isaiah 52

Arise, and sit down, O Jerusalem;
Loose thyself from the bands of thy neck,
O captive daughter of Zion.

3. For thus saith the LORD:
Ye were sold for nought;
And ye shall be redeemed without money.
4. For thus saith the Lord GOD:
My people went down aforetime into Egypt to sojourn there;
And the Assyrian oppressed them without cause.
5. Now therefore, what do I here, saith the LORD,
Seeing that My people is taken away for nought?
They that rule over them do howl, saith the LORD,
And My name continually all the day is blasphemed.
6. Therefore My people shall know My name;
Therefore they shall know in that day
That I, even He that spoke, behold, here I am.
7. How beautiful upon the mountains
Are the feet of the messenger of good tidings,
That announceth peace, the harbinger of good tidings,
That announceth salvation;
That saith unto Zion:
'Thy God reigneth!'

52 : 3 *Sold for nought ... redeemed without money.* Rashi interprets it as follows: You were sold because of your worthless sins (i.e., as our English word "naughty" or "naught" means "of no worth") and you will be redeemed not by money but by your repentance. But Ibn Ezra says: I sold you not for money, as a captor usually does; so I will redeem you without receiving money for it. Malbim agrees with this interpretation.

52 : 4 *Egypt to sojourn ... Assyrian ... without cause.* Rashi understands the verse to express a distinction between those two oppressions. The Egyptians had some vague justification. Israel of its own accord had entered Egypt and settled there (though, as Kimchi says, this did not justify the harsh servitude). But Assyria had no justification at all (for enslaving the Ten Tribes).

52 : 5 *What do I here, saith the Lord.* Rashi, Kimchi, and Krauss: Why am I delaying to help My children?

Isaiah 52

8. Hark, thy watchmen! they lift up the voice,
Together do they sing;
For they shall see, eye to eye,
The Lord returning to Zion.
9. Break forth into joy, sing together,
Ye waste places of Jerusalem;
For the Lord hath comforted His people,
He hath redeemed Jerusalem.
10. The Lord hath made bare His holy arm
In the eyes of all the nations;
And all the ends of the earth shall see
The salvation of our God.
11. Depart ye, depart ye, go ye out from thence,
Touch no unclean thing;
Go ye out of the midst of her; be ye clean,
Ye that bear the vessels of the Lord.

52 : 8 *Hark, thy watchmen!* Rashi: The watchmen who stand on the city walls as lookouts. But Kimchi, evidently realizing that the exiles cannot be described as having watchmen to guard their city, says the verse refers to the prophets, for the prophets are also called "watchmen," as in the Prophet Ezekiel: "I have appointed thee a watchman to the house of Israel." (3:17)

52 : 11 *Depart . . . touch no unclean thing . . . ye that bear the vessels of the Lord.* Kimchi takes the word for "vessels" to mean "weapons." He interprets the verse symbolically: When you leave the exile, you will need no weapons. It is God's mercy which will protect you. Krauss, however, explains that it refers to the sacred vessels of the Temple that had been carried away to Babylon by Nebuchadnezzar. Now the priests will carry them back and therefore they must be clean.

52 : 12 *The Lord will go before you . . . your rearward.* God will protect you as an army is protected by both a vanguard and a rear guard.

12. For ye shall not go out in haste,
    Neither shall ye go by flight;
    For the LORD will go before you,
    And the God of Israel will be your rearward.
13. Behold, My servant shall prosper,
    He shall be exalted and lifted up, and shall be very high.
14. According as many were appalled at thee—
    So marred was his visage unlike that of a man,
    And his form unlike that of the sons of men—
15. So shall he startle many nations,
    Kings shall shut their mouths because of him;
    For that which had not been told them shall they see,
    And that which they had not heard shall they perceive.

Isaiah 52

52 : 13-15 *My servant shall prosper . . . marred was his visage.*

This, together with Chapter 53, is considered to be the last of the Servant Songs. Its theme is the suffering of the servant, a theme which is developed more fully in the next chapter. The people of Israel, the servant of God, so distorted by his suffering that he astonishes the beholders. This suffering servant of God will yet prosper.

Ibn Ezra calls attention to the fact that Christians traditionally consider this suffering servant of God as being Jesus. He then also cites Saadia who makes a complete parallel between the suffering of the Prophet Jeremiah and the description here of the suffering servant of God. This identification has influenced some modern scholarly opinion that the career of Jeremiah was that of a suffering servant of God. Therefore the career of Jeremiah served as a sort of model for Israel, the servant of God. This explanation is strengthened by the fact that Jeremiah still was alive in the early days of the Exile, and his biography may well have been known to the author of this part of Isaiah.

53

IN OUR ENGLISH translation Chapter 53 begins with a quotation which concludes at the end of Verse 9. It is delivered by one speaker. But who is the speaker who describes the suffering of God's servant? Both Rashi and Kimchi (and also Krauss) agree that it is the gentile nations that here participate in the conversation. This identification of the speaker as the nations fits well with the introductory part of this "servant's song." In the preceding chapter the closing verse says that many nations and their kings were astounded at the sight of Israel distorted (Verse 14: "So marred was his visage") by the tortures of exile. So Chapter 53 logically gives voice to their surprise. Understanding that it is the gentile nations who are here describing the meaning of the miseries of Israel as they see it clarifies much of the chapter. In essence what the nations are saying is that at first they thought that the miseries of Israel were due to God's contempt for Israel; but now they see that Israel's suffering is undeserved. Israel is a vicarious substitute for the suffering which was actually deserved by the nations themselves. In other words, the nations will be redeemed and ennobled because Israel is suffering for them.

Isaiah 53

1. 'Who would have believed our report?
And to whom hath the arm of the LORD been revealed?

53 : 1 *Who would have believed our report?* The nations say that the sight of Israel's suffering is unbelievable and must be explained.

2. For he shot up right forth as a sapling,
   And as a root out of a dry ground;
   He had no form nor comeliness, that we should look upon him,
   Nor beauty that we should delight in him.
3. He was despised, and forsaken of men,
   A man of pains, and acquainted with disease,
   And as one from whom men hide their face:
   He was despised, and we esteemed him not.
4. Surely our diseases he did bear, and our pains he carried;
   Whereas we did esteem him stricken,

Isaiah 53

To whom hath the arm of the Lord been revealed? Kimchi says that this is a scornful statement on the part of the nations, as if to say: To what an insignificant people God has revealed His power.

53 : 2 *Shot up . . . as a sapling . . . no form nor comeliness.* The nations say: This people shot up suddenly like a weed and has no particular beauty which can be admired. (Rashi)

53 : 3 *He was despised, and we esteemed him not.* The nations continue thus to describe their indifference and contempt for Israel and his sufferings. Ibn Ezra adds here ruefully: Even in our day there are people who turn aside at the sight of a Jew, lest they be obliged to assist him.

53 : 4 *Surely our diseases did he bear . . . we did esteem him stricken . . . of God.* The commentators agree that "we did esteem him stricken of God" represents here a further statement of the nations saying that they have changed their mind about Israel. They say: We thought that God punished him for his own sins, but we do not think that now; we rather believe "our diseases doth he bear." Ibn Ezra says that means: They say that it was not God who afflicted Israel but it was we in our cruelty who put these "diseases," these sufferings upon Israel. But Rashi and Kimchi both take it to mean: It is the suffering that should have come to us (the heathen nations) which God has inflicted upon Israel; Israel is bearing our punishment. Although Kimchi gives this explanation, he is somewhat troubled by it, because the Prophet Ezekiel in Chapter 18 said that no one will be punished for the sins of others (not the son for the father, etc.). Then he

Isaiah 53

Smitten of God, and afflicted.
5. But he was wounded because of our transgressions,
   He was crushed because of our iniquities:
   The chastisement of our welfare was upon him,
   And with his stripes we were healed.
6. All we like sheep did go astray,
   We turned every one to his own way;
   And the LORD hath made to light on him
   The iniquity of us all.
7. He was oppressed, though he humbled himself
   And opened not his mouth;
   As a lamb that is led to the slaughter,
   And as a sheep that before her shearers is dumb;
   Yea, he opened not his mouth.
8. By oppression and judgment he was taken away,
   And with his generation who did reason?

explains the difficulty by saying that while this type of vicarious punishment is really wrong (according to Judaism) the heathens, however, believed in it and so they explain Israel's suffering on this basis.

53 : 5 *The chastisement of our welfare was upon him.* Kimchi takes this to mean: The punishment that we deserve for our idolatry was visited upon Israel. But Ibn Ezra stresses the word "welfare" and says: Our punishment will come when God redeems Israel. As long as Israel is still being punished, we will remain unpunished and thus it is to our welfare that Israel is still afflicted.

53 : 6 *All we like sheep did go astray.* We acknowledge now (say the nations) that we were in error when we thought that it was for his own sins that Israel was punished, "to light on him," i.e., to "alight," "to come down" on him (i.e., on Israel).

53 : 7 *A lamb ... led to the slaughter.* This verse continues the metaphor of sheep but it is applied now to Israel who is led in his innocence to the slaughter and does not offer resistance. An analogous metaphor is used in Proverbs 7:22: "As an ox goeth to the slaughter."

53 : 8 *With his generation who did reason?* Ibn Ezra: Who could have foretold to that generation that all this suffering would come upon it? The Malbim gives a similar but somewhat

For he was cut off out of the land of the living,
For the transgression of my people to whom the stroke was due.
9. And they made his grave with the wicked,
And with the rich his tomb;
Although he had done no violence,
Neither was any deceit in his mouth.'
10. Yet it pleased the LORD to crush him by disease;
To see if his soul would offer itself in restitution,
That he might see his seed, prolong his days,
And that the purpose of the LORD might prosper by his hand:
11. Of the travail of his soul he shall see to the full, even My servant,
Who by his knowledge did justify the Righteous One to the many,

Isaiah 53

fuller explanation: Who could explain to this generation of Israel that it was "for the transgression of My people" (i.e., the gentile people) that all this suffering came?

53:9 *With the rich his tomb.* Kimchi says this refers to the rich of Israel who were slain for their wealth. But Ibn Ezra takes the "rich" here to mean the powerful of the nations and says that the verse means that in their suffering the children of Israel longed for death and said, Let us die with these powerful ones, i.e., in our exile; and he cites as an analogy the blinded, despairing Samson saying: "Let me die with the Philistines." (Judges 16:20)

53:10 *If his soul would offer itself.* With this sentence (as in our English edition the paragraphing indicates) the speech of the gentile nations has ended; and from here on God speaks through the prophet. The phrase means to see whether Israel will accept this suffering. If he does, then he will have a future and "prolong his days."

53:11 *Travail of his soul ... even My servant.* This sentence is somewhat disarranged and its difficult sequence is carried over into this translation. It would be easier to follow if the sentence began as follows: It is My servant who by the travail of his soul did justify the Righteous One.

As for the phrase, "travail of his soul," Rashi takes this physically and says that it means: By his own labor did Israel live

275

Isaiah 53

And their iniquities he did bear.

12. Therefore will I divide him a portion among the great,
And he shall divide the spoil with the mighty;
Because he bared his soul unto death,
And was numbered with the transgressors;
Yet he bore the sin of many,
And made intercession for the transgressors.

and not by the exploitation of others. But Kimchi takes it spiritually: By his own sufferings which he endures patiently will he justify God's justice.

Their iniquities he did bear. Rashi: The righteous of every generation always bear the burden of the sins of their time, as was said of Aaron and his sons: "Thou and thy sons shall bear the iniquity of the Sanctuary." (Numbers 18:1)

53:12 *Therefore will I divide him a portion ... with the mighty.* Because he endured the burden of the sins of mankind, I the Lord will reward him.

The mighty. According to Rashi that means that Israel will share the blessings which God promised the mighty, i.e., the patriarchs.

54

THE PROPHET calls upon Zion (the people of Israel) to rejoice at the coming deliverance. Zion will be blessed with many children. God promises also that He will never be enraged against them and that every enemy that rises against her will be defeated.

Isaiah 54

1. Sing, O barren, thou that didst not bear,
   Break forth into singing, and cry aloud, thou that didst not travail;
   For more are the children of the desolate
   Than the children of the married wife, saith the LORD.
2. Enlarge the place of thy tent,
   And let them stretch forth the curtains of thy habitations, spare not;
   Lengthen thy cords, and strengthen thy stakes.

54 : 1 *Sing, O barren.* Israel in exile is described as a childless woman who now will be blessed with children. This metaphor of Israel as a wife and God as a husband has already been used by the prophet in Chapter 50. (See commentary note there.)

Than the children of the married wife. If Israel is the childless wife, who is the "married wife"? Both Rashi and Kimchi say that this refers to the now well-established heathen nations.

Isaiah 54

3. For thou shalt spread abroad on the right hand and on the left;
And thy seed shall possess the nations,
And make the desolate cities to be inhabited.
4. Fear not, for thou shalt not be ashamed.
Neither be thou confounded, for thou shalt not be put to shame;
For thou shalt forget the shame of thy youth,
And the reproach of thy widowhood shalt thou remember no more.
5. For thy Maker is thy husband,
The LORD of hosts is His name;
And the Holy One of Israel is thy Redeemer,
The God of the whole earth shall He be called.
6. For the LORD hath called thee
As a wife forsaken and grieved in spirit;
And a wife of youth, can she be rejected?
Saith thy God.
7. For a small moment have I forsaken thee;
But with great compassion will I gather thee.
8. In a little wrath I hid My face from thee for a moment;
But with everlasting kindness will I have compassion on thee,
Saith the LORD thy Redeemer.
9. For this is as the waters of Noah unto Me;
For as I have sworn that the waters of Noah
Should no more go over the earth,
So have I sworn that I would not be wroth with thee,
Nor rebuke thee.

54 : 3 *Shall possess the nations.* This means: Your land will spread east and west. (Kimchi)

54 : 4-6 *Thy widowhood . . . thy Maker is thy husband.* The general metaphor that God is the husband makes it difficult for the use of the idea of widowhood to be taken literally. It means the time of your loneliness (grass widowhood) as in Verse 6, "a wife forsaken, can she be rejected?"

54 : 9 *As the waters of Noah.* As God made a covenant with mankind after the flood that He would not again destroy the inhabitants of the earth, so He now promises that He will never again reject Israel.

Isaiah 54

10. For the mountains may depart,
    And the hills be removed;
    But My kindness shall not depart from thee,
    Neither shall My covenant of peace be removed,
    Saith the LORD that hath compassion on thee.
11. O thou afflicted, tossed with tempest,
    And not comforted,
    Behold, I will set thy stones in fair colours,
    And lay thy foundations with sapphires.
12. And I will make thy pinnacles of rubies,
    And thy gates of carbuncles,
    And all thy border of precious stones.
13. And all thy children shall be taught of the LORD;
    And great shall be the peace of thy children.
14. In righteousness shalt thou be established;
    Be thou far from oppression, for thou shalt not fear,
    And from ruin, for it shall not come near thee.
15. Behold, they may gather together, but not by Me;
    Whosoever shall gather together against thee shall fall because of thee.
16. Behold, I have created the smith
    That bloweth the fire of coals,
    And bringeth forth a weapon for his work;
    And I have created the waster to destroy.
17. No weapon that is formed against thee shall prosper;
    And every tongue that shall rise against thee in judgment thou shalt condemn.
    This is the heritage of the servants of the LORD,
    And their due reward from Me, saith the LORD.

54 : 11-13 *Thy foundations with sapphires.* A poetic description of the radiant beauty of Zion rebuilt.

54 : 14 *In righteousness shalt thou be established.* The grandest splendor of Zion rebuilt will be moral excellence of the nation.

54 : 15-17 *Whosoever shall gather together.* In the future there may still be enemies who gather together against you, but they will never destroy you. Verse 17: "No weapon that is formed against thee shall prosper." Ibn Ezra adds: In that time (the messianic time) the nations will abandon their idolatry and accept the religion of Israel (the Torah) and this is the meaning of "the heritage of the servants of the Lord." (Verse 17)

55

THIS IS CONSIDERED by most scholars to be the concluding chapter of the Second Isaiah. As is usually the case with such an address or series of addresses, it ends up with an appeal. The prophet tells the people to come nearer to God and to be sure that God's promises will be fulfilled.

Isaiah 55

1. Ho, every one that thirsteth, come ye for water,
And he that hath no money;
Come ye, buy, and eat;
Yea, come, buy wine and milk
Without money and without price.
2. Wherefore do ye spend money for that which is not bread?
And your gain for that which satisfieth not?
Hearken diligently unto Me, and eat ye that which is good,
And let your soul delight itself in fatness.

55:1 *Every one that thirsteth.* The Targum gives the meaning by paraphrasing the sentence: Let every one who wishes to learn come and learn. Rashi simply says that this means: Come to the Torah. And Kimchi calls special attention to this verse: "Not a thirst for water, but for hearing the words of the Lord." (Amos 8:11)

3. Incline your ear, and come unto Me;
   Hear, and your soul shall live;
   And I will make an everlasting covenant with you,
   Even the sure mercies of David.
4. Behold, I have given him for a witness to the peoples,
   A prince and commander to the peoples.
5. Behold, thou shalt call a nation that thou knowest not,
   And a nation that knew not thee shall run unto thee;
   Because of the LORD thy God,
   And for the Holy One of Israel, for He hath glorified thee.
6. Seek ye the LORD while He may be found,
   Call ye upon Him while He is near;
7. Let the wicked forsake his way,
   And the man of iniquity his thoughts;
   And let him return unto the LORD, and He will have compassion upon him,
   And to our God, for He will abundantly pardon.
8. For My thoughts are not your thoughts,
   Neither are your ways My ways, saith the LORD.
9. For as the heavens are higher than the earth,
   So are My ways higher than your ways,
   And My thoughts than your thoughts.

Isaiah 55

55 : 3-5 *The sure mercies of David.* Ibn Ezra first offers the explanation that this refers to the promise which God made to David: "I will keep My mercy for him forevermore." (Psalm 89: 29) His second explanation is that this is a reference to the Messiah, descendant of David, since the idea of the Messiah fits better with the statement in Verse 4 that he will be "a prince . . . to the people."

Verse 5 is also messianic: "A nation . . . shall run unto thee."

55 : 6 *While He may be found.* The Targum says this means: While you are still alive. But Kimchi says he follows his father's explanation which takes the verse to mean: Seek ye the Lord *in the way* He may be found (i.e., with all your heart). Ibn Ezra connects this with "Let the wicked forsake his way" (Verse 7) and says it means: Seek the Lord with righteous conduct.

Isaiah 55

10. For as the rain cometh down and the snow from heaven,
    And returneth not thither,
    Except it water the earth,
    And make it bring forth and bud,
    And give seed to the sower and bread to the eater;
11. So shall My word be that goeth forth out of My mouth:
    It shall not return unto Me void,
    Except it accomplish that which I please,
    And make the thing whereto I sent it prosper.
12. For ye shall go out with joy,
    And be led forth with peace;
    The mountains and the hills shall break forth before you into singing,
    And all the trees of the field shall clap their hands.
13. Instead of the thorn shall come up the cypress,
    And instead of the brier shall come up the myrtle;
    And it shall be to the LORD for a memorial,
    For an everlasting sign that shall not be cut off.

---

55 : 8-11 *My thoughts are not your thoughts ... My word ... shall not return unto Me void.* Human thoughts and human plans often fail of success, but God's plans and intentions never fail.

55 : 12 *Go out with joy ... the trees ... will clap their hands.* Kimchi: This is a metaphor that all of nature will rejoice at Israel's redemption.

55 : 13 *Instead of the brier.* Rashi cites the rabbinic explanation: Instead of the brier, will come up the myrtle, that in the blessed future there will be no wicked ones but only righteous. (See Megillah 10b.)

Krauss says that the removing of the thorns and the briers are really a description of the way in which God will prepare the road for the returning exiles. Thus he says this part of the book, which began with a description in Chapter 40 of the highway for the redeemed, ends consistently with the same thought. Krauss does not believe that this chapter ends the work of Deutero-Isaiah. He believes that the rest of the book was also written by him.

56

CHAPTERS 56 to 66 form what many scholars call "Trito-Isaiah," meaning thereby that they were not written by the unknown prophet we call Deutero-Isaiah (the second Isaiah) but by still another unknown prophet whose works were appended to the Book of Isaiah. In fact some scholars even say that these chapters are not a unit but a composite, deriving from many different authors. However, the majority of scholars, while seeing some differences in ideas between "Deutero-Isaiah" and "Trito-Isaiah," observe that there are many similarities in writing between the two books and therefore, while Chapters 56 to 66 were not written by the author of Chapters 40 to 55, they were however written by his disciples. But Krauss believes that Chapters 40 through 66 are one unit and that Deutero-Isaiah was the author of all of them.

The thought of Chapter 56 is that the prophet calls upon the people to live righteously and to observe the Sabbath in preparation for their coming deliverance. Then the prophet gives especial assurance to proselytes and to eunuchs that they are welcome to become part of the redeemed community. The chapter ends with a denunciation of the neglectful and evil leaders of the people.

1. Thus saith the LORD:
    Keep ye justice, and do righteousness;
    For My salvation is near to come,
    And My favour to be revealed.

Isaiah 56

2. Happy is the man that doeth this,
   And the son of man that holdeth fast by it:
   That keepeth the sabbath from profaning it,
   And keepeth his hand from doing any evil.
3. Neither let the alien,
   That hath joined himself to the LORD, speak, saying:
   'The LORD will surely separate me from His people';
   Neither let the eunuch say:
   'Behold, I am a dry tree.'
4. For thus saith the LORD
   Concerning the eunuchs that keep My sabbaths,
   And choose the things that please Me,
   And hold fast by My covenant:
5. Even unto them will I give in My house
   And within My walls a monument and a memorial
   Better than sons and daughters;
   I will give them an everlasting memorial,
   That shall not be cut off.

56 : 2 *Happy the man . . . that keepeth the sabbath.* Those who hold to the separate authorship of these chapters (i.e., who speak of a "Trito-Isaiah") call attention to the fact that nowhere in Chapters 40 through 55 is there a call for the observance of any ritual commandment such as the Sabbath and the proper mood of conducting the fast day (as in Chapter 58). But as to the Sabbath, Kimchi says: This being the most important of the commandments, it is specifically mentioned; but the prophet calls for obedience to all the commandments. Malbim calls attention to the two ideas in this verse—to keep the Sabbath and to keep from doing evil. To keep from evil is our proper relationship with our fellow man. To observe the Sabbath is our relationship, our covenant with God.

56 : 3 *The alien . . . the eunuch.* Kimchi says that the alien had no portion in the land of Israel (since the land was distributed to the Twelve Tribes) and the eunuch has no descendants. Nevertheless the prophet says God will bless them otherwise. Krauss calls attention to the fact that the prophet here evidently did not hold with the legislation mentioned in Deuteronomy 23:2 that eunuchs may not enter the community of the Lord. Perhaps the reason was that some of the Judean noblemen and even the royal

6. Also the aliens, that join themselves to the Lord, to minister unto Him,
And to love the name of the Lord,
To be His servants,
Every one that keepeth the sabbath from profaning it,
And holdeth fast by My covenant:
7. Even them will I bring to My holy mountain,
And make them joyful in My house of prayer;
Their burnt-offerings and their sacrifices
Shall be acceptable upon Mine altar;
For My house shall be called
A house of prayer for all peoples.
8. Saith the Lord God who gathereth the dispersed of Israel:
Yet will I gather others to him, beside those of him that are gathered.
9. All ye beasts of the field, come to devour,

Isaiah 56

family may have been made to serve as eunuchs in the palace of the Babylonian kings. Isaiah 39:7 reads (God speaking to Hezekiah): "Thy sons shall they take away [into captivity] and they shall be officers ["sarisim"—the word can be translated here as "eunuchs"] in the palace of the king of Babylon." Malbim says (explaining the welcoming of the eunuchs) that righteousness and the ennoblement of personal character is more important than the perpetuation of the race.

56:4-8 *Also the aliens.* All who will obey God's law are welcome to join the community. Their sacrifices will be accepted in the Temple for "My house shall be called a house of prayer for all peoples." (Verse 7) Kimchi calls attention to Solomon's prayer at the dedication of the Temple (I Kings 8:41) at which he asks God to listen to the prayer of strangers. Kimchi says further that if God's house is a house in which prayers of strangers are welcome how much more welcome are those who actually become full proselytes.

56:9 *All ye beasts of the field.* This sentence seems to break the sequence of the thought. But Kimchi, who explains most of these prophetic promises as applying to the time of the Messiah, says that this refers to the great premessianic wars of Gog and Magog,

Isaiah 56

Yea, all ye beasts in the forest.
10. His watchmen are all blind,
    Without knowledge;
    They are all dumb dogs,
    They cannot bark;
    Raving, lying down, loving to slumber.
11. Yea, the dogs are greedy,
    They know not when they have enough;
    And these are shepherds
    That cannot understand;
    They all turn to their own way,
    Each one to his gain, one and all.
12. 'Come ye, I will fetch wine,
    And we will fill ourselves with strong drink;
    And to-morrow shall be as this day,
    And much more abundant.'

with regard to which Ezekiel says that the beasts of the field will feed on the slain in those great battles. (39:17ff.) But Malbim counts this verse as introductory to the next sentences and says it is the false prophets who fail to rebuke the people who really devour them like beasts.

56 : 10-12 *Watchmen ... dogs ... shepherds.* The false leaders of the people are here described as blind watchmen, greedy dogs, irresponsible shepherds. (See Rashi and Kimchi.) The dogs mentioned here must be taken as relating to the watchmen and not with the shepherds. Therefore he rebukes the dogs as being unable to bark and warn of the approach of a marauder or a thief or an enemy. There is no reference in the Bible to dogs being used to aid the shepherd, as they were used in Europe to round up the sheep. In the East the sheep were trained to follow the shepherd. Hence Psalm 23 says: "He leadeth me." In the West the shepherd follows the sheep and the dogs run ahead to keep them together. If a Western shepherd had written the psalm, he would have said, "He driveth me."

57

THE PROPHET continues the theme of denunciation which closed the last chapter, i.e., against the blind watchmen, the greedy shepherds. Now he describes the evil deeds of the leaders (and of the people) for which they merited the punishments they now endure. The prophet speaks of them as idolatrous and their idolatry involved sexual indulgence and even the slaughter of children. The chapter concludes with a declaration of God's forgiveness and ends with the favorite theme of the prophet, a new highway for the pardoned people who will return home from exile.

1. The righteous perisheth,
   And no man layeth it to heart,
   And godly men are taken away,
   None considering
   That the righteous is taken away from the evil to come.

57 : 1 *The righteous perisheth . . . from the evil to come.* The prophet describes the corrupt conditions which were the cause of the exile. Ibn Ezra indicates that the verse means the death of the righteous is not a misfortune but a reward, that God let the righteous die so that they may not witness the inevitable calamity. A similar meaning is found in Rashi and Malbim who also say that it refers to the death of the righteous before the exile. He cites the example of the good king Josiah who died before the exile occurred.

Isaiah 57

2. He entereth into peace,
   They rest in their beds,
   Each one that walketh in his uprightness.
3. But draw near hither,
   Ye sons of the sorceress,
   The seed of the adulterer and the harlot.
4. Against whom do ye sport yourselves?
   Against whom make ye a wide mouth,
   And draw out the tongue?
   Are ye not children of transgression,
   A seed of falsehood,
5. Ye that inflame yourselves among the terebinths,
   Under every leafy tree;
   That slay the children in the valleys,
   Under the clefts of the rocks?
6. Among the smooth stones of the valley is thy portion;
   They, they are thy lot;
   Even to them hast thou poured a drink-offering,
   Thou hast offered a meal-offering.

57 : 2 *He entereth into peace ... that walketh in his uprightness.* This verse fits well with the interpretation of Rashi and Malbim that the righteous died before the exile and so were spared the experience of the calamity.

57 : 3-6 *Sorceress ... harlot ... slay children ... to them (i. e., the idols) ... a meal-offering.* The idolatry which they had adopted from their heathen neighbors always involved witchcraft, sexual license, and child sacrifices.

57 : 6 *Smooth stones of the valley thy portion.* Rashi: The smooth stones upon which you offered sacrifices will some day be the instrument of your doom ("thy portion"). There will come a time when you will be stoned by them.

Should I pacify Myself? God says: Should I take such things calmly? The verb translated here as "pacify" can also mean "repent," and Kimchi takes this second meaning. He cites the verse in Jonah 3:10, where this same verb is used and means "God repented of the evil which He said He would do to them" (i.e., God decided not to punish the city of Nineveh after all).

Should I pacify Myself for these things?
7. Upon a high and lofty mountain
Hast thou set thy bed;
Thither also wentest thou up
To offer sacrifice.
8. And behind the doors and the posts
Hast thou set up thy symbol;
For thou hast uncovered, and art gone up from Me,
Thou hast enlarged thy bed,
And chosen thee of them
Whose bed thou lovedst,
Whose hand thou sawest.
9. And thou wentest to the king with ointment,
And didst increase thy perfumes,
And didst send thine ambassadors far off,
Even down to the nether-world.
10. Thou wast wearied with the length of thy way;
Yet saidst thou not: 'There is no hope';
Thou didst find a renewal of thy strength,
Therefore thou wast not affected.

Isaiah 57

Therefore Kimchi and Ibn Ezra say this verse means: Should I repent of My intended punishment and forgive you?

57 : 8 *Whose hand thou sawest.* Ibn Ezra says that the word "hand" here simply means "place." So the phrase means: In whatever place thou didst see, thou didst commit thy sins. Your harlotry (i.e., your idolatry) took place all over the land. But see Krauss who cites the modern commentators to the effect that the word "hand" here is a sexual euphemism.

57 : 9 *Didst send thine ambassadors . . . to the nether-world.* Our translation means to say: You sent your ambassadors and messengers (seeking alliances described here in the simile of sexual relationships) as far as the nether-world. But Kimchi and Ibn Ezra agree on an entirely different translation: You sent your messengers everywhere pleading for alliances; thus you humbled yourself until you were as low as the nether-world.

57 : 10 *Renewal of . . . strength . . . not affected.* All these efforts to find alliances did not seem to weary you. You always seemed to renew your strength to seek further alliances.

Isaiah 57

11. And of whom hast thou been afraid and in fear,
    That thou wouldest fail?
    And as for Me, thou hast not remembered Me,
    Nor laid it to thy heart.
    Have not I held My peace even of long time?
    Therefore thou fearest Me not.
12. I will declare thy righteousness;
    Thy works also —they shall not profit thee.
13. When thou criest, let them that thou hast gathered deliver thee;
    But the wind shall carry them all away,
    A breath shall bear them off;
    But he that taketh refuge in Me shall possess the land,
    And shall inherit My holy mountain.
14. And He will say:
    Cast ye up, cast ye up, clear the way,
    Take up the stumblingblock out of the way of My people.

57 : 11   *I held My peace ... thou fearest Me not.*   Because I was patient, you grew over-confident. You no longer feared My punishment and so you continued on your evil ways.

57 : 12   *I will declare thy righteousness ... they shall not profit thee.*   Rashi takes the verse to mean the following: I have always declared (God says) what righteous actions you should have performed. You ignored My teachings. Therefore your actions will not protect you in the day of calamity. Kimchi takes the verse as follows: I note your self-declared righteousness. It will not profit thee. I contrast it with your actual deeds. Krauss takes the word "righteousness" here to mean, as it frequently means, vindication or deliverance and translates the verse as follows: I, says the Lord, am able to bring about your deliverance; but your own deeds cannot profit you at all. This explanation of Krauss fits well with the following verse which says, scornfully, "Call to your idols and see if they can deliver you. Only those who take refuge in Me shall be vindicated."

57 : 14-21   Here the mood of the chapter changes.   The theme recounting Israel's misdeeds is now succeeded by descriptions of the deliverance.

57 : 14   *Cast ye up ... clear the way, take up the stumblingblock.*

Isaiah 57

15. For thus saith the High and Lofty One
    That inhabiteth eternity, whose name is Holy:
    I dwell in the high and holy place,
    With him also that is of a contrite and humble spirit,
    To revive the spirit of the humble,
    And to revive the heart of the contrite ones.
16. For I will not contend for ever,
    Neither will I be always wroth;
    For the spirit that enwrappeth itself is from Me,
    And the souls which I have made.
17. For the iniquity of his covetousness was I wroth and smote him,
    I hid Me and was wroth;
    And he went on frowardly in the way of his heart.
18. I have seen his ways, and will heal him;
    I will lead him also, and requite with comforts him and his mourners.
19. Peace, peace, to him that is far off and to him that is near,

Prepare the road for the return of the redeemed. This is the same theme with which Deutero-Isaiah began: "Clear ye a highway . . ." (40:2-3) (See also commentary note to 55:13.)

57 : 16 *The spirit that enwrappeth itself.* Rashi translates the word for "enwrappeth" as meaning "to humble oneself," and thus connects it with the beginning of the sentence as follows: I will not always be angry; the spirit of man will become humble and I will forgive. This interpretation would fit with Verse 15: "I dwell . . . with him that is of a . . . humble spirit." But Kimchi translates the word as in our translation, "enwrappeth," and says the verse means: I will forgive them because the spirit which comes from Me enwrappeth itself in the body and can lead the body onto the right path.

57 : 17 *Frowardly.* The word is taken from the King James version and is defined as "contrary to what should be expected or perverse." Ibn Ezra says that the word (translated here "frowardly") can also be translated "in repentance," but he says the word "shovav" here is used in a bad sense, namely, that instead of returning to God they returned to their evil ways.

57 : 19 *Createth the fruit of the lips.* Kimchi, as he frequently does, interprets this verse as referring to the messianic days when

Isaiah 57

Saith the LORD that createth the fruit of the lips;
And I will heal him.
20. But the wicked are like the troubled sea;
For it cannot rest,
And its waters cast up mire and dirt.
21. There is no peace,
Saith my God concerning the wicked.

wars shall cease and people will then use a phrase which is new, "peace to the far and near."

57 : 20-21 *Wicked ... like the troubled sea ... no peace.* This is the same sentence which ends Chapter 48, except that another name for God is used. Rashi says that this refers to those who will not repent. Ibn Ezra takes the verse psychologically and says: The wicked never have peace. They are always like the troubled sea.

58

THE PROPHET is called upon to "declare to My people their sins." Their daily prayers, their fasts are unacceptable to God because these are not accompanied by social justice. The whole chapter reflects the words of Micah where the same verb "to declare" is used: "It hath been told (declared to) thee, O man, what is good: to do justly, to love mercy . . . " (Micah 6:8) Two rituals are discussed in this chapter, fasting and (as in Chapter 56) the Sabbath. This chapter is traditionally the prophetical reading for Yom Kippur. (Cf. Megillah 31a.)

1. Cry aloud, spare not,
   Lift up thy voice like a horn,
   And declare unto My people their transgression,
   And to the house of Jacob their sins.
2. Yet they seek Me daily,
   And delight to know My ways;
   As a nation that did righteousness,
   And forsook not the ordinance of their God,
   They ask of Me righteous ordinances,

Isaiah 58

58:1 *Spare not.* Do not hold back. Kimchi says it means: Do not stop; keep on rebuking them.

58:2 *Seek Me daily . . . delight to know My ways.* Rashi: They ask for guidance, pretending that they are going to obey.

Isaiah 58

They delight to draw near unto God.
3. 'Wherefore have we fasted, and Thou seest not?
   Wherefore have we afflicted our soul, and Thou takest no knowledge?'—
   Behold, in the day of your fast ye pursue your business,
   And exact all your labours.
4. Behold, ye fast for strife and contention,
   And to smite with the fist of wickedness;
   Ye fast not this day
   So as to make your voice to be heard on high.
5. Is such the fast that I have chosen?
   The day for a man to afflict his soul?
   Is it to bow down his head as a bulrush,
   And to spread sackcloth and ashes under him?
   Wilt thou call this a fast,
   And an acceptable day to the LORD?
6. Is not this the fast that I have chosen?
   To loose the fetters of wickedness,
   To undo the bands of the yoke,
   And to let the oppressed go free,
   And that ye break every yoke?
7. Is it not to deal thy bread to the hungry,
   And that thou bring the poor that are cast out to thy house?
   When thou seest the naked, that thou cover him,
   And that thou hide not thyself from thine own flesh?
8. Then shall thy light break forth as the morning,

Kimchi and Ibn Ezra: They seek God with words but not with their hearts.

58:3 *Exact all your labours.* Rashi and Ibn Ezra: You force payment for the money owed you.

58:5 *To afflict his soul.* This is the classic term for fasting on Yom Kippur: It (Yom Kippur) is a Sabbath of solemn rest and ye shall afflict your souls. (See Leviticus 16:31.)

58:7 *Hide not ... from thine own flesh.* Rashi: From thine own kinfolk. Ibn Ezra calls attention to the words of Judah referring to their brother Joseph: "He is our brother, our flesh." (Genesis 37:27)

And thy healing shall spring forth speedily;
And thy righteousness shall go before thee,
The glory of the LORD shall be thy rearward.
9. Then shalt thou call, and the LORD will answer;
Thou shalt cry, and He will say: 'Here I am.'
If thou take away from the midst of thee the yoke,
The putting forth of the finger, and speaking wickedness;
10. And if thou draw out thy soul to the hungry,
And satisfy the afflicted soul;
Then shall thy light rise in darkness,
And thy gloom be as the noonday;
11. And the LORD will guide thee continually,
And satisfy thy soul in drought,
And make strong thy bones;
And thou shalt be like a watered garden,
And like a spring of water, whose waters fail not.
12. And they that shall be of thee shall build the old waste places,
Thou shalt raise up the foundations of many generations;
And thou shalt be called The repairer of the breach,
The restorer of paths to dwell in.
13. If thou turn away thy foot because of the sabbath,
From pursuing thy business on My holy day;
And call the sabbath a delight,
And the holy of the LORD honourable;
And shalt honour it, not doing thy wonted ways,

Isaiah
58

Scripture does not express kinship by the word "blood" (as we say "blood kin") but by the word "flesh"—we are of one flesh. Malbim here says: This does not refer only to one's relatives; all human beings are of one flesh. Therefore the verse means: Do not withhold help from anybody.

58 : 8 *Thy rearward.* The rear guard which protects an army from hostile pursuit. (See commentary note to 52:12.)

58 : 13 *Call the sabbath a delight.* Repeats the call to observe the Sabbath as in Chapter 56, Verse 2. Here the word "oneg" is used. It became a classic term for the mood of the Sabbath, "Oneg Shabbat," "delight or joy in the Sabbath."

Isaiah 58

Nor pursuing thy business, nor speaking thereof;
14. Then shalt thou delight thyself in the Lord,
And I will make thee to ride upon the high places of the earth,
And I will feed thee with the heritage of Jacob thy father;
For the mouth of the Lord hath spoken it.

59

THE PEOPLE complain that their deliverance is slow in coming. The prophet answers them by saying: If the deliverance is slow in coming, it is not because God is too weak to save you, it is your sins which have brought this punishment upon you. Nevertheless God will redeem you and establish an everlasting covenant.

1. Behold, the LORD's hand is not shortened, that it cannot save,
   Neither His ear heavy, that it cannot hear;
2. But your iniquities have separated
   Between you and your God,
   And your sins have hid His face from you,
   That He will not hear.
3. For your hands are defiled with blood,
   And your fingers with iniquity;
   Your lips have spoken lies,
   Your tongue muttereth wickedness.

Isaiah 59

59:1 *The Lord's hand is not shortened, that it cannot save.* Kimchi connects this statement with the complaint of the people in the preceding chapter: "Why have we fasted and afflicted our souls and Thou takest no knowledge?" (58:3) This now is the prophet's answer to their complaint: God is able to help you, but "your sins have hid His face from you."

Isaiah 59

4. None sueth in righteousness,
   And none pleadeth in truth;
   They trust in vanity, and speak lies,
   They conceive mischief, and bring forth iniquity.
5. They hatch basilisks' eggs,
   And weave the spider's web;
   He that eateth of their eggs dieth,
   And that which is crushed breaketh out into a viper.
6. Their webs shall not become garments,
   Neither shall men cover themselves with their works;
   Their works are works of iniquity,
   And the act of violence is in their hands.
7. Their feet run to evil,
   And they make haste to shed innocent blood;
   Their thoughts are thoughts of iniquity,
   Desolation and destruction are in their paths.
8. The way of peace they know not,
   And there is no right in their goings;
   They have made them crooked paths,
   Whosoever goeth therein doth not know peace.
9. Therefore is justice far from us,
   Neither doth righteousness overtake us;
   We look for light, but behold darkness,
   For brightness, but we walk in gloom.
10. We grope for the wall like the blind,
    Yea, as they that have no eyes do we grope;

---

59 : 5-6 *Hatch basilisks' eggs ... spider's web.* The evil that they do is either poisonous like viper's eggs or as useless for weaving cloth as spider webs.

59 : 8 *Crooked paths ... doth not know peace.* This thought is the same as in the closing sentence for both Chapters 48 and 57: "There is no peace, saith the Lord, for the wicked."

59 : 9 *Therefore is justice far from us.* From Verse 9 to Verse 15, the people continue to speak, but they speak now in a different mood as if convinced by the prophet's words. They understand now and they acknowledge here the reason why they suffer. They have merited their misfortunes, or as Kimchi states it: The prophet quoting the new insight of the people, as did the Prophet Jeremiah who put into words the repentance of the people: "We

We stumble at noonday as in the twilight;
We are in dark places like the dead.
11. We all growl like bears,
And mourn sore like doves;
We look for right, but there is none;
For salvation, but it is far off from us.
12. For our transgressions are multiplied before Thee,
And our sins testify against us;
For our transgressions are present to us,
And as for our iniquities, we know them:
13. Transgressing and denying the LORD,
And turning away from following our God,
Speaking oppression and perverseness,
Conceiving and uttering from the heart words of falsehood.
14. And justice is turned away backward,
And righteousness standeth afar off;
For truth hath stumbled in the broad place,
And uprightness cannot enter.
15. And truth is lacking,
And he that departeth from evil maketh himself a prey.
And the LORD saw it, and it displeased Him
That there was no justice;
16. And He saw that there was no man,
And was astonished that there was no intercessor;

Isaiah 59

acknowledge, O Lord, our wickedness. We have sinned against Thee." (Jeremiah 14:20)

59:11 *Growl like bears . . . mourn . . . like doves.* "Mourning like doves" is a good simile for the mood of repentance, but not "growling like bears." Krauss emends the word for "bears" to "bees." We murmur or hum like bees.

59:15 *He that departeth from evil maketh himself a prey.* The Targum takes the sentence as it is translated here: The righteous man is robbed and despoiled. But the word for "prey" can be translated as "insane" or "bereft of one's senses." So both Rashi and Ibn Ezra take the sentence to mean that in an evil society a righteous man is considered to be insane.

59:16 *No man . . . no intercessor.* God sees that there is no

Isaiah 59

Therefore His own arm brought salvation unto Him;
And His righteousness, it sustained Him;

17. And He put on righteousness as a coat of mail,
And a helmet of salvation upon His head,
And He put on garments of vengeance for clothing,
And was clad with zeal as a cloak.
18. According to their deeds, accordingly He will repay,
Fury to His adversaries, recompense to His enemies;
To the islands He will repay recompense.
19. So shall they fear the name of the LORD from the west,
And His glory from the rising of the sun;

man among the people righteous enough to plead for them. So God himself on His own accord (for His mercy's sake) interceded for His people.

59 : 17 *Righteousness as a coat of mail . . . helmet of salvation.* The metaphor here is that of a warrior putting on his armor. Here, of course, the helmet and armor are described as the spiritual armor of righteousness and justice.

59 : 19 *Distress will come in like a flood.* Rashi says: Calamities will come like a flood against the enemies of God; but our translation is akin to that of Ibn Ezra's, that there will come times of

For distress will come in like a flood,
Which the breath of the Lord driveth.
20. And a redeemer will come to Zion,
And unto them that turn from transgression in Jacob,
Saith the Lord.
21. And as for Me, this is My covenant with them, saith the Lord; My spirit that is upon thee, and My words which I have put in thy mouth, shall not depart out of thy mouth, nor out of the mouth of thy seed, nor out of the mouth of thy seed's seed, saith the Lord, from henceforth and for ever.

Isaiah
59

great trouble but Israel will be saved, as the next verse declares.

59 : 20 *A redeemer will come to Zion.* Ibn Ezra and Kimchi connect Verses 19 and 20: In the times of great distress, a redeemer will come to Zion.

59 : 21 *My spirit ... My words.* Kimchi says it means that the spirit which God gives to His prophets will now enter into the soul of the entire people of Israel. He cites the words of Jeremiah: "Behold, this is the covenant I shall make with the house of Israel ... and in their heart will I write it." (Jeremiah 31:33)

60

THE PROPHET rhapsodizes upon the radiant future of Zion restored and declares that all people shall come to Zion, for it will be the world center of spiritual light.

Isaiah 60

1. Arise, shine, for thy light is come,
   And the glory of the Lord is risen upon thee.
2. For, behold, darkness shall cover the earth,
   And gross darkness the peoples;
   But upon thee the Lord will arise,
   And His glory shall be seen upon thee.
3. And nations shall walk at thy light,
   And kings at the brightness of thy rising.
4. Lift up thine eyes round about, and see:
   They all are gathered together, and come to thee;
   Thy sons come from far,

60 : 2 *Darkness shall cover the earth.* Even though it will be a time of trouble for the whole world, the deliverance will surely come.

60 : 3 *Nations shall walk at thy light.* Kimchi cites the verse in Isaiah, Chapter 2, Verse 3: "Many people will come and say, 'Let us go up to the mountain of the Lord.'"

60 : 4 *Thy sons come from afar ... daughters ... borne on the side.* This is the same thought as in Chapter 49, Verse 23:

And thy daughters are borne on the side.
5. Then thou shalt see and be radiant,
And thy heart shall throb and be enlarged;
Because the abundance of the sea shall be turned
  unto thee,
The wealth of the nations shall come unto thee.
6. The caravan of camels shall cover thee,
And of the young camels of Midian and Ephah,
All coming from Sheba;
They shall bring gold and frankincense,
And shall proclaim the praises of the LORD.
7. All the flocks of Kedar shall be gathered together
  unto thee,
The rams of Nebaioth shall minister unto thee;
They shall come up with acceptance on Mine altar,
And I will glorify My glorious house.
8. Who are these that fly as a cloud,
And as the doves to their cotes?
9. Surely the isles shall wait for Me,
And the ships of Tarshish first,
To bring thy sons from far,
Their silver and their gold with them,
For the name of the LORD thy God,
And for the Holy One of Israel, because He hath
  glorified thee.
10. And aliens shall build up thy walls,
And their kings shall minister unto thee;
For in My wrath I smote thee,
But in My favour have I had compassion on thee.
11. Thy gates also shall be open continually,
Day and night, they shall not be shut;

Isaiah 60

Kings and queens shall take care of thy children and nurture them. As for the expression, "borne on the side," Krauss calls attention to the fact that it is customary in the East for mothers to carry their infants on their hips.

60:7 *The rams . . . shall minister.* The rams themselves can hardly minister. Kimchi translates it: With the rams as offerings, the people shall minister unto thee.

60:11 *Thy gates shall be open . . . day and night.* There will

Isaiah 60

That men may bring unto thee the wealth of the nations,
And their kings in procession.

12. For that nation and kingdom that will not serve thee shall perish;
Yea, those nations shall be utterly wasted.

13. The glory of Lebanon shall come unto thee,
The cypress, the plane-tree, and the larch together;
To beautify the place of My sanctuary,
And I will make the place of My feet glorious.

14. And the sons of them that afflicted thee
Shall come bending unto thee,
And all they that despised thee shall bow down
At the soles of thy feet;
And they shall call thee The city of the LORD,
The Zion of the Holy One of Israel.

15. Whereas thou hast been forsaken and hated,
So that no man passed through thee,
I will make thee an eternal excellency,
A joy of many generations.

16. Thou shalt also suck the milk of the nations,
And shalt suck the breast of kings;
And thou shalt know that I the LORD am thy Saviour,
And I, the Mighty One of Jacob, thy Redeemer.

17. For brass I will bring gold,

---

be no need any more to close the gates of the cities, because there will never again be any danger of war.

60:13 *The place of My feet.* The Targum characteristically paraphrases this anthropomorphism thus: The place where My presence (Shechinah) rests. But this is the same metaphor that is used in Isaiah, Chapter 66, Verse 1: "The heaven is My throne, the earth is My footstool."

60:16 *Suck the milk of nations . . . kings.* Again this is the same thought as in Chapter 49, Verse 23: "Kings shall be thy foster fathers and queens thy nursing mothers."

60:17 *Thy officers peace, and righteousness thy magistrates.*

And for iron I will bring silver,
And for wood brass,
And for stones iron;
I will also make thy officers peace,
And righteousness thy magistrates.
18. Violence shall no more be heard in thy land,
Desolation nor destruction within thy borders;
But thou shalt call thy walls Salvation,
And thy gates Praise.
19. The sun shall be no more thy light by day,
Neither for brightness shall the moon give light unto thee;
But the LORD shall be unto thee an everlasting light,
And thy God thy glory.
20. Thy sun shall no more go down,
Neither shall thy moon withdraw itself;
For the LORD shall be thine everlasting light,
And the days of thy mourning shall be ended.
21. Thy people also shall be all righteous,
They shall inherit the land for ever;
The branch of My planting, the work of My hands,
Wherein I glory.
22. The smallest shall become a thousand,
And the least a mighty nation;
I the LORD will hasten it in its time.

Isaiah
60

Malbim explains that in messianic days your influence over the nations will not be by force or oppression but it will be based upon peace and justice.

60 : 19 *The sun ... no more.* The rhapsody continues: In those days they will not need sun or moon but they will live by God's eternal radiance. (Verse 21: "Thy people shall be all righteous.")

60 : 22 *Will hasten it in its time.* The sentence seems illogical. If God will hasten the deliverance, it cannot be "in its time"; it will be before its time. Rashi therefore calls attention to the rabbinic interpretation of this verse. (Sanhedrin 98a) God says to Israel: If you will be worthy, I will hasten the deliverance, but if not it will come in the time (which I have previously set for it).

305

61

Isaiah 61

THIS CHAPTER and the following one are a unit. The prophet describes his mission and his consecration to it. This theme is found in the works of many of the prophets as, for example, in Isaiah, Chapter 6 and Jeremiah, Chapter 1.

1. The spirit of the Lord GOD is upon me;
   Because the LORD hath anointed me
   To bring good tidings unto the humble;
   He hath sent me to bind up the broken-hearted,
   To proclaim liberty to the captives,
   And the opening of the eyes to them that are bound;
2. To proclaim the year of the LORD's good pleasure,
   And the day of vengeance of our God;
   To comfort all that mourn;

61 : 1 *The Lord hath anointed me . . . to bind up the broken-hearted.* In other prophetic literature, the prophet in his consecration sermons tells that he is appointed to rebuke Israel for its sins and to threaten punishment. But, here, this prophet is to speak to Israel in exile and is therefore summoned to console and to strengthen.

61 : 2 *Day of vengeance.* Kimchi, who explains most of these prophecies as pertaining to the messianic days, says that the day of vengeance refers to the bloody wars of Gog and Magog in Ezekiel, Chapter 38, which will precede the "end of days."

3. To appoint unto them that mourn in Zion,
   To give unto them a garland for ashes,
   The oil of joy for mourning,
   The mantle of praise for the spirit of heaviness;
   That they might be called terebinths of righteousness,
   The planting of the LORD, wherein He might glory.
4. And they shall build the old wastes,
   They shall raise up the former desolations,
   And they shall renew the waste cities,
   The desolations of many generations.
5. And strangers shall stand and feed your flocks,
   And aliens shall be your plowmen and your vinedressers.
6. But ye shall be named the priests of the LORD,
   Men shall call you the ministers of our God;
   Ye shall eat the wealth of the nations,
   And in their splendour shall ye revel.
7. For your shame which was double,
   And for that they rejoiced: 'Confusion is their portion';
   Therefore in their land they shall possess double,
   Everlasting joy shall be unto them.

Isaiah 61

61 : 3 *A garland for ashes.* This is exactly the opposite to the dire prediction of Isaiah ben Amoz that the daughters of Zion would get, "instead of spices, rottenness, instead of a girdle, rags." (Isaiah 3:24)

Terebinths . . . the planting of the Lord. A metaphor for Israel redeemed; a noble tree planted by God himself. Kimchi calls attention to the parallel thought in Chapter 60, Verse 21: "The branch of My planting."

61 : 6 *Priests of the Lord.* Kimchi says: Since "strangers shall stand and feed your flocks," (Verse 5) Israel will now have time to devote itself entirely to sacred tasks. (Cf. Exodus 19:6: "Ye shall be to Me a kingdom of priests.")

61 : 7 *That they rejoiced.* Their enemies laughed and mocked them during their exile, saying, "Confusion is their portion." But Kimchi comments on this differently and says that the subject of "rejoice" is Israel, translating the sentence as follows: Instead

Isaiah 61

8. For I the Lord love justice,
   I hate robbery with iniquity;
   And I will give them their recompense in truth,
   And I will make an everlasting covenant with them.
9. And their seed shall be known among the nations,
   And their offspring among the peoples;
   All that see them shall acknowledge them,
   That they are the seed which the Lord hath blessed.
10. I will greatly rejoice in the Lord,
    My soul shall be joyful in my God;
    For He hath clothed me with the garments of salvation,
    He hath covered me with the robe of victory,
    As a bridegroom putteth on a priestly diadem,
    And as a bride adorneth herself with her jewels.
11. For as the earth bringeth forth her growth,
    And as the garden causeth the things that are sown in it to spring forth;
    So the Lord God will cause victory and glory
    To spring forth before all the nations.

of the double portion of shame which they had, Israel now will be able to rejoice in its portion.

62

THE PROPHET continues his description of the restoration.

Isaiah 62

1. For Zion's sake will I not hold My peace,
   And for Jerusalem's sake I will not rest,
   Until her triumph go forth as brightness,
   And her salvation as a torch that burneth.
2. And the nations shall see thy triumph,
   And all kings thy glory;
   And thou shalt be called by a new name,
   Which the mouth of the LORD shall mark out.
3. Thou shalt also be a crown of beauty in the hand of the LORD,

62 : 1 *For Zion's sake I will not hold My peace.* Both Rashi and Kimchi says that these words are spoken by God; but Krauss, who considers that this and the preceding chapter are the words of the prophet expressing his dedication to his task, explains that the prophet says: I will not cease to speak and to pray until Zion is redeemed. These opening sentences are the inspiration for Blake's famous lines: "I will not cease from mental fight . . . till we have built Jerusalem."

62 : 2 *Called by a new name.* A new name is a symbol of a new and a better life. Thus in this chapter God gives a number of new names to Israel. For example in Verse 4: "Thou shalt no more be termed Forsaken, but . . . Espoused."

Isaiah 62

And a royal diadem in the open hand of thy God.
4. Thou shalt no more be termed Forsaken,
Neither shall thy land any more be termed Desolate;
But thou shalt be called, My delight is in her,
And thy land, Espoused;
For the LORD delighteth in thee,
And thy land shall be espoused.
5. For as a young man espouseth a virgin,
So shall thy sons espouse thee;
And as the bridegroom rejoiceth over the bride,
So shall thy God rejoice over thee.
6. I have set watchmen
Upon thy walls, O Jerusalem,
They shall never hold their peace
Day nor night:
'Ye that are the LORD's remembrancers,
Take ye no rest,
7. And give Him no rest,
Till He establish,
And till He make Jerusalem
A praise in the earth.'
8. The LORD hath sworn by His right hand,
And by the arm of His strength:

62 : 4 *My delight is in her.* This new name in Hebrew is Cheftzivah (Hephzibah in English). In the same verse, the new name in Hebrew for "Espoused" is Beulah.

62 : 6 *The Lord's remembrancers.* Rashi: They will not cease to remind God of the merit of the fathers. Ibn Ezra: Recalls another verse speaking of reminding God, "Put Me in remembrance ... that thou mayest be justified." (Isaiah 43:26)

Surely I will no more give thy corn
To be food for thine enemies;
And strangers shall not drink thy wine,
For which thou hast laboured;
9. But they that have garnered it shall eat it,
And praise the LORD,
And they that have gathered it shall drink it
In the courts of My sanctuary.
10. Go through, go through the gates,
Clear ye the way of the people;
Cast up, cast up the highway,
Gather out the stones;
Lift up an ensign over the peoples.
11. Behold, the LORD hath proclaimed
Unto the end of the earth:
Say ye to the daughter of Zion:
'Behold, thy salvation cometh;
Behold, His reward is with Him,
And His recompense before Him.'
12. And they shall call them The holy people,
The redeemed of the LORD;
And thou shalt be called Sought out,
A city not forsaken.

Isaiah 62

62 : 10 *Go through the gates.* Ibn Ezra says (and Krauss, too) that it means: Go through gates of city after city to tell of God's deliverance.

Cast up the highway. This is the same thought as in Isaiah, Chapter 40: "Prepare the road for the redeemed."

62 : 12 *Sought out.* The Hebrew of this new name of blessedness is Derushah.

63

A VIVID picture of the destruction of Edom and its capital city Bozrah. Edom is the arch enemy of Israel. God is described here as a warrior returning from battle. The thought of the chapter then moves to God's protection of Israel in the past, specifically in the Exodus from Egypt, and ends with the plea that God come again to the deliverance of Israel.

Isaiah 63

1. 'Who is this that cometh from Edom,
   With crimsoned garments from Bozrah?
   This that is glorious in his apparel,

63 : 1 *Who ... cometh from Edom ... ?* The prophet asks this rhetorical question and gives the answer: It is God who is coming victorious from Edom. Since this whole chapter speaks of the redemption from Egypt as a precedent for which the people now ask for God's return as a Deliverer, His victory over the Egyptians becomes parallel to His victory over the present-day enemies (exemplified by Edom). Since, in the ancient song at the Red Sea, God is described as "a Man of war" (Exodus 15:3-4), here too He is described in military terms. The poet wishes to say that God comes victorious from battle with His garments blood-stained. Then the prophet softens the metaphor by comparing it to a wine press in which the garments of the wine presser is wine spattered. The whole metaphor, "trodden the

Stately in the greatness of his strength?'—
'I that speak in victory, mighty to save.'—
2. 'Wherefore is Thine apparel red,
And Thy garments like his that treadeth in the winevat?'—
3. 'I have trodden the winepress alone,
And of the peoples there was no man with Me;
Yea, I trod them in Mine anger,
And trampled them in My fury;
And their lifeblood is dashed against My garments,
And I have stained all My raiment.
4. For the day of vengeance that was in My heart,
And My year of redemption are come.
5. And I looked, and there was none to help,
And I beheld in astonishment, and there was none to uphold;
Therefore Mine own arm brought salvation unto Me,
And My fury, it upheld Me.
6. And I trod down the peoples in Mine anger,
And made them drunk with My fury,
And I poured out their lifeblood on the earth.'
7. I will make mention of the mercies of the LORD,
And the praises of the LORD,
According to all that the LORD hath bestowed on us;
And the great goodness toward the house of Israel,
Which He hath bestowed on them according to His compassions,
And according to the multitude of His mercies.
8. For He said: 'Surely, they are My people,

Isaiah 63

winepress . . . in Mine anger," is the inspiration of Julia Ward Howe in her *Battle Hymn of the Republic*, "Mine eyes have seen the glory of the coming of the Lord, He is trampling out the vintage where the grapes of wrath are stored. . . ."

63 : 5 *I looked, and there was none to help.* Ibn Ezra says it means there was no human agency to come to the help of Israel, so God himself has saved them.

63 : 8 *Children that will not deal falsely.* Although God knows that they will indeed sin, yet He thinks of them as His children who can still be trusted. (Rashi) Kimchi: I have taken them to be

Isaiah 63

Children that will not deal falsely';
So He was their Saviour.
9. In all their affliction He was afflicted,
And the angel of His presence saved them;
In His love and in His pity He redeemed them;
And He bore them, and carried them all the days of old.
10. But they rebelled, and grieved His holy spirit;
Therefore He was turned to be their enemy,
Himself fought against them.
11. Then His people remembered the days of old, the days of Moses:
'Where is He that brought them up out of the sea
With the shepherds of His flock?
Where is He that put His holy spirit
In the midst of them?
12. That caused His glorious arm to go

My people. They will not be permanently sinful. Ibn Ezra: I knew they would be trustworthy; that is why I adopted them.

63 : 9 *In all their affliction He was afflicted.* The word "lo" in the text can be read as meaning "to Him" or as meaning "not." This is one of the many cases in Scripture where there is a difference between the spelling (ketiv) and the pronunciation (keri) and the difference, of course, between the two affects the meaning of the text. Our translation here follows the pronunciation "keri" and therefore translates, "There was affliction to Him"; but Rashi takes the spelling (ketiv) and translates the word as "not." Therefore the verse as read by Rashi is: In their affliction He did not afflict them as much as they deserved. Kimchi calls attention to both possible meanings. Ibn Ezra (as does our translation) follows the pronunciation "keri" and translates: He was afflicted. Ibn Ezra cites as a parallel Verse 16 in Chapter 10 of Judges which also speaks of God saddened by the suffering of Israel: "His soul was grieved for the misery of Israel."

Angel of His presence. Rashi says this is the Archangel Michael. Ibn Ezra calls attention to a parallel idea in Verse 16, Chapter 20 of Numbers: "Moses sent a messenger to the king of Moab and said, 'God sent an angel and brought us forth out of Egypt.'"

Isaiah 63

At the right hand of Moses?
That divided the water before them,
To make Himself an everlasting name?
13. That led them through the deep,
    As a horse in the wilderness, without stumbling?
14. As the cattle that go down into the valley,
    The spirit of the LORD caused them to rest;
    So didst Thou lead Thy people,
    To make Thyself a glorious name.'
15. Look down from heaven, and see,
    Even from Thy holy and glorious habitation;
    Where is Thy zeal and Thy mighty acts,
    The yearning of Thy heart and Thy compassions,
    Now restrained toward me?
16. For Thou art our Father;
    For Abraham knoweth us not,
    And Israel doth not acknowledge us;

He bore them. God carried them as a father carries his child. An analogous thought is used with regard to the Exodus from Egypt. (Exodus 19:4: "I carried you as on eagle's wings.")

63 : 11 *His people remembered . . . 'Where is He . . .'* After God had turned against them, they recalled the help He had given them when He delivered them from Egypt, and they wondered where the God is who once helped them.

63 : 13-14 *Horse in the wilderness . . . cattle . . . into the valley.* The prophet compares their easy march through the Red Sea to that of a horse galloping over the desert where he finds no fences or other obstacles or as cattle ambling without effort down a sloping field.

63 : 15-19 The people plead to God to renew His help as of old.

63 : 16 *Thou art our Father; for Abraham knoweth us not, and Israel doth not acknowledge us.* The Targum, avoiding as usual the anthropomorphical idea of God as a human father, reads the sentence as follows: As a Father to His children, so great are Thy mercies toward us. It was not Abraham who rescued us from Egypt, nor Jacob who saved us in the wilderness; it was only Thou. Rashi adopts this entire explanation. But Kimchi calls attention to Verse 10 in Chapter 27 of Psalms: "Though father and mother have forsaken me, the Lord will take me up." The

Isaiah 63

Thou, O Lord, art our Father,
Our Redeemer from everlasting is Thy name.
17. O Lord, why dost Thou make us to err from Thy ways,
And hardenest our heart from Thy fear?
Return for Thy servants' sake,
The tribes of Thine inheritance.
18. Thy holy people they have well nigh driven out,
Our adversaries have trodden down Thy sanctuary.
19. We are become as they over whom Thou never borest rule,
As they that were not called by Thy name.
Oh that Thou wouldest rend the heavens, that Thou wouldest come down,
That the mountains might quake at Thy presence,

meaning of the psalm is applicable here: Ultimately all parents must forsake their children when they die; but God alone is our eternal help.

63 : 17 *Why dost Thou make us to err...?* Rashi: You, O Lord, could have removed entirely the evil impulse from us. Kimchi: Because You have brought us to this state in which we see the prosperity of the evil ones and our own misery, we are led away from our faith in Thee.

63 : 19 *They over whom Thou never borest rule.* Here, in our misery, we have become like men over whom Thou hast never ruled (Ibn Ezra), i.e., we have become like men whom Thou hast never taught through Thy prophets.

Rend the heavens... mountains... quake. Rashi: Rescue us again as Thou didst in Egypt.

The rescue of Egypt is described as follows: When Israel came out of Egypt, the mountains skipped like rams. (Psalms 14) Krauss: "When God delivered, the mountains did tremble." (Psalms 18:9)

64

THIS CHAPTER continues the theme with which the last chapter ended, pleading with God to come and save the people of Israel; it then proceeds to describe its miseries in exile. "O that Thou wouldst come down, that the mountains might quake at Thy presence." (63:19)

1. As when fire kindleth the brushwood,
   And the fire causeth the waters to boil;
   To make Thy name known to Thine adversaries,
   That the nations might tremble at Thy presence,
2. When Thou didst tremendous things
   Which we looked not for—
   Oh that Thou wouldest come down, that the mountains might quake at Thy presence!—

Isaiah 64

64 : 1-2 *As when fire kindleth . . . to make Thy name known.* According to the ancient Greek and Latin versions, this chapter should begin with the last verse of the preceding chapter. The sequence would then be clear: "Oh that Thou wouldst come down . . . that the mountains might quake . . . as when fire kindleth . . ." All this describes the earthquake and fire when God descends to earth, as it was described when God came to Mount Sinai.

64 : 2 *When Thou didst tremendous things.* As in the last chapter, the tremendous things are a reference to the redemption from Egypt. (Rashi) (See commentary note to 63:19.)

317

Isaiah 64

3. And whereof from of old men have not heard, nor perceived by the ear,
Neither hath the eye seen a God beside Thee,
Who worketh for him that waiteth for Him.
4. Thou didst take away him that joyfully worked righteousness,
Those that remembered Thee in Thy ways—
Behold, Thou wast wroth, and we sinned—
Upon them have we stayed of old, that we might be saved.
5. And we are all become as one that is unclean,
And all our righteousnesses are as a polluted garment;
And we all do fade as a leaf,
And our iniquities, like the wind, take us away.
6. And there is none that calleth upon Thy name,
That stirreth up himself to take hold of Thee;
For Thou hast hid Thy face from us,

64 : 3 *Whereof from of old men have not heard.* People had never before seen such wonders as Thou didst perform in the Exodus from Egypt.

64 : 4 *Thou didst take away him.* Those noble men who might now in our exile have interceded with You in our behalf are all gone by now. (Rashi and Kimchi) But Ibn Ezra translates the verb "have gone" or "departed" to mean "to meet"; and he interprets the verse as follows: In the past when we had sinned, Thou wouldst meet the righteous (such as Moses) who would intercede for us. Now there is no one who can meet You to plead for us.

Behold, Thou wast wroth . . . upon them have we stayed. "Upon them" (the righteous men) have we stayed, i.e., we have relied of old. The thought will be clearer if we invert the order

And hast consumed us by means of our iniquities.
7. But now, O LORD, Thou art our Father;
We are the clay, and Thou our potter,
And we all are the work of Thy hand.
8. Be not wroth very sore, O LORD,
Neither remember iniquity for ever;
Behold, look, we beseech Thee, we are all Thy people.
9. Thy holy cities are become a wilderness,
Zion is become a wilderness,
Jerusalem a desolation.
10. Our holy and our beautiful house,
Where our fathers praised Thee,
Is burned with fire;
And all our pleasant things are laid waste.
11. Wilt Thou refrain Thyself for these things, O LORD?
Wilt Thou hold Thy peace, and afflict us very sore?

Isaiah 64

of these two phrases as follows: the righteous (as in Verse 4) upon whom we had relied in the past are now gone. Now we have sinned (Verse 5) and have all become unclean and (Verse 6) there is none that calleth upon Thy name (in our behalf).

64 : 7 *We are the clay, and Thou our potter.* Kimchi cites as parallel the same metaphor in Verses 1 through 6 of Chapter 16 of Jeremiah: "Whenever the vessel was marred in the hands of the potter, He made it again into another vessel." So he explains this verse as follows: The potter can change the clay from shape to shape. If we have sinned, we are in Thy hands; Thou canst change us.

64 : 11 *Wilt Thou hold Thy peace?* How canst Thou, O Lord, keep from interfering in our behalf, when the beautiful Temple "our beautiful house" (Verse 10) where our fathers praised Thee is now in ashes?

65

THE PROPHET in God's name contrasts the miserable future of those who turn to idolatry with the happy destiny of those who are loyal to God. The loyal ones will be restored. A modern scholar, N. H. Snaith, dates these two chapters to the time when the exiles had already returned from Babylon and found that those who had remained in Judea and had never been in the Exile had lapsed into the idolatry of the heathen people of the land. The returning exiles, according to Snaith, considered themselves the true Israel and those who had remained were considered the sinners; and it is to them that the denunciations in Chapters 65 and 66 are addressed.

Isaiah 65

1. I gave access to them that asked not for Me,
   I was at hand to them that sought Me not;
   I said: 'Behold Me, behold Me,'
   Unto a nation that was not called by My name.
2. I have spread out My hands all the day
   Unto a rebellious people,

65 : 1 *Gave access to them that asked not for Me.* According to Rashi and Kimchi this is the response to the plea of the exiles and their complaint that they have no one worthy to intercede for them. God answers: Your fathers did not seek Me, yet I was accessible to them. Therefore they deserved the punishment of exile.

65 : 2 *I have spread out My hands.* Rashi and Kimchi: In order to receive them in repentance.

Isaiah 65

    That walk in a way that is not good,
    After their own thoughts;
3. A people that provoke Me
    To My face continually,
    That sacrifice in gardens,
    And burn incense upon bricks;
4. That sit among the graves,
    And lodge in the vaults;
    That eat swine's flesh,
    And broth of abominable things is in their vessels;
5. That say: 'Stand by thyself,
    Come not near to me, for I am holier than thou';
    These are a smoke in My nose,
    A fire that burneth all the day.
6. Behold, it is written before Me;
    I will not keep silence, except I have requited,
    Yea, I will requite into their bosom,
7. Your own iniquities, and the iniquities of your fathers together,
    Saith the LORD,
    That have offered upon the mountains,
    And blasphemed Me upon the hills;
    Therefore will I first measure their wage into their bosom.

65: 3-7   The sins of the past generation for which they have incurred punishment. According to Snaith, the sins of those children of Israel who had remained in the land and lapsed into idolatry.

65 : 4   *Sit among the graves.*   Kimchi: To invoke the ghosts of the dead.

    Swine's flesh.   This is the third ritual commandment mentioned in these chapters; the Sabbath, fasting, and, now, the forbidden foods.

65 : 5   *That say: '... I am holier than thou.'*   Those who eat the swine's flesh are self-righteous. They consider themselves holier than those who observe the law. (Kimchi and Ibn Ezra)

65 : 6   *It is written before Me.*   Their sins are recorded; they will not be erased. (Rashi and Kimchi)

65 : 7   *Offered upon the mountains.*   The high places where altars were set up for idol worshipers.

Isaiah 65

8. Thus saith the LORD:
As, when wine is found in the cluster,
One saith: 'Destroy it not,
For a blessing is in it';
So will I do for My servants' sakes,
That I may not destroy all.

9. And I will bring forth a seed out of Jacob,
And out of Judah an inheritor of My mountains;
And Mine elect shall inherit it,
And My servants shall dwell there.

10. And Sharon shall be a fold of flocks,
And the valley of Achor a place for herds to lie down in,
For My people that have sought Me

11. But ye that forsake the LORD,
That forget My holy mountain,
That prepare a table for Fortune,
And that offer mingled wine in full measure unto Destiny,

12. I will destine you to the sword,
And ye shall all bow down to the slaughter;
Because when I called, ye did not answer,
When I spoke, ye did not hear;
But ye did that which was evil in Mine eyes,
And chose that wherein I delighted not.

65 : 8 *Wine ... in the cluster ... 'Destroy it not ...'* The Targum says: As the righteous Noah was found in the evil generation (i.e., he was the "wine" in the cluster). Rashi, taking the Targum's explanation, says it means: For the sake of the righteous few among them, the generation will not be destroyed. Kimchi elaborates this by saying: God says to the exiles, Although I shall punish the evil ones among you, do not despair; there is enough good wine in the cluster for Me to redeem you.

65 : 11 *A table for Fortune ... Destiny.* The gods of Fortune and of Fate, idols who were worshiped by setting out a table in their honor. (See Krauss)

65 : 12 *When I called, ye did not answer.* This verse reechoes the opening sentence of the chapter: "I was accessible and they did not call upon Me."

13. Therefore thus saith the Lord God:
    Behold, My servants shall eat,
    But ye shall be hungry;
    Behold, My servants shall drink,
    But ye shall be thirsty;
    Behold, My servants shall rejoice,
    But ye shall be ashamed;
14. Behold, My servants shall sing
    For joy of heart,
    But ye shall cry for sorrow of heart,
    And shall wail for vexation of spirit.
15. And ye shall leave your name for a curse unto
    Mine elect:
    'So may the Lord God slay thee';
    But He shall call His servants by another name;
16. So that he who blesseth himself in the earth
    Shall bless himself by the God of truth;
    And he that sweareth in the earth
    Shall swear by the God of truth;
    Because the former troubles are forgotten,
    And because they are hid from Mine eyes.
17. For, behold, I create new heavens
    And a new earth;
    And the former things shall not be remembered,
    Nor come into mind.
18. But be ye glad and rejoice for ever

Isaiah 65

65:15 *Ye shall leave your name for a curse.* God addresses the evil ones and says: Your punishment will be so great that in the future, when people will want to curse somebody, they will think of how heavily you were punished and will say to the person whom they wish to curse, In this way may the Lord slay thee. (See Kimchi.)

Ibn Ezra gives the same explanation and cites two illustrative verses. The first is: "The Lord make thee a curse and an oath among thy people." (Numbers 5:21) And the second is: "The Lord make thee like Zedekiah and like Ahab, whom the king of Babylon roasted in the fire." (Jeremiah 29:22)

His servants by another name. A name of blessing. (Cf. commentary note to 62:2.)

Isaiah 65

In that which I create;
For, behold, I create Jerusalem a rejoicing,
And her people a joy.
19. And I will rejoice in Jerusalem,
And joy in My people;
And the voice of weeping shall be no more heard in her,
Nor the voice of crying.
20. There shall be no more thence an infant of days, nor an old man,
That hath not filled his days;
For the youngest shall die a hundred years old,
And the sinner being a hundred years old shall be accursed.
21. And they shall build houses, and inhabit them;
And they shall plant vineyards, and eat the fruit of them.
22. They shall not build, and another inhabit,

65 : 20 *An infant of days.* In those blessed times all will live long and no one will die in infancy.

Sinner being a hundred years. If a man in those days will die at the age of a hundred, he will be considered short-lived, punished because he was a sinner.

65 : 25 *The wolf and the lamb.* This recalls the ideal picture

> They shall not plant, and another eat;
> For as the days of a tree shall be the days of My people,
> And Mine elect shall long enjoy the work of their hands.
> 23. They shall not labour in vain,
> Nor bring forth for terror;
> For they are the seed blessed of the Lord,
> And their offspring with them.
> 24. And it shall come to pass that, before they call, I will answer,
> And while they are yet speaking, I will hear.
> 25. The wolf and the lamb shall feed together,
> And the lion shall eat straw like the ox;
> And dust shall be the serpent's food.
> They shall not hurt nor destroy
> In all My holy mountain,
> Saith the Lord.

of Isaiah when all of nature will be at peace: "They shall not hurt nor destroy." (11:6)

Dust shall be the serpent's food. Even the serpents will be content to eat dust and will not bite live creatures for food. (Kimchi)

66

KRAUSS assigns this chapter and the preceding one to an earlier date than does Snaith. He says it belongs to the time when Cyrus had given permission for the exiles to return and rebuild the Temple. So he explains Chapter 65 to be a denunciation of those who preferred to stay in Babylon and had become attached to Babylonian superstitions. This chapter is primarily addressed to those who have decided that they were going to return and build the Temple. God, therefore, says to them that since He does not need an earthly dwelling place with its animal sacrifices He let them remember that the ritual they will reestablish must be accompanied by sincerity of heart and righteousness.

Isaiah
66

1. Thus saith the LORD:
The heaven is My throne,
And the earth is My footstool;
Where is the house that ye may build unto Me?

66 : 1 *The heaven is My throne ... the earth My footstool.* The same thought was expressed by Solomon when he dedicated the Temple: "But will God in very truth dwell on earth? Behold, the heaven of heavens cannot contain Thee. How much less this house that I have builded." (I Kings 8:27) Rashi: I do not need your sanctuary for a dwelling place. Kimchi is more specific and says: These words were addressed to the wicked ones whose sac-

And where is the place that may be My resting-place?

2. For all these things hath My hand made,
And so all these things came to be,
Saith the LORD;
But on this man will I look,
Even on him that is poor and of a contrite spirit,
And trembleth at My word.
3. He that killeth an ox is as if he slew a man;
He that sacrificeth a lamb, as if he broke a dog's neck;
He that offereth a meal-offering, as if he offered swine's blood;
He that maketh a memorial-offering of frankincense, as if he blessed an idol;
According as they have chosen their own ways,
And their soul delighteth in their abominations;
4. Even so I will choose their mockings,
And will bring their fears upon them;
Because when I called, none did answer;
When I spoke, they did not hear,
But they did that which was evil in Mine eyes,
And chose that in which I delighted not.
5. Hear the word of the LORD,
Ye that tremble at His word:
Your brethren that hate you, that cast you out for My name's sake, have said:
'Let the LORD be glorified,

Isaiah 66

rifices are displeasing to God because of their evil life. (Isaiah 1:11: "To what purpose is the multitude of your sacrifices unto Me? ..." Isaiah 1:15: "Your hands are full of blood.")

66 : 2-3 *I look ... on him that is ... of a contrite spirit ... he that killeth an ox.* It is easier to read these two phrases in reverse order, as Ibn Ezra does: I do not look at him who sacrifices animals but lives evilly. I am with him who is of a humble spirit.

66 : 5-9 God reassures the righteous. The restoration may seem to be unbelievable but it will nevertheless surely come.

66 : 5 *'Let the Lord be glorified, that we may gaze ...'* Your enemies say these words scornfully: Let us just see whether God

Isaiah 66

That we may gaze upon your joy,'
But they shall be ashamed.

6. Hark! an uproar from the city,
Hark! it cometh from the temple,
Hark! the LORD rendereth recompense to His enemies.

7. Before she travailed, she brought forth;
Before her pain came,
She was delivered of a man-child.

8. Who hath heard such a thing?
Who hath seen such things?
Is a land born in one day?
Is a nation brought forth at once?
For as soon as Zion travailed,
She brought forth her children.

9. Shall I bring to the birth, and not cause to bring forth?
Saith the LORD;
Shall I that cause to bring forth shut the womb?
Saith thy God.

10. Rejoice ye with Jerusalem,
And be glad with her, all ye that love her;
Rejoice for joy with her,
All ye that mourn for her;

11. That ye may suck, and be satisfied
With the breast of her consolations;
That ye may drink deeply with delight
Of the abundance of her glory.

12. For thus saith the LORD:
Behold, I will extend peace to her like a river,

---

will show His glory and make you happy. Those who say this will be ashamed for the deliverance will surely come.

66 : 7 *Before she travailed, she brought forth.* A metaphor for the miraculous deliverance of Zion. She will bring forth her children without birth pains.

66 : 13 *As one whom his mother comforteth.* Kimchi: As a mother comforts her child for pains that have been endured, so will God comfort you in Jerusalem for the sorrows of the Exile.

66 : 15 *The Lord will come in fire ... His chariots.* Once again

And the wealth of the nations like an overflowing stream,
And ye shall suck thereof;
Ye shall be borne upon the side,
And shall be dandled upon the knees.
13. As one whom his mother comforteth,
So will I comfort you;
And ye shall be comforted in Jerusalem.
14. And when ye see this, your heart shall rejoice,
And your bones shall flourish like young grass;
And the hand of the Lord shall be known toward His servants,
And He will have indignation against His enemies.
15. For, behold, the Lord will come in fire,
And His chariots shall be like the whirlwind;
To render His anger with fury,
And His rebuke with flames of fire.
16. For by fire will the Lord contend,
And by His sword with all flesh;
And the slain of the Lord shall be many.
17. They that sanctify themselves and purify themselves
To go unto the gardens,
Behind one in the midst,
Eating swine's flesh, and the detestable thing, and the mouse,
Shall be consumed together, saith the Lord.
18. For I [know] their works and their thoughts; [the time] cometh, that I will gather all nations and tongues; and they shall come, and shall see My glory. 19. And I will work a sign among them, and

Isaiah 66

the metaphor of God coming as a victorious soldier. (See commentary note to 63:1.)

66:17 *They that sanctify themselves.* The idolators prepare themselves with careful ritual. Kimchi says they imagine that they are sanctified but they are really defiled.

66:18-21 *For I [know] their works . . . [the time] cometh.* I am aware of their evil works. Nevertheless the time will come when I will gather My children from all the distant lands of their exile. These exiles from distant lands will bring their gifts and I

Isaiah 66

I will send such as escape of them unto the nations, to Tarshish, Pul and Lud, that draw the bow, to Tubal and Javan, to the isles afar off, that have not heard My fame, neither have seen My glory; and they shall declare My glory among the nations. 20. And they shall bring all your brethren out of all the nations for an offering unto the LORD, upon horses, and in chariots, and in litters, and upon mules, and upon swift beasts, to My holy mountain Jerusalem, saith the LORD, as the children of Israel bring their offering in a clean vessel into the house of the LORD. 21. And of them also will I take for the priests and for the Levites, saith the LORD. 22. For as the new heavens and the new earth, which I will make, shall remain before Me, saith the LORD, so shall your seed and your name remain.

will choose Kohanim (priests) and Levites from among them to serve in My sanctuary.

66 : 23 *Shall all flesh come to worship.* This verse describes the glorious future under "the new heavens and the new earth" when all mankind will come regularly (on Sabbath and new moons) to worship God.

66 : 24 *Carcasses of the men that have rebelled.* Chapter 66 ends with the same somber description as did Chapters 48 and 57 ("No peace for the wicked"); but, since this chapter ends the entire Book of Isaiah, traditional feeling was against ending on such a somber note and Verse 23 was repeated as a happier ending of the book.

23. And it shall come to pass,
    That from one new moon to another,
    And from one sabbath to another,
    Shall all flesh come to worship before Me,
    Saith the Lord.
24. And they shall go forth, and look
    Upon the carcasses of the men that have rebelled against Me;
    For their worm shall not die,
    Neither shall their fire be quenched;
    And they shall be an abhorring unto all flesh.

Isaiah 66

And it shall come to pass,
That from one new moon to another,
And from one sabbath to another,
Shall all flesh come to worship before Me,
Saith the Lord.

Ibn Ezra wrote his commentary on Isaiah during his long wanderings over Europe. He was in the city of Lucca, Italy, when he completed his commentary and wrote the following poem at the conclusion.

Finished is the Book of Isaiah the Prophet,
Thanks without number to the God of my father,
Who taught me the book of his prophet,
And gave my heart wisdom.
May he hold my right hand that I may finish my writing,
Iyar 905 (i.e., 1145) in Lucca, the city of my habitation.

Bibliography

Blank, Sheldon, *Prophetic Faith in Isaiah*, New York, 1958
Buttenwieser, Moses, "Where did Deutero-Isaiah Live?" *Journal of Biblical Literature*, Vol. 38 (1919), pp. 94-112
Ehrlich, Arnold B., *Randglossen*, Leipzig, 1912
Eissfeldt, Otto, *The Old Testament*, New York, 1965
Friedlander, M., *Commentary of Ibn Ezra on Isaiah*, London, 1873, p. 232, note 6
Gray, George Buchanan, *International Critical Commentary on Isaiah*, New York, 1912
Haran, Menachem, *Behn Reshonos L'Chadoshos*, Hebrew University Series, Jerusalem, 1963
Kaminka, A., *Mechkarim*, Vol. I, pp. 8 ff.
Krauss, Samuel, *Commentary on Sefer Isaiah*, Kahana Series, Warsaw (n.d.)
Liebreich, L. J., *Jewish Quarterly Review*, New Series, Vols. 46-47
Morgenstern, Julian, *Message of Deutero-Isaiah*, Cincinnati, 1961
Orlinsky, Harry, *Supplement to Vetus Testamentum*, Vol. 14, pp. 1-133
Snaith, *Supplement to Vetus Testamentum*, Vol. 14, pp. 135-264
Tur-Sinai, N. T., *P'Shuto Shel Mikro*, Jerusalem, 1967
Yellin, David, *Chikreh Mikra, Isaiah*, Jerusalem, 1939

COMMISSION ON

JEWISH EDUCATION

of the UNION OF AMERICAN HEBREW CONGREGATIONS
and CENTRAL CONFERENCE OF AMERICAN RABBIS

AS OF 1972

JACOB P. RUDIN, *Chairman*
MARTIN S. ROZENBERG, *Vice Chairman*
SOLOMON B. FREEHOF, *Honorary Chairman*

DR. DOROTHY G. AXELROTH	MORTIMER MAY
DAVID BARISH	SAMUEL A. NEMZOFF
ALAN D. BENNETT	SEYMOUR PRYSTOWSKY
WILLIAM C. CUTTER	ELLIOT D. ROSENSTOCK
HARVEY J. FIELDS	MRS. CECIL B. RUDNICK
LEON C. FRAM	DR. LENORE SANDEL
HILLEL GAMORAN	FREDERICK C. SCHWARTZ
ROLAND B. GITTELSOHN	SYLVAN D. SCHWARTZMAN
SAMUEL C. GLASNER	HAROLD S. SILVER
JOSHUA O. HABERMAN	MRS. M. M. SINGER
DAVID S. HACHEN	L. WILLIAM SPEAR
LESLIE A. HART	PAUL M. STEINBERG
LEON A. JICK	MARVIN S. WALTS
BERNARD KLIGFELD	HEINZ WARSCHAUER
MRS. DAVID M. LEVITT	ALFRED C. WOLF
LOUIS LISTER	

MAURICE N. EISENDRATH, *Secretary*

Ex Officio

DAVID POLISH   JOSEPH B. GLASER

UNION EDUCATION SERIES

EDITED BY

JACK D. SPIRO, *National Director of Education*
UNION OF AMERICAN HEBREW CONGREGATIONS

Associate Director of Education,
Director of Continuing Education
ABRAHAM SEGAL

Director of Professional Education
MANUEL GOLD

Editor of Keeping Posted
EDITH SAMUEL

Associate Editor
MYRNA POLLAK

Director of Publications
RALPH DAVIS